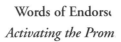

In *Activating the Promises of God*, Dee Chernicky addresses present-day problems candidly and compassionately. Then she does the work of searching out specific Scriptures that lead to spiritual breakthrough. Each chapter includes promises that will restore your hope and awaken you to life-giving faith in God's unconditional love and never-ending mercy.

—GERMAINE COPELAND, author of the Prayers That Avail Much® book
series, president and founder of Word Ministries, Inc.

*Activating the Promises of God* will strengthen your knowledge of the Word and show you how to implement the Word in everyday issues. Refreshing and empowering! A must-have book besides the Bible.

—AMBER ANDERSON, first lady and a co-founder of Bridgeway
Community Church, Columbia, Maryland

*Activating the Promises of God* can be used as prayer guide, study guide, or daily devotional. It is an excellent topical handbook that offers hope, instruction, and comfort to anyone facing challenges and suffering. Each subject, conveniently alphabetized, offers easy reference for prayer. You will find this book to be a great blessing because it points you to Christ and His all-sufficient Word.

—MICHAEL MORELLI, Morelli Ministries International, Tulsa, Oklahoma

Dee Chernicky not only shares her keen insight into capturing the heart of God through His Word, but she also provides practical steps to empower your life with an infusion of His promises. This book is a perfect resource for all, from the seasoned counselor to the new seeker.

—PASTOR LARRY MAURIELLO, Committed Ministries, Dallas, Texas

*Activating the Promises of God* is a powerful tool that enables you to walk fully in the promise of God's power. Covering many of the issues that hold us captive, this book reminds us of how relevant God's Word is for the issues we face today. It exposes God's heart as it personalizes the power of the living Word, enabling you to take captive God's thoughts, overcome the unthinkable, and perform the impossible. Be prepared to draw your sword as you become fully armed with a mighty offensive weapon in the warfare of daily living.

 —Dr. Kimberly P. Ray-Thomas, licensed psychologist

The words on these pages will find their way into your heart. You will find yourself, like a deer panting for water, longing for a more passionate pursuit of God.

 —Pastor Steve Vaggalis, lead pastor at Destiny Worship Center,
  Miramar, Florida

When *Activating the Promises of God* was placed in my hands, my heart immediately connected with the writer—her love for Jesus, her love for God's Word, and her commitment to seeing people's lives transformed. Be encouraged and challenged as you read on. This book will inspire you to fulfill your God-given destiny.

 —Valerie Peterson, licensed mental health counselor

*Activating the Promises of God* is a wonderful and effective tool for anyone who wants to combat the life issues that affect all of us. As you read this collection of Scriptures, let the truth of God's Word heal your body, mind, and heart.

 —Jennifer Crow, pastor of Victory Church, Oklahoma City, Oklahoma

# ACTIVATING
## THE PROMISES OF GOD

Unlock the Power of the Bible & Empower Your Life

**Over 1,600 Topically Arranged Scripture Verses
with Insight & Encouragement on Today's Real Life Issues**

# Dee Chernicky

ACTIVATING THE PROMISES OF GOD
PUBLISHED BY DEE CHERNICKY MINISTRIES

ISBN 978-0-615-36630-2

Printed in the United States of America
2010—First Edition

10 9 8 7 6 5 4 3 2 1

*To my former pastor Billy Joe Daugherty of Victory Christian Center
in Tulsa, Oklahoma, who is now at home in the presence
of the One he so faithfully and passionately served*

Thanks be to God!
He gives us the victory
through our Lord Jesus Christ.

—1 CORINTHIANS 15:57, NIV

# Contents

# CONTENTS

# CONTENTS

# INTRODUCTION

In a recent telephone conversation with my son Jonathan, I asked him for directions to a certain electronics store. I was out of town and wasn't familiar with the area. Since he was near his computer, it would be easy for him to look up the store's Web site and get directions. Instead, he said, "Mom, don't you have a GPS on your phone that you could use?"

I did have GPS on my phone, but the phone was fairly new and I hadn't taken the time to learn how to use it. As I had to admit to Jonathan, I had the resource in my hands—yet I couldn't activate it.

It is the same with God's Word. We all have the resource of the Scriptures, but many of us do not know to activate it for direction, wisdom, or divine health in our bodies, finances, and relationships.

Yet, "the Word of God is living and powerful, and sharper than any two-edged sword, piercing even to the division of soul and spirit, and of joints and marrow, and is a discerner of the thoughts and intents of the heart" (Hebrews 4:12, NKJV). When God gave us His Word, He gave us His power. He also gave us the responsibility of digging into His Word and pulling out that power.

My heart's passion is to teach you how to activate God's promises through unlocking the power of the Bible. I believe in the power of God's Word because I have seen His power manifested in my life and in the lives of others time and time again.

## KNOWING GOD AND HIS WORD

I am in awe when I think of the verse "Come unto me" (Matthew 11:28). The Creator of the universe, the Almighty, the King of Glory, and the Eternal God says to you and to me, "Come." He is calling us into His presence.

You activate the promises of God by *knowing God* and *knowing His Word*. True fellowship with God comes when you know Him personally through the Bible He has given you.

Will you yield yourself to God's invitation? Will you answer the call of His love that constantly beckons you? When you do, you will be empowered to overcome in this world. You will experience the fullness and pleasure of who God really is!

## OBEYING GOD'S WORD

You can know God and know His Word, but in order to unlock the power of the Bible, you must be "careful to do everything written in it [God's Word]. Then you will be prosperous and successful" (Joshua 1:8, NIV).

God shows His love for you by keeping His Word to you. The greatest example of this is God sending the promised Savior as foretold by His prophets (Romans 1:2-4). Your love for Him is shown through obeying His Word (John 14:23-24). God has put the responsibility of activating His promises in your hands when you choose to obey or disobey His Word.

## BELIEVING GOD'S WORD

To see the promises of God come to pass in your life, you must believe in Him and believe in His Word. The writer of Hebrews distinguishes between those who believe in the Word they hear and those who do not: "The gospel was preached to us as well as to them; but the word which they heard did not profit them, not being mixed with faith in those who heard it" (Hebrews 4:2, NKJV). One of the greatest victories you will ever have is when you *believe* God's Word more than what you see or feel in the natural world.

You will not find any other book or power source as effective at overcoming life's issues as the Word of God. There are countless self-help books, seminars, and Web sites that offer the latest and greatest solutions to your financial, relational and spiritual problems. Beware of such offers independent of God! Only the Word of God has the power to heal, deliver from bondage, and bring truth to the human heart.

When you know this truth deep in your soul, you will find that true belief leads to faith in action. Faith includes hearing, believing, praying, receiving, confessing, meditating, praising, and *doing!* "Be doers of the word, and not hearers only, deceiving yourselves" (James 1:22, NKJV). If you are in faith and you believe with all your heart, acting on your belief as a doer of the Word, God will produce living fruit of His Word in your life.

## SPEAKING GOD'S WORD

Everything that God created came into being as a result of His words, which are filled with faith, authority, and power. "The worlds were framed [formed] by the word of God, so that the things which are seen were not made of things which are visible" (Hebrews 11:3, NKJV). This is why God's power is released in your life when you *speak* His Word, in faith, over your circumstances.

God says that you will enjoy things after your mouth has spoken them: "A man's stomach shall be satisfied from the fruit of his mouth; from the produce of his lips he shall be filled" (Proverbs 18:20, NKJV). Your mouth is the power source that releases the supernatural in your life! When you speak and declare God's Word out of your mouth, you activate the very angels of God on your behalf. "Bless the LORD, you His angels, who excel in strength, who do His word, heeding the voice of His word" (Psalm 103:20, NKJV). The words of your mouth are vital to activating God's promises in your life.

## EXERCISING YOUR GOD-GIVEN AUTHORITY

Activating God's promises also means *exercising your authority* from God. When God gave you His Word, He gave you His power because God's power is "in and for us who believe" (Ephesians 1:19, AMP). In other words, the same power that created the heavens and the earth and raised Christ from the dead dwells in *you* (Romans 8:11).

From the beginning, God's desire was for His people to have dominion over the earth (Genesis 1:26). That means we are to govern in a way that allows each creation to fulfill its God-given purpose. God would not have created us with the responsibility of having dominion over the earth without giving us the resource to do it. His Word is your resource!

In the Bible, serpents and scorpions are symbolic of the power of the devil. God has given you all authority "to trample on snakes and scorpions and to overcome all the power of the enemy" (Luke 10:19). That means that the devil doesn't have authority over any area of your life! "And having disarmed the powers and authorities, he made a public spectacle of them, triumphing over them by the cross" (Colossians 2:15).

The Word tells us that we will be tried and tested, but some of our circumstances are from the natural consequences of our misled choices. When you exercise authority over the devil by speaking the Word, you have the right to expect the Word to come to pass. You have the right to demand circumstances to line up with the Word of God. You are demanding this of *Satan,* the one who is controlling the circumstances because he is the god of this world (2 Corinthians 4:4). The schemes of the devil no longer need to dominate you or those you are praying for.

In order to exercise your authority effectively, you have to know and walk in the knowledge of who you are in Christ and know that God lives in you. The stronger the Word of God in you, the stronger your authority.

## HAVING DONE ALL—STAND

When you've done all that you know how to do and you're still waiting for the manifestation of the promises of God to enter your life or the life of the person you are praying for, having done all, *stand* (from Ephesians 6:13). When you've obeyed God's Word, prayed, fasted, praised, quoted Scriptures, rebuked the devil, surrendered your will, read books, forgiven, and been reconciled with everyone who could have a problem with you, *stand.*

The Christian life is a paradox of doing and surrendering. Ultimately, "God's gift is not a question of human will and human effort, but of God's mercy. It depends not on one's own willingness nor on his strenuous exertion as in running a race, but on God's having mercy on him" (Romans 9:16, AMP). Standing means staying strong in your faith, receiving God's mercy as a gift to you, and believing that God's Word will come to pass in its time. As Jesus told His disciples, we are to "always pray and not give up" (Luke 18:1, NIV).

## HOW TO USE THIS BOOK

Reading through Scriptures on a particular topic and not knowing how to use them in faith is like getting a bicycle in a box and not knowing how to assemble it and use it.

*Activating the Promises of God* will encourage you and instruct you on *how* to use God's Word. It is designed to help you *know* God more intimately through His Word, *obey* His Word, *believe* in His Word, *speak* His Word, *exercise* the authority He gives through personal application of His Word, and finally *stand* in faith and submission to God's mercy.

Even though the Bible was not written topically, God provides a Scripture for every need that you have. *Activating the Promises of God* is a compilation of Scriptures that can be applied to each personal need. As you pray these Scriptures over your life and the lives of your loved ones, God will watch over His Word to perform it (Isaiah 55:11). You have all of heaven behind you when you pray His Word!

This book begins with verses of *praise.* The Lord is so deserving of our praise, and in order to activate God's promises and put His words "in remembrance" (Isaiah 43:26), you should first offer praises to the One who is worthy: "Enter his gates with thanksgiving and his courts with praise; give thanks to him and praise his name" (Psalm 100:4). When you go into the presence of someone above you, you acknowledge that person's authority with a reverential spirit. The same protocol exists when you go into the presence of your heavenly Father. Praise God for what He has done in your life, for all that He is currently doing in your life, and for what He promises to do in the future.

After verses of praise in the beginning of this book, you will find a list of the names of God. Begin your prayer by acknowledging God for who He is. Read through each of the names of God with worshipful consideration. God chose those names for Himself because He longs for you to know His full character. He wants you to acknowledge Him for who He is. I find that when I begin prayer with praise, worship, and an acknowledgment of who God really is, who I really am comes to light. Almost inevitably, the things that were concerning me suddenly come into a different perspective.

Following the list of the names of God, you will find a list of who *you* are in God's sight. Prayerfully read through this list, speaking the truth out loud about your true identity in Christ.

Finally, seek God's Word for the specific area of your life in which you need His wisdom *right now*. If you are uncertain as to whether a Scripture is for the need you have, ask the Holy Spirit to reveal it to you, and He will. "When the Spirit of truth comes, he will guide you into all truth" (John 16:13 NIV)

Prayerfully read through the introduction to the subject, then slowly read the verses. When one verse stands out to you or touches your spirit, stop and ask God what He wants to speak to you through those words. Speak God's promises aloud back to Him, for yourself and those you are praying for. Pray for His revelation through that verse.

Consider writing verses that you want to memorize (and stand on) on note cards or in the back of this book. Memorizing Scripture is a powerful way to keep God's Word in your mind always. Remember that God is not impressed or moved because of the *amount* of Scriptures that you memorize or declare. He is moved when you humbly trust, rely on, and believe in His Word.

When you meditate on the Word, it will focus your thoughts on God's ability to help you rather than your own inability to help yourself (based on Joshua 1:8). When we meditate, we think about God's ways and align our hearts with His will and purpose. It is an act that takes place in our heart. Therefore, David prays, "With my whole heart I have sought You; oh, let me not wander from Your commandments!" (Psalm 119:10, NKJV). Meditation brings understanding and it brings remembrance of the Word of God.

## THE POWER OF GOD'S WORD

Ephesians 5:1 tells us, "Be imitators of God, therefore, as dearly loved children" (NIV). How can you do that unless you know His Word and have been touched by His intimate presence? He wants your life to reflect Him based on His Word.

The amount of time you "spend with God" every day is not as important as your heart attitude toward Him as you pray, act, and speak. Even if you start with ten minutes here or there it will be honoring to Him if your heart is right. Your relationship with God will grow and become an intimate love relationship.

God's will is that you live your life as a strong and confident Christian—a person of great influence and spiritual wealth, a resource who draws others to God. You will come to understand this truth more deeply as you know His Word more and more. A knowledge of God's Word will equip you to fulfill His purposes, to overcome, to take dominion, to prosper, to walk in health, and to be victorious in every area of your life!

My desire is to encourage you to get into the habit of going to God and His Word for help, instruction, encouragement, insight, and daily, practical wisdom.

My prayer is that, throughout your lifetime, the timeless Word of God will be your wise counsel and that you will have one heart and one voice with God your Creator.

Many well-researched Bible translations reflect the heart of God's Word. I have prayerfully chosen several to use in *Activating the Promises of God*. Each Scripture reference in the book includes a translation abbreviation in case you want to study the passage more yourself. (For more information about these translations, please see the copyright page.)

AMP: Amplified Bible.

CEV: Contemporary English Version

ESV: English Standard Version

KJV: King James Version

MSG: The Message

NASB: New American Standard Bible

NCV: New Century Version

NIV: New International Version

NKJV: New King James Version

NLT: New Living Translation

# Come into His Gates—
# Opening with Praise

Exodus 18:11, NKJV

Now I know that the LORD is greater than all the gods.

Psalm 5:7, NIV

But I, by your great mercy, will come into your house; in reverence will I bow down toward your holy temple.

Psalm 29:2, NKJV

Give unto the LORD the glory due to His name; worship the LORD in the beauty of holiness.

Psalm 66:4-5, NCV

All the earth worships you and sings praises to you. They sing praises to your name. Come and see what God has done, the amazing things he has done for people.

Psalm 83:18, NLT

You alone are the Most High, supreme over all the earth.

Psalm 84:1-2, NIV

How lovely is your dwelling place, O LORD Almighty! My soul yearns, even faints, for the courts of the LORD; my heart and my flesh cry out for the living God.

Psalm 86:12, NIV

I will praise you, O LORD my God, with all my heart; I will glorify your name forever.

| | |
|---|---|
| Psalm 100:4, NIV | Enter his gates with thanksgiving and his courts with praise; give thanks to him and praise his name. |
| Psalm 145:1-3, NIV | I will exalt you, my God the King; I will praise your name for ever and ever. Every day I will praise you and extol your name for ever and ever. Great is the LORD and most worthy of praise; his greatness no one can fathom. |
| Psalm 145:10-12, NCV | LORD, everything you have made will praise you; those who belong to you will bless you. They will tell about the glory of your kingdom and will speak about your power. Then everyone will know the mighty things you do and the glory and majesty of your kingdom. |
| Psalm 146:2, NIV | I will praise the LORD all my life; I will sing praise to my God as long as I live. |
| Isaiah 25:1, NIV | O LORD, you are my God; I will exalt you and praise your name, for in perfect faithfulness you have done marvelous things, things planned long ago. |
| Matthew 6:10, NKJV | Your kingdom come. Your will be done on earth as it is in heaven. |

# The Names of God—
# Acknowledging God's Presence

**Names of God • Meaning**
**Pronunciation • Scripture Reference**

YHWH • The Self-Existent One
YAH-way • Genesis 2:4

El Roi • The God Who Sees Me
el ROY • Genesis 6:11-14

Jehovah-jireh • The Lord Will Provide
jeh-HO-vah JAHY-rah • Genesis 22:1

El Shaddai • The All-Sufficient One
el sha-DIE • Genesis 35:11

Jehovah • The Great I Am
jeh-HO-vah • Exodus 3:14

Jehovah-nissi • The Lord Our Banner
jeh-HO-vah NEE-see • Exodus 17:15

Adonai • My Great Lord
ah-doe-NAHY • Joshua 5:14

Jehovah-shalom • The Lord Our Peace
jeh-HO-vah sha-LOME • Judges 6:24

Jehovah-rapha • The Lord Who Heals
jeh-HO-vah RAH-fah • Psalm 103:3

Immanuel • The God Who Is with Us
ih-MAN-u-el • Isaiah 7:14

Jehovah-tsidkenu • The Lord Our Righteousness
jeh-HO-vah tsid-KAY-noo • Jeremiah 23:6

Jehovah-shammah • The Lord Is There
jeh-HO-vah SHA-mah • Ezekiel 48:35

Jehovah-rohi • The Lord Is My Shepherd
jeh-HO-vah ROW-hee • Psalm 23

# "I AM…"

Christians have used "I am" statements for centuries to acknowledge who they are before God. The references following each statement provide background for each truth about your identity in Christ.

I am a child of God. *Romans 8:16*

I am not my own, I am bought with a price. *1 Corinthians 6:19-20*

I am redeemed from the hand of the enemy. *Psalm 107:2*

I am crucified with Christ. *Galatians 2:20*

I am dead with Christ. *Colossians 3:3*

I am buried with Christ. *Colossians 2:11*

I am risen with Christ. *Colossians 2:13*

I am forgiven. *Colossians 1:13-14*

I am washed. *1 Corinthians 6:11*

I am saved by grace through faith. *Ephesians 2:8*

I am justified by faith and have peace with God through our Lord Jesus Christ. *Romans 3:24*

I am born again. *1 Peter 1:2-3*

I am sanctified. *1 Corinthians 6:11*

I am His workmanship. *Ephesians 2:10*

I am a partaker of His divine nature. *2 Peter 1:4*

I am pure. *1 Peter 1:22*

I am holy. *Hebrews 3:11*

I am a saint. *Colossians 1:11*

I am in His hand. *John 10:28-29*

I am delivered from powers of darkness. *Colossians 1:13*

I am redeemed from the curse of the law. *Galatians 3:13*

I am translated into the kingdom of His dear Son. *Colossians 1:13*

I am His sheep and He is my Shepherd. *Psalm 23:1*

I am led by the Spirit of God. *Romans 8:14*

I am a son of God. *Romans 8:14*

I am protected by the hands of angels wherever I go. *Psalm 91:11*

I am getting all my needs met by Jesus. *Philippians 4:19*

I am casting all my cares on Him because He cares for me. *1 Peter 5:7*

I am above only and not beneath. *Deuteronomy 28:13*

I am strong in the Lord and in the power of His might. *Ephesians 6:10*

I am receiving power to get wealth. *Deuteronomy 8:18*

I am doing all things through Christ who strengthens me. *Philippians 4:13*

I am speaking the truth in love. *Ephesians 4:15*

I am my Beloved's and He is mine. *Song of Solomon 6:3*

I am delighting myself in Jesus. *Psalm 37:4*

I am acknowledging Him in all things. *Proverbs 3:6*

I am an heir of God and joint heir with Jesus. *Romans 8:17*

I am seated with Christ in heavenly places. *Ephesians 2:6*

I am heir to the blessings of Abraham. *Galatians 3:13-14*

I am observing and doing the Lord's commandments. *Deuteronomy 28:13*

I am an inheritor of eternal life. *1 John 5:11-12*

I am blessed with all spiritual blessing in heavenly places in Christ Jesus. *Ephesians 1:3*

I am healed by His stripes. *1 Peter 2:24*

I am prosperous. *3 John, 2*

I am reigning in life through the one Jesus Christ. *Romans 5:17*

I am blessed coming in and blessed going out. *Deuteronomy 28:6*

I am above principalities and powers. *Luke 9:1*

I am more than a conqueror through Christ who loves me. *Romans 8:37*

I am possessing by my confessing. *Mark 11:23-24*

I am daily overcoming the devil because the One in me is greater than the one in the world. *1 John 4:4*

# Abortion—
# Should I Choose Abortion?

Do you feel as if you're being pulled one way and your heart and conscience are going in another direction? You're facing a difficult decision. What do you do next? What does God say about abortion? Does He address such a personal issue?

When you look to God's Word you will find His heart. You will discover His plan for you and the unborn child you are carrying.

God's Word tells us that He creates our "inmost being," knitting us together in the womb (Psalm 139:13, NIV). "Children are a gift from the LORD; they are a reward from him" (Psalm 127:3, NLT). Even if the circumstances of your pregnancy are grim, God can bring good out of a difficult situation.

The child inside you already has a soul, a beating heart, and a purpose. You also have a purpose. Even now, when life seems dark, God wants to breathe new life into you, just as He has breathed His breath of life into all living beings (Genesis 2:7). Others may not have comfort or understanding. God does. You may not have a sense of direction. God does. Go to Him. He's waiting with outstretched arms.

You are probably experiencing a range of emotions: fear, anger, confusion, even guilt. You are not a bad person for feeling overwhelmed. God is on your side. And in the midst of all your feelings, you have the opportunity to choose life for a child. Hope is possible for that child *and* for you—not just someday, but today.

God tells us, "This day...I have set before you life and death, blessings and curses. Now choose life, so that you and your children may live" (Deuteronomy 30:19, NIV). You will not regret choosing life. There are many people who are called by God to help you and to support your decision to have your baby. Will you pray and ask God to show you who those people are?

*For other helpful categories, see pages 115, 153, 350, 428, 437.*

| | |
|---|---|
| Genesis 2:7, NIV | The LORD God formed the man from the dust of the ground and breathed into his nostrils the breath of life, and the man became a living being. |
| Deuteronomy 30:19, NIV | This day I call heaven and earth as witnesses against you that I have set before you life and death, blessings and curses. Now choose life, so that you and your children may live. |
| Psalm 1:1, NIV | Blessed is the man who does not walk in the counsel of the wicked or stand in the way of sinners or sit in the seat of mockers. |
| Psalm 82:2-4, NKJV | Defend the poor and fatherless. Do justice to the afflicted and needy. Deliver the poor and needy. Free them from the hand of the wicked. |
| Psalm 127:3, NLT | Children are a gift from the LORD; they are a reward from him. |
| Psalm 139:13, NIV | You created my inmost being; you knit me together in my mother's womb. |
| Psalm 139:16, NIV | Your eyes saw my unformed body. All the days ordained for me were written in your book before one of them came to be. |
| Psalm 143:8, NIV | Show me the way I should go, for to you I lift up my soul. |
| Proverbs 6:16-19, NIV | There are six things the LORD hates, seven that are detestable to him: haughty eyes, a lying tongue, hands that shed innocent blood, a heart |

that devises wicked schemes, feet that are quick
to rush into evil, a false witness who pours out
lies and a man who stirs up dissension among
brothers.

Proverbs 31:8, NIV — Speak up for those who cannot speak for
themselves.

Isaiah 1:15, NIV — When you spread out your hands in prayer, I will
hide my eyes from you; even if you offer many
prayers, I will not listen. Your hands are full of
blood.

Jeremiah 1:5, NIV — Before I formed you in the womb I knew you,
before you were born I set you apart.

John 10:10, NIV — The thief comes only to steal and kill and destroy;
I have come that they may have life, and have it
to the full.

Acts 5:29, NIV — We must obey God rather than men!

Romans 2:8, NIV — But for those who are self-seeking and who reject
the truth and follow evil, there will be wrath and
anger.

Romans 12:21, NIV — Do not be overcome by evil, but overcome evil
with good.

Romans 16:17, NIV — I urge you, brothers, to watch out for those who
cause divisions and put obstacles in your way that
are contrary to the teaching you have learned.
Keep away from them.

| | |
|---|---|
| Hebrews 4:13, NIV | Nothing in all creation is hidden from God's sight. Everything is uncovered and laid bare before the eyes of him to whom we must give account. |
| 1 Peter 3:17, NIV | It is better, if it is God's will, to suffer for doing good than for doing evil. |
| 3 John, 11, NIV | Do not imitate what is evil but what is good. Anyone who does what is good is from God. Anyone who does what is evil has not seen God. |

# ABORTION—
# HEALING AFTER ABORTION

Abortion is not beyond the reach of God's love and forgiveness. This hope, not past decisions, can define your days if you let it. Ask God for forgiveness. Believe that one day new life will come again.

No matter how long ago you had an abortion (or abortions), you might still struggle with the physical or emotional aftermath of that decision. If the decision was forced upon you, or if you were given incomplete information about abortion, you might feel deeply angry. You might find yourself wondering about who this child would have been. If you have other children, you might experience new waves of grief as you carry a pregnancy full-term. You might feel guilty, even if you didn't want to have an abortion when you did.

But there is hope. And hope is healing.

God tells us that He does not treat us as our sins deserve or pay us back in full for our wrongs. When grief, regret, or shame comes back to you, remember that "as high as the heavens are above the earth, so great is his love for those who fear him" (Psalm 103:11, NIV).

Many women find comfort in the image of their children waiting for them in heaven. You might not have known them, but God does (Jeremiah 1:5). And one day He will delight to see you holding them in your arms.

*For other helpful categories, see pages 171, 174, 223, 236.*

| | |
|---|---|
| Psalm 25:3, NIV | No one whose hope is in you will ever be put to shame, but they will be put to shame who are treacherous without excuse. |
| Psalm 25:5, NIV | Guide me in your truth and teach me, for you are God my Savior, and my hope is in you all day long. |
| Psalm 34:5, NIV | Those who look to him are radiant; their faces are never covered with shame. |
| Psalm 51:2, NCV | Wash away all my guilt and make me clean again. |
| Psalm 103:10, NIV | He does not treat us as our sins deserve or repay us according to our iniquities. |
| Psalm 103:11, NIV | For as high as the heavens are above the earth, so great is His love for those who fear him. |
| Psalm 103:12, NCV | He has taken our sins away from us as far as the east is from west. |
| Jeremiah 1:5, NIV | Before I formed you in the womb I knew you, before you were born I set you apart. |
| Jeremiah 31:18, NIV | Restore me, and I will return, because you are the LORD my God. |
| Jeremiah 33:8, NIV | I will cleanse them from all the sin they have committed against me and will forgive all their sins of rebellion against me. |

| | |
|---|---|
| Matthew 26:28, NIV | This is my blood of the covenant, which is poured out for many for the forgiveness of sins. |
| Acts 13:38, NIV | Through Jesus the forgiveness of sins is proclaimed to you. |
| Romans 2:4, NIV | God's kindness leads you toward repentance. |
| Romans 4:7, NIV | Blessed are they whose transgressions are forgiven, whose sins are covered. |
| Romans 8:1, NIV | Therefore, there is now no condemnation for those who are in Christ Jesus. |
| Ephesians 1:7, NIV | In him we have redemption through his blood, the forgiveness of sins, in accordance with the riches of God's grace. |
| 1 John 1:9, NKJV | If we confess our sins, He is faithful and just to forgive us our sins and to cleanse us from all unrighteousness. |

# ABUSE—CHILD ABUSE

If you experienced abuse as a child, hearing that God knows your pain now is not enough. Where was God when you were being abused? The truth is, God knew your pain even as you did. He grieved with you. He was angry for you. One day He will judge those who hurt you (Romans 12:19).

Perhaps you don't know how to name what you experienced as a child. Abuse is any inappropriate activity initiated by a peer or adult without your consent. It could have been physical, verbal, visual, or sexual.

God understands what you experienced, because Jesus was also abused. He was mistreated though He did nothing wrong. We read that Jesus "did not retaliate when he was insulted, nor threaten revenge when he suffered. He left his case in the hands of God, who always judges fairly" (1 Peter 2:23, NLT).

As difficult as it may sound, ask God to help you forgive and release the person who has abused you, as well as the circumstances surrounding the abuse. The consequences of unforgiveness can produce even further destruction. Forgiveness is the key to living free from shame, guilt, humiliation, and feelings of betrayal. It will unlock the healing power of restoration in your life (Matthew 18:21-35).

Your abuser cannot change God's power in your life. God's power, through His Word, will bring healing that no one can take away. Are you ready to move forward?

*For other helpful categories, see pages 13, 103, 174, 223, 329.*

Leviticus 18:6, NIV — No one is to approach any close relative to have sexual relations. I am the LORD.

Psalm 25:3, NIV — No one whose hope is in you will ever be put to shame, but they will be put to shame who are treacherous without excuse.

Psalm 73:26, NIV — My flesh and my heart may fail, but God is the strength of my heart and my portion forever.

Psalm 94:1, NLT — O LORD, the God of vengeance, O God of vengeance, let your glorious justice shine forth!

Psalm 119:156, NKJV — Great are Your tender mercies, O LORD; revive me according to Your judgments.

Matthew 18:21-22, NLT — Then Peter came to Jesus and asked, "Lord, how often should I forgive someone who sins against me? Seven times?" "No, not seven times," Jesus replied, "but seventy times seven!"

Mark 11:25, NIV — When you stand praying, if you hold anything against anyone, forgive him, so that your Father in heaven may forgive you your sins.

Luke 17:1-2, NKJV — It is impossible that no offenses should come, but woe to him through whom they do come! It would be better for him if a millstone were hung around his neck, and he were thrown into the sea, than that he should offend one of these little ones.

Acts 7:34, CEV

With my own eyes I have seen the suffering of my people in Egypt. I have heard their groans and have come down to rescue them. Now I am sending you back to Egypt.

Romans 12:19, NCV

My friends, do not try to punish others when they wrong you, but wait for God to punish them with his anger. It is written: "I will punish those who do wrong; I will repay them," says the Lord.

Romans 15:13, NIV

May the God of hope fill you with all joy and peace as you trust in him, so that you may overflow with hope by the power of the Holy Spirit.

1 Peter 2:23, NLT

He did not retaliate when he was insulted, nor threaten revenge when he suffered. He left his case in the hands of God, who always judges fairly.

# ABUSE—SPOUSAL ABUSE

If your spouse is abusing you verbally, sexually, or physically, you probably feel incredibly lonely. The person you trusted most has become someone you fear. You might feel you can't tell others. You might even feel *you* are doing something wrong.

The Psalms tell us, "Pour out your heart to [God]" (Psalm 62:8, NLT). You do not need to guard your words with God. You do not need to feel ashamed in front of Him. You are *beautiful* to Him.

Pouring out your heart to God means telling Him all your anger, fears, guilt, and confusion. It might mean asking Him why He seems far away. It might mean crying without words.

Right now, your spouse has a lot of control over your feelings and actions. God can help you be in charge of your life again. Healing and wholeness is not only possible but inevitable when you choose to overcome the victim mentality and work to become a survivor.

Find a safe place physically, get counsel and help from an experienced source, then pray for your spouse. The Bible says that after Job prayed for the people who had hurt him, "the LORD made him prosperous again and gave him twice as much as he had before" (Job 42:10, NIV). Together, you and God can take the next step toward your healing. You don't need to feel alone anymore.

*For other helpful categories, see pages 13, 174, 223, 236, 437.*

Job 42:10, NIV

After Job had prayed for his friends, the LORD made him prosperous again and gave him twice as much as he had before.

Psalm 18:48, NKJV

He delivers me from my enemies. You also lift me up above those who rise against me; you have delivered me from the violent man.

Psalm 62:8, NLT

O my people, trust in him at all times. Pour out your heart to him, for God is our refuge.

Psalm 121:8, NLT

The LORD keeps watch over you as you come and go, both now and forever.

Proverbs 22:10, AMP

Drive out the scoffer, and contention will go out; yes, strife and abuse will cease.

Joel 2:25, NKJV

I will restore to you the years that the swarming locust has eaten.

Malachi 2:16, AMP

For the LORD, the God of Israel, says: I hate divorce and marital separation and him who covers his garment [his wife] with violence. Therefore keep a watch upon your spirit [that it may be controlled by My Spirit], that you deal not treacherously and faithlessly [with your marriage mate].

Luke 6:28, NCV

Bless those who curse you, pray for those who are cruel to you.

Acts 7:26, AMP

Then on the next day Moses suddenly appeared to some who were quarreling and fighting among

themselves, and he urged them to make peace
and become reconciled, saying, Men, you are
brethren; why do you abuse and wrong one
another?

1 Corinthians 3:16-17, NIV    Don't you know that you yourselves are God's
temple and that God's Spirit lives in you? If
anyone destroys God's temple, God will destroy
him; for God's temple is sacred, and you are that
temple.

Colossians 3:8, AMP    But now put away and rid yourselves [completely]
of all these things: anger, rage, bad feeling toward
others, curses and slander, and foulmouthed abuse
and shameful utterances from your lips!

1 Peter 2:23, NLT    He did not retaliate when he was insulted, nor
threaten revenge when he suffered. He left his
case in the hands of God, who always judges
fairly.

# ABUSE—VERBAL ABUSE

Whether you are facing verbal abuse in your home, in your workplace, or from a parent or child, God has words of healing for you.

There is a difference between constructive criticism and verbal abuse. Verbal abuse undermines the *truth* of who you are in God's eyes. It is more a reflection on the person speaking to you than it is a reflection on you, but it is still painful. The greatest danger is beginning to believe what is being spoken to you. If a parent tells a child he is "stupid" long enough, he begins to doubt his abilities. He begins to behave according to the words spoken over him. Soon it becomes the way he thinks of himself.

The initial way to respond to verbal abuse is to remember how *God* speaks to you: "I have loved you with an everlasting love" (Jeremiah 31:3, NKJV). "I will never leave you nor forsake you" (Hebrews 13:5, NKJV). "I have summoned you by name; you are mine" (Isaiah 43:1, NIV).

Your abuser may remind you of your past. Scripture tells you that God remembers your sin "no more" (Hebrews 8:12, ESV). Your abuser may tell you that you're worthless. Scripture tells you that you are "precious and honored in [God's] sight" (Isaiah 43:4, NIV). Your abuser may tell you that you can't do anything right. Scripture tells you that you "can do all things through Christ" (Philippians 4:13, NKJV).

God's words are more powerful than any human words. Renew your mind with them, so that when these hurtful words of the accuser come your way, you can release them with what your loving God has to say. You will find new strength, power, and confidence in who you really are (Romans 12:2).

*For other helpful categories, see pages 13, 174, 196, 236, 445.*

Psalm 62:8, NIV

Trust in the Lord at all times, O people; pour out your hearts to him, for God is our refuge.

Psalm 118:5, NLT

In my distress I prayed to the LORD, and the LORD answered me and set me free.

Proverbs 4:23, NIV

Above all else, guard your heart, for it is the wellspring of life.

Proverbs 20:22, NIV

Do not say, "I'll pay you back for this wrong!" Wait for the LORD, and he will deliver you.

Isaiah 43:1, NCV

This is what the LORD says. He created you, people of Jacob; he formed you, people of Israel. He says, "Don't be afraid, because I have saved you. I have called you by name, and you are mine.

Isaiah 54:17, NKJV

No weapon formed against you shall prosper, and every tongue which rises against you in judgment you shall condemn. This is the heritage of the servants of the LORD, and their righteousness is from Me," says the LORD.

Matthew 6:14-15, NLT

If you forgive those who sin against you, your heavenly Father will forgive you. But if you refuse to forgive others, your Father will not forgive your sins.

Romans 12:2, NKJV

Do not be conformed to this world, but be transformed by the renewing of your mind, that you may prove what is that good and acceptable and perfect will of God.

| | |
|---|---|
| Romans 12:19, NIV | Do not take revenge, my friends, but leave room for God's wrath, for it is written: "It is mine to avenge; I will repay," says the Lord. |
| Philippians 3:13-14, NIV | One thing I do: Forgetting what is behind and straining toward what is ahead, I press on toward the goal to win the prize for which God has called me heavenward in Christ Jesus. |
| Hebrews 4:13, NCV | Nothing in all the world can be hidden from God. Everything is clear and lies open before him. And to him we must explain the way we have lived. |
| Hebrews 13:5, NKJV | I will never leave you nor forsake you. |

# Addiction—Overcoming Drug and Alcohol Addiction

If you have repeatedly and with no success tried to reduce or control the use of a substance, you already know that overcoming addiction requires time, commitment, and outside support. Addiction is a powerful deception that traps you into believing you need a substance to secure comfort, relief, or success as you navigate life. It becomes your means of coping, keeping you from becoming the purposeful person God intends you to be.

When you struggle with an addiction that seems bigger than yourself, remember: *God is for you* (Romans 8:31). He is in you to help you overcome whatever physical, mental, or emotional compulsion is troubling your life. And He is there to help you find and fulfill your purpose and destiny. God has a good plan for your life (Jeremiah 29:11).

Do you see yourself overcoming this addiction? Or do you replay the images in your mind of the person who constantly gave in to desire? Meditate on the truth of what the Scriptures say about you. Let God's love remind you that you are not a failure. You will never be a lost cause to God. You are a child of God, and the Holy Spirit will help you with your weaknesses (Romans 8:26).

There is great power in surrendering your limitations to God. You cannot overcome in your own strength and you cannot overcome in a single day. Be patient and forgive yourself for your shortcomings. Surround yourself with godly support. By acknowledging that God is bigger than your addiction, you are moving toward a life of freedom and joy.

*For other helpful categories, see pages 13, 196, 336, 343, 402, 411, 421, 428.*

| | |
|---|---|
| Proverbs 23:20-21, NIV | Do not join those who drink too much wine or gorge themselves on meat, for drunkards and gluttons become poor, and drowsiness clothes them in rags. |
| Proverbs 23:31-32, NIV | Do not gaze at wine when it is red, when it sparkles in the cup, when it goes down smoothly! In the end it bites like a snake and poisons like a viper. |
| Isaiah 5:22, NIV | Woe to those who are heroes at drinking wine and champions at mixing drinks. |
| John 8:32, NIV | Then you will know the truth, and the truth will set you free. |
| Romans 8:26, NIV | The Spirit helps us in our weakness. We do not know what we ought to pray for, but the Spirit himself intercedes for us with groans that words cannot express. |
| Romans 8:31, KJV | What shall we then say to these things? If God be for us, who can be against us? |
| Romans 12:2, NIV | Do not conform any longer to the pattern of this world, but be transformed by the renewing of your mind. Then you will be able to test and approve what God's will is—his good, pleasing and perfect will. |
| Romans 13:12-14, NIV | Let us put aside the deeds of darkness and put on the armor of light. Let us behave decently, as in the daytime, not in orgies and *drunkenness*, not in sexual immorality and debauchery, not in |

dissension and jealousy. Rather, clothe yourselves with the Lord Jesus Christ, and do not think about how to gratify the desires of the sinful nature.

1 Corinthians 6:19-20, NIV — Do you not know that your body is a temple of the Holy Spirit, who is in you, whom you have received from God? You are not your own; you were bought at a price. Therefore honor God with your body.

1 Corinthians 15:34, AMP — Awake [from your drunken stupor and return] to sober sense and your right minds, and sin no more.

Galatians 5:19-21, NIV — The acts of the sinful nature are obvious: sexual immorality, impurity and debauchery; idolatry and witchcraft; hatred, discord, jealousy, fits of rage, selfish ambition, dissensions, factions and envy; *drunkenness,* orgies, and the like. I warn you, as I did before, that those who live like this will not inherit the kingdom of God.

Ephesians 5:18, NIV — Do not get drunk on wine, which leads to debauchery. Instead, be filled with the Spirit.

Philippians 4:13, NKJV — I can do all things through Christ who strengthens me.

2 Peter 2:19, NIV — For a man is a slave to whatever has mastered him.

1 John 4:4, KJV — Greater is he that is in you, than he that is in the world.

# ADDICTION—
# STAYING FREE FROM ADDICTION

Addiction is powerfully relentless. Overcoming addiction requires a *process*. As you work to stay free from addiction, do not allow the enemy to tally your past failures against you. God's mercy is new every morning (Lamentations 3:23).

We learn over and over again in Scripture that our future is not based on our past. Moses murdered a man (Exodus 2:12), yet God used him to lead the Israelites into the Promised Land. David committed adultery (2 Samuel 11:4), yet he was called a man after God's own heart (Acts 13:22). Matthew, as a tax collector in that day, was a cheat and a liar, yet Jesus welcomed him as a disciple (Matthew 9:9).

You might hear these stories and forget how they apply to you. You might think, *That worked for him, but I've done too much to make a clean start now.* Don't let those thoughts turn into actions. Instead, replace those lies with God's truth. Renew your mind and memorize His Word one Scripture at a time. Changing your thoughts will have a profound effect on your behavior and will help you to stay clean and strong through your recovery.

You did not have the strength on your own to overcome your addiction. But God's strength was in you. The Word tells you, "For the LORD your God is he who goes with you to fight for you against your enemies, to give you the victory" (Deuteronomy 20:4, ESV). Believe that this is your season of victory and restoration. God will bring you through one day at a time!

*For other helpful categories, see pages 13, 199, 236, 289, 314, 329, 346, 398, 421.*

Deuteronomy 20:4, ESV     For the LORD your God is he who goes with you to fight for you against your enemies, to give you the victory.

Psalm 18:32, NIV     It is God who arms me with strength and makes my way perfect.

Psalm 34:19, NKJV     Many are the afflictions of the righteous: but the LORD delivers him out of them all.

Psalm 119:45, NLT     I will walk in freedom, for I have devoted myself to your commandments.

Psalm 138:3, CEV     When I asked for your help, you answered my prayer and gave me courage.

Proverbs 4:23, NCV     Be careful what you think, because your thoughts run your life.

Proverbs 21:16, CEV     If you stop using good sense, you will find yourself in the grave.

Micah 7:8, NIV     Do not gloat over me, my enemy! Though I have fallen, I will rise.

Romans 7:15, NIV     I do not understand what I do. For what I want to do I do not do, but what I hate I do.

1 Corinthians 3:16-17, NIV     Don't you know that you yourselves are God's temple and that God's Spirit lives in you? If anyone destroys God's temple, God will destroy him; for God's temple is sacred, and you are that temple.

| 1 Corinthians 5:11, NIV | You must not associate with anyone who calls himself a brother but is sexually immoral or greedy, an idolater or a slanderer, a *drunkard* or a swindler. With such a man do not even eat. |
| --- | --- |
| 1 Corinthians 10:13, NIV | No temptation has seized you except what is common to man. And God is faithful; he will not let you be tempted beyond what you can bear. But when you are tempted, he will also provide a way out so that you can stand up under it. |
| 2 Corinthians 1:21, NIV | It is God who makes both us and you stand firm in Christ. He anointed us, set his seal of owner-ship on us, and put his Spirit in our hearts. |
| Galatians 5:1, NIV | It is for freedom that Christ has set us free. Stand firm, then, and do not let yourselves be burdened again by a yoke of slavery. |
| Philippians 2:13, NIV | It is God who works in you to will and to act according to his good purpose. |
| Philippians 4:13, NKJV | I can do all things through Christ who strengthens me. |
| Colossians 3:2, NLT | Think about the things of heaven, not the things of earth. |
| 2 Timothy 1:7, NKJV | God has not given us a spirit of fear, but of power and of love and of a sound mind. |
| Titus 2:11-12, NIV | The grace of God that brings salvation has appeared to all men. It teaches us to say "No" to |

ungodliness and worldly passions, and to live self-controlled, upright and godly lives in this present age.

1 Peter 4:1-2, NCV

Since Christ suffered while he was in his body, strengthen yourselves with the same way of thinking Christ had. The person who has suffered in the body is finished with sin. Strengthen yourselves so that you will live here on earth doing what God wants, not the evil things people want.

1 Peter 5:8, NIV

Be self-controlled and alert. Your enemy the devil prowls around like a roaring lion looking for someone to devour.

1 Peter 5:9, NCV

Refuse to give in to [the devil], by standing strong in your faith. You know that your Christian family all over the world is having the same kinds of suffering.

2 Peter 2:9, AMP

The Lord knows how to rescue the godly out of temptations and trials.

# ADULTERY—IF YOU ARE IN AN ADULTEROUS RELATIONSHIP

Adultery can start with a playful or flirtatious look (Matthew 5:28). It can come through an online Web site or by an unhealthy emotional attachment to someone other than your spouse.

You may have begun an adulterous relationship for many reasons. You probably have a void in your life that you are seeking to fill. Another person may temporarily fill that void, but God alone is the healing source for every need you have.

Sin has a season of pleasure (Hebrews 11:25). You might feel the thrill or adrenaline rush that can come from doing something wrong. But the truth is, that feeling cannot last forever.

Being in an affair is like living in a situation of controlled chaos. It is exciting but ultimately wearing on your spirit. You must get out of it. "A man who commits adultery…destroys himself" (Proverbs 6:32, NIV).

Read the Scriptures in this section and pray for God's strength, forgiveness, and restoration. Step back and take a look at what you are really longing for. You are not beyond God's help. His love and forgiveness are reaching out to you now. Will you respond by drawing near and asking Him to set your heart free? Your heart can find a safe place in Him.

*For other helpful categories, see pages 13, 121, 196, 218, 402, 421, 437, 441.*

| | |
|---|---|
| Exodus 20:14, NIV | You shall not commit adultery. |
| Proverbs 5:15, NIV | Drink water from your own cistern, running water from your own well. |
| Proverbs 6:25, NIV | Do not lust in your heart after a woman's beauty or let her captivate you with her eyes. |
| Proverbs 6:32, NIV | But a man who commits adultery lacks judgment; whoever does so destroys himself. |
| Matthew 5:27-28, NIV | You have heard that it was said, "Do not commit adultery." But I tell you that anyone who looks at a woman lustfully has already committed adultery with her in his heart. |
| Matthew 5:32, NIV | But I tell you that anyone who divorces his wife, except for marital unfaithfulness, causes her to become an adulteress, and anyone who marries the divorced woman commits adultery. |
| Matthew 15:19, NIV | For out of the heart come evil thoughts, murder, *adultery*, sexual immorality, theft, false testimony, slander. |
| Matthew 19:19, MSG | Jesus said, "Don't murder, don't commit adultery, don't steal, don't lie, honor your father and mother, and love your neighbor as you do yourself." |
| Acts 3:19, NIV | Repent, then, and turn to God, so that your sins may be wiped out, that times of refreshing may come from the Lord. |

1 Corinthians 6:9-10, NCV    Surely you know that the people who do wrong will not inherit God's kingdom. Do not be fooled. Those who sin sexually, worship idols, take part in adultery, those who are male prostitutes, or men who have sexual relations with other men, those who steal, are greedy, get drunk, lie about others, or rob—these people will not inherit God's kingdom.

1 Corinthians 6:18-20, NKJV    Flee sexual immorality. Every sin that a man does is outside the body, but he who commits sexual immorality sins against his own body. Or do you not know that your body is the temple of the Holy Spirit who is in you, whom you have from God, and you are not your own? For you were bought at a price; therefore glorify God in your body and in your spirit, which are God's.

Ephesians 5:3, NKJV    But fornication and all uncleanness or covetousness, let it not even be named among you, as is fitting for saints.

Hebrews 11:25, KJV    Choosing rather to suffer affliction with the people of God, than to enjoy the pleasures of sin for a season.

Hebrews 13:4, NIV    Marriage should be honored by all, and the marriage bed kept pure, for God will judge the adulterer and all the sexually immoral.

# ADULTERY—

# IF YOU HAVE COMMITTED ADULTERY

No sin is beyond God's healing. God's grace is always available to you if you are ready to receive it. True repentance is the key to living your life free from guilt, shame, and embarrassment. Godly, sorrowful repentance is not being sorry you were caught, it is true sorrow for the sin committed against the One who gave the gift of marriage.

Part of God's grace is the opportunity to restore your relationship with your spouse and your family. What do you need to do for those relationships? Pray for God's wisdom as you take practical steps with the future in mind. Pray for patience as your spouse begins his or her own difficult journey of healing.

It takes humility to ask for and receive forgiveness—first from God and then from others. It takes courage to turn away from sinful desires. But the Bible tells you, "If anyone is in Christ, he is a new creation; the old has gone, the new has come!" (2 Corinthians 5:17, NIV). Your former desires do not need to hold you any longer. Your former actions do not need to define your marriage.

God's work in you is a process. He is continually creating you to be more like Him. Use this time in your life to open yourself to how God wants to mold and shape you (Isaiah 64:8). Though you strayed from God in the past, He can still hold your future. Forgive yourself and move forward!

*For other helpful categories, see pages 136, 171, 174, 196, 269, 340.*

| | |
|---|---|
| Psalm 51:1, NIV | Have mercy on me, O God, according to your unfailing love; according to your great compassion blot out my transgressions. |
| Psalm 130:3-4, NIV | If you, O LORD, kept a record of sins, O LORD, who could stand? But with you there is forgiveness; therefore you are feared. |
| Isaiah 1:18, NIV | Though your sins are like scarlet, they shall be as white as snow; though they are red as crimson, they shall be like wool. |
| Isaiah 43:25, NIV | I, even I, am he who blots out your transgressions, for my own sake, and remembers your sins no more. |
| Isaiah 64:8, NKJV | But now, O LORD, You are our Father; we are the clay, and You our potter; and all we are the work of Your hand. |
| Daniel 9:9, NLT | The LORD our God is merciful and forgiving, even though we have rebelled against him. |
| Joel 2:25, KJV | I will restore to you the years that the locust hath eaten. |
| Romans 6:14, NIV | Sin shall not be your master, because you are not under law, but under grace. |
| 2 Corinthians 5:17, NIV | If anyone is in Christ, he is a new creation; the old has gone, the new has come! |

| | |
|---|---|
| Galatians 6:1, NIV | If someone is caught in a sin, you who are spiritual should restore him gently. But watch yourself, or you also may be tempted. |
| Ephesians 1:7, NIV | In him we have redemption through his blood, the forgiveness of sins, in accordance with the riches of God's grace. |
| 1 John 1:9, NKJV | If we confess our sins, He is faithful and just to forgive us our sins and to cleanse us from all unrighteousness. |
| Revelation 21:5, KJV | Behold, I make all things new. |

# ADULTERY—
# HEALING AFTER ADULTERY

The book of Hosea in the Bible is built around the commitment a husband has for a wife who left him for other men. Yet the husband loves his wife, just as God loves you and your spouse. God is not giving up on you. He is not giving up on your marriage.

How do you rebuild a marriage after the devastation of adultery? By first realizing that your relationship *can be* rebuilt—if you are both willing to work at rebuilding it.

Instead of turning away from you, God is calling you to a new commitment—to each other and to Him. He promises to "make the Valley of [Trouble] a door of hope" (Hosea 2:15, NIV). In other words, your struggle can become something *hopeful.* Your relationship can be a reminder to yourself and others of the healing God can bring about.

You and your spouse have the opportunity to demonstrate God's unconditional love to each other, to give and receive grace. Come stand on God's Word for healing and wholeness. Watch God lead you through the door of hope.

*For other helpful categories, see pages 13, 144, 171, 174, 196, 207, 223, 269, 311, 340.*

Joshua 1:8, NKJV

This Book of the Law shall not depart from your mouth, but you shall meditate in it day and night, that you may observe to do according to all that is written in it. For then you will make your way prosperous, and then you will have good success.

2 Chronicles 7:14, NIV

If my people, who are called by my name, will humble themselves and pray and seek my face and turn from their wicked ways, then will I hear from heaven and will forgive their sin and will heal their land.

Psalm 46:1, NIV

God is our refuge and strength, an ever-present help in trouble.

Psalm 147:3, NIV

He heals the brokenhearted and binds up their wounds.

Proverbs 2:6-7, NKJV

For the LORD gives wisdom; from His mouth come knowledge and understanding; He stores up sound wisdom for the upright; He is a shield to those who walk uprightly.

Song of Songs 7:10, NIV

I belong to my lover, and his desire is for me.

Hosea 2:15, NIV

There I will give her back her vineyards, and will make the Valley of Achor a door of hope. There she will sing as in the days of her youth.

Hosea 3:1, NIV

The LORD said to me, "Go, show your love to your wife again, though she is loved by another and is an adulteress. Love her as the LORD loves the Israelites, though they turn to other gods and love the sacred raisin cakes."

| | |
|---|---|
| Matthew 5:43-45, NIV | You have heard that it was said, "Love your neighbor and hate your enemy." But I tell you: Love your enemies and pray for those who persecute you, that you may be sons of your Father in heaven. |
| Romans 5:8, NIV | God demonstrates his own love for us in this: While we were still sinners, Christ died for us. |
| 1 Corinthians 13:7-8, NLT | Love never gives up, never loses faith, is always hopeful, and endures through every circumstance. Love never fails. |
| Ephesians 4:32, NIV | Be kind and compassionate to one another, forgiving each other, just as in Christ God forgave you. |
| Philippians 4:19, NIV | My God will meet all your needs according to his glorious riches in Christ Jesus. |
| Hebrews 4:13, NLT | Nothing in all creation is hidden from God. Everything is naked and exposed before his eyes, and he is the one to whom we are accountable. |
| Hebrews 8:12, NLT | I will forgive their wickedness, and I will never again remember their sins. |
| 1 Peter 5:5, NIV | All of you, clothe yourselves with humility toward one another, because, "God opposes the proud but gives grace to the humble." |

# Aging—
## Strength for the Elderly

If you are older, you might resist being called "elderly"—after all, you are the same person you have always been! The labels of our culture can be limiting. In fact, the Bible reveals a view of the elderly that is dramatically at odds with the dominant attitude of our culture. In God's perspective, older men and women are of great value and are worthy of much honor.

Whatever age you are, you are made in the image of God and therefore important to Him (Genesis 1:27). The image of God doesn't fade in you as you age, and neither does your dignity as God's special creation.

If you are a widow, be comforted with the words of Timothy: "Now she who is a widow indeed and who has been left alone, has fixed her hope on God and continues in entreaties and prayers night and day" (1 Timothy 5:5, NASB). God is aware of you and continues to call you to His side.

Whatever your circumstances, the Bible associates your age with wisdom. As the book of Job tells us, "Wisdom is with aged men, and with length of days, understanding" (Job 12:12, NKJV). Although time may take away some of your physical capabilities, as you age, you gain a more thoughtful understanding of the ways of God and life.

Don't trust in what our culture says about the elderly. Trust in what the Word says. Remind God of His promise of wisdom and pray for opportunities to share your words and experience with others. Your hope for eternity gives you youth in your spirit, even if your body doesn't reflect it. Look to God as your source of strength as you age gracefully under His loving care.

*For other helpful categories, see pages 13, 84, 207, 226, 230, 263, 375, 434.*

| | |
|---|---|
| Genesis 1:27, NKJV | God created man in His own image; in the image of God He created him; male and female He created them. |
| Deuteronomy 31:6, NKJV | Be strong and of good courage, do not fear nor be afraid of them; for the LORD your God, He is the One who goes with you. He will not leave you nor forsake you. |
| Job 12:12, NKJV | Wisdom is with aged men, and with length of days, understanding. |
| Psalm 68:6, NIV | God sets the lonely in families. |
| Psalm 68:19, NIV | Praise be to the Lord, to God our Savior, who daily bears our burdens. |
| Psalm 71:18, NIV | Even when I am old and gray, do not forsake me, O God, till I declare your power to the next generation, your might to all who are to come. |
| Psalm 112:7, NIV | They will have no fear of bad news; his heart is steadfast, trusting in the LORD. |
| Psalm 138:7, NIV | Though I walk in the midst of trouble, you preserve my life; you stretch out your hand against the anger of my foes, with your right hand you save me. |
| Psalm 146:8, CEV | He heals blind eyes. He gives a helping hand to everyone who falls. The LORD loves good people. |

| | |
|---|---|
| Proverbs 3:24, NIV | When you lie down, you will not be afraid; when you lie down, your sleep will be sweet. |
| Proverbs 13:22, NIV | A good man leaves an inheritance for his children's children, but a sinner's wealth is stored up for the righteous. |
| Proverbs 16:31, NKJV | The silver-haired head is a crown of glory, if it is found in the way of righteousness. |
| Isaiah 40:29, NIV | He gives strength to the weary and increases the power of the weak. |
| Isaiah 46:4, NIV | Even to your old age and gray hairs I am he, I am he who will sustain you. I have made you and I will carry you; I will sustain you and I will rescue you. |
| Jeremiah 30:17, NKJV | "I will restore health to you and heal you of your wounds," says the LORD. |
| John 11:25-26, NKJV | Jesus said to her, "I am the resurrection and the life. He who believes in Me, though he may die, he shall live. And whoever lives and believes in Me shall never die. Do you believe this?" |
| Acts 2:17, NIV | "In the last days," God says, "I will pour out my Spirit on all people. Your sons and daughters will prophesy, your young men will see visions, your old men will dream dreams." |

# Aging—Caring
## for Someone Who Is Elderly

The Bible gives a different perspective on the elderly than our culture does. They are not a burden on society—they are a treasure!

The Bible is also realistic about the physical challenges of old age. The latter stage of life can be a time of failing eyesight (Genesis 27:1), failing feet (1 Kings 15:23), and declining overall bodily health (1 Kings 1:1).

It's not easy to grow old. And it's not easy to take care of people who are older. But it is still a privilege.

If you're a caregiver for someone who is elderly, perhaps a parent, then know that God will reward your hard, repetitive labor. You're doing godly work by honoring your elders. The Lord won't overlook it.

Scripture says that God gives strength, patience, and endurance to those who ask for it (Isaiah 40:29). Believe it, and He will.

*For other helpful categories, see pages 144, 180, 314, 411, 428.*

Genesis 27:1, NKJV — Isaac was old and his eyes were so dim that he could not see.

Leviticus 19:32, NCV — Show respect to old people; stand up in their presence. Show respect also to your God. I am the LORD.

1 Kings 1:1, NKJV — Now King David was old, advanced in years; and they put covers on him, but he could not get warm.

Psalm 40:1, NCV — I waited patiently for the LORD; he turned to me and heard my cry.

Psalm 68:19, NIV — Praise be to the Lord, to God our Savior, who daily bears our burdens.

Psalm 121:1-2, ESV — I lift up my eyes to the hills. From where does my help come? My help comes from the LORD, who made heaven and earth.

Proverbs 21:13, NLT — Those who shut their ears to the cries of the poor will be ignored in their own time of need.

Isaiah 40:29, NKJV — He gives power to the weak, and to those who have no might He increases strength.

Matthew 11:28-29, NCV — Come to me, all of you who are tired and have heavy loads, and I will give you rest. Accept my teachings and learn from me, because I am gentle and humble in spirit, and you will find rest for your lives.

| | |
|---|---|
| Mark 10:45, NIV | The Son of Man did not come to be served, but to serve, and to give his life as a ransom for many. |
| John 15:13, ESV | Greater love has no one than this, that someone lay down his life for his friends. |
| Philippians 2:13, NASB | For it is God who is at work in you, both to will and to work for His good pleasure. |
| 1 Timothy 5:1-2, NLT | Never speak harshly to an older man, but appeal to him respectfully as you would to your own father. |
| 1 Timothy 5:4, CEV | If a widow has children or grandchildren, they should learn to serve God by taking care of her, as she once took care of them. This is what God wants them to do. |
| 1 Timothy 5:8, NCV | Whoever does not care for his own relatives, especially his own family members, has turned against the faith and is worse than someone who does not believe in God. |

# ANGER

Anger is not sin in itself. What determines whether our anger will become sin or not is what we do with it. Jesus got angry, yet he "knew no sin" (2 Corinthians 5:21, NKJV).

The danger appears when anger becomes a stronghold in your life. Is anger your first reaction to a difficult situation? Are you always justifying your anger to yourself and others? Has anger become a way of life? In that case, your anger is probably a mask for pride. It stems from an attitude of "I deserve better than this."

Anger at its best is a *signal* to you that something needs to be addressed in your heart. It should never be the end result.

Chronic anger reveals a lack of faith that God is in control—and you're not. If anger has taken over your thoughts and words, you might have trouble seeing this truth. As God's Word says, "Anger will not help you live the right kind of life God wants" (James 1:20, NCV).

This is why it's so important to turn to Scripture. Scripture can speak truth to your soul when anger overwhelms you. God's Word will help you move past your anger before it turns into a downward spiral of unforgiveness and resentment. Take time to renew your mind with His Word and let His Sprit renew your thoughts and attitudes (Ephesians 4:23).

We read in Ephesians, "Be angry, and do not sin" (Ephesians 4:26, NKJV). God's truth can help us see the purpose in our anger—and keep anger from leading us into sin.

*For other helpful categories, see pages 13, 153, 174, 180, 289, 311, 428.*

| | |
|---|---|
| Psalm 37:8, NIV | Refrain from anger and turn from wrath; do not fret—it leads only to evil. |
| Psalm 103:8, NIV | The LORD is compassionate and gracious, slow to anger, abounding in love. |
| Proverbs 15:1, NCV | A gentle answer will calm a person's anger, but an unkind answer will cause more anger. |
| Proverbs 16:32, NCV | Patience is better than strength. Controlling your temper is better than capturing a city. |
| Proverbs 19:11, AMP | Good sense makes a man restrain his anger, and it is his glory to overlook a transgression or an offense. |
| Proverbs 21:19, NKJV | Better to dwell in the wilderness, than with a contentious and angry woman. |
| Proverbs 22:24, NIV | Do not make friends with a hot-tempered man, do not associate with one easily angered. |
| Proverbs 25:28, NCV | Those who do not control themselves are like a city whose walls are broken down. |
| Proverbs 29:22, NASB | An angry man stirs up strife, and a hot-tempered man abounds in transgression. |
| Ecclesiastes 7:9, NLT | Control your temper, for anger labels you a fool. |
| 2 Corinthians 5:21, NKJV | He made Him who knew no sin to be sin for us, that we might become the righteousness of God in Him. |

| | |
|---|---|
| Ephesians 4:23, NLT | Let the Spirit renew your thoughts and attitudes. |
| Ephesians 4:26-27, NKJV | Be angry, and do not sin. Do not let the sun go down on your wrath, nor give place to the devil. |
| Ephesians 4:31, NKJV | Let all bitterness, wrath, anger, clamor, and evil speaking be put away from you, with all malice. |
| James 1:19-20, NCV | My dear brothers and sisters, always be willing to listen and slow to speak. Do not become angry easily, because anger will not help you live the right kind of life God wants. |

# ANIMALS AND PETS

God loves the animals He created. Throughout Scripture, God shows us that animals matter to Him.

At the beginning of the world, God created the whole animal kingdom and called it good (Genesis 1:20-25). Psalm 36:6 tells us that God cares for animals! Scripture also shows God's love and care for animals through Noah at the time of the Flood; Noah was specifically commanded to save the animals from harm (Genesis 6 and 7).

Animal companions can become a part of our family. We love our pets, and for good reason—they are a source of comfort and companionship offering unconditional love and acceptance.

Most children view their pets as the best of friends. A family pet is often one of the first introductions a child has to nurturing another living being. Learning how to think about the pet's needs and feelings is a good way for children to get invaluable training in learning to treat people with kindness. If a pet dies, the grieving process can help children learn how to cope with other losses throughout life. Being sensitive to their pain will help them heal as they learn to cope with this difficult loss.

Even for adults, losing a pet for whatever reason can be like losing a family member. If your pet is lost or sick, remember that prayer can make a difference in the outcome of that situation. Praying God's Word is powerful. It doesn't matter whether you are praying for a pet or a person—God wants you to know that He cares about everything that concerns you. He wants you to put your faith and trust in His Word.

*For other helpful categories, see pages 118, 196, 223, 428.*

Genesis 1:25, NCV

So God made the wild animals, the tame animals, and all the small crawling animals to produce more of their own kind. God saw that this was good.

Genesis 6:19-20, NIV

You are to bring into the ark two of all living creatures, male and female, to keep them alive with you. Two of every kind of bird, of every kind of animal and of every kind of creature that moves along the ground will come to you to be kept alive.

Genesis 7:2-3, NLT

Take with you seven pairs—male and female—of each animal I have approved for eating and for sacrifice, and take one pair of each of the others. Also take seven pairs of every kind of bird. There must be a male and a female in each pair to en-sure that all life will survive on the earth after the flood.

Psalm 36:6, NKJV

Your righteousness is like the great moun-tains; Your judgments are a great deep; O LORD, You preserve man and beast.

Psalm 50:10-11, ESV

Every beast of the forest is Mine, the cattle on a thousand hills. I know all the birds of the hills, and all that moves in the field is mine.

Proverbs 12:10, NIV

A righteous man cares for the needs of his animal, but the kindest acts of the wicked are cruel.

Proverbs 27:23, NKJV

Be diligent to know the state of your flocks, and attend to your herds.

| | |
|---|---|
| Ecclesiastes 3:19-20, NKJV | What happens to the sons of men also happens to animals; one thing befalls them: as one dies, so dies the other. Surely, they all have one breath; man has no advantage over animals, for all is vanity. All go to one place: all are from the dust, and all return to dust. |
| Matthew 6:26, NIV | Look at the birds of the air; they do not sow or reap or store away in barns, and yet your heavenly Father feeds them. |
| Matthew 10:29, NIV | Are not two sparrows sold for a penny? Yet not one of them will fall to the ground apart from the will of your Father. |
| Revelation 5:13, NKJV | Every creature which is in heaven and on the earth and under the earth and such as are in the sea, and all that are in them, I heard saying: "Blessing and honor and glory and power be to Him who sits on the throne, and to the Lamb, forever and ever!" |
| Revelation 19:11, NKJV | I saw heaven opened, and behold, a white horse. And He who sat on him was called Faithful and True. |

# ANOINTING

The title *Christ* means "Anointed One." Just as Jesus was filled by the Holy Spirit, so are we filled by the Holy Spirit. This anointing is a divine enablement for you to accomplish God's unique purposes for you on earth.

Some are called into full-time ministry and others are not. Some are called to the service industry and some are called into the medical community. No matter what God has destined for you to do in life, your anointing empowers you for that specific task.

Whatever your vocation, your anointing means you are to do what Jesus did (1 John 2:20). Scripture says of Jesus: "The Spirit of the Sovereign LORD is on me, because the LORD has anointed me to preach good news to the poor. He has sent me to bind up the brokenhearted, to proclaim freedom for the captives and release from darkness for the prisoners" (Isaiah 61:1 and Luke 4:18, NIV).

Ask God for a revelation of the power you already have through Christ. Look for opportunities all around you to "preach good news to the poor" and "bind up the brokenhearted" because you are anointed already. What a privilege it is to be able to continue Christ's work on earth! It is the greatest calling you will ever know.

*For other helpful categories, see pages 13, 65, 88, 239, 257, 384.*

| | |
|---|---|
| Exodus 40:15, NIV | Anoint them just as you anointed their father, so they may serve me as priests. Their anointing will be to a priesthood that will continue for all generations to come. |
| Psalm 20:6, NKJV | I know that the LORD saves his anointed; He will answer him from His holy heaven with the saving strength of His right hand. |
| Psalm 84:9, NIV | Look upon our shield, O God; look with favor on your anointed one. |
| Isaiah 10:27, NKJV | It shall come to pass in that day that their burden will be taken away from your shoulder, and his yoke from your neck, and the yoke will be destroyed because of the anointing oil. |
| Isaiah 61:1, NIV | The Spirit of the Sovereign LORD is on me, because the LORD has anointed me to preach good news to the poor. He has sent me to bind up the brokenhearted, to proclaim freedom for the captives and release from darkness for the prisoners. |
| Mark 6:13, NKJV | They cast out many demons, and anointed with oil many who were sick, and healed them. |
| Acts 10:38, NKJV | God anointed Jesus of Nazareth with the Holy Spirit and with power, who went about doing good and healing all who were oppressed by the devil, for God was with Him. |

2 Corinthians 1:21-22, NIV   It is God who makes both us and you stand firm in Christ. He anointed us and set his seal of ownership on us.

1 John 2:20, NIV   You have an anointing from the Holy One, and all of you know the truth.

1 John 2:27, NIV   As for you, the anointing you received from him remains in you, and you do not need anyone to teach you. But as his anointing teaches you about all things and as that anointing is real, not counterfeit—just as it has taught you, remain in him.

# Anxiety and Worry

God wants you to live a life of peace, joy, and confidence. Even if worry and anxiety are deeply ingrained habits in your life, you *can* overcome them. Every small decision you make not to worry strengthens your ability to follow the unchanging wisdom of God's Word.

Worry leads to an unproductive life. As Jesus said, "Who of you by worrying can add a single hour to his life?" (Luke 12:25, NIV). Not only do the majority of things you worry about never happen, but also worry robs you of life-giving faith. It is like a poison that seeps into your thoughts and keeps you from seeing God's purpose because you are so concerned about what may or may not happen tomorrow.

When circumstances are dire, it might seem strange *not* to worry about something. But God offers a "peace which surpasses all understanding" (Philippians 4:7, NKJV). The more you receive that peace, the more you will see how pointless worry is and how powerful God's truth is. It may be "beyond understanding" to the world, but as God changes your heart, worry will have no place in your life.

*For other helpful categories, see pages 13, 132, 153, 180, 218, 236, 311.*

Psalm 86:7, NKJV

In the day of my trouble I will call upon You, for You will answer me.

Psalm 94:19, NIV

When anxiety was great within me, your consolation brought joy to my soul.

Psalm 107:28-30, NIV

They cried out to the LORD in their trouble, and he brought them out of their distress. He stilled the storm to a whisper; the waves of the sea were hushed. They were glad when it grew calm, and he guided them to their desired haven.

Matthew 6:27, NIV

Who of you by worrying can add a single hour to his life?

Matthew 6:28-29, NCV

Why do you worry about clothes? Look at how the lilies in the field grow. They don't work or make clothes for themselves. But I tell that even Solomon with all his riches was not dressed as beautifully as one of these flowers.

Matthew 6:31-33, NIV

Do not worry, saying, "What shall we eat?" or "What shall we drink?" or "What shall we wear?" For the pagans run after all these things, and your heavenly Father knows that you need them. But seek first his kingdom and his righteousness, and all these things will be given to you as well.

Matthew 6:34, NIV

Do not worry about tomorrow, for tomorrow will worry about itself. Each day has enough trouble of its own.

| | |
|---|---|
| Matthew 28:20, NKJV | I am with you always, even to the end of the age. |
| John 14:1, NIV | Do not let your hearts be troubled. Trust in God; trust also in me. |
| Philippians 4:6-7, NKJV | Be anxious for nothing, but in everything by prayer and supplication, with thanksgiving, let your requests be made known to God; and the peace of God, which surpasses all understanding, will guard your hearts and minds through Christ Jesus. |
| 1 Peter 5:7, NIV | Cast all your anxiety on him because he cares for you. |

# THE AUTHORITY OF THE BELIEVER

As an ambassador of Christ (2 Corinthians 5:20), you continue the work of Christ. As Jesus said, "these signs will follow those who believe: In My name they will cast out demons; they will speak with new tongues; they will take up serpents; and if they drink anything deadly, it will by no means hurt them; they will lay hands on the sick, and they will recover" (Mark 16:17-18, NKJV).

Satan once had authority, but Jesus gave it back to the church (Colossians 2:15). That means you have the authority of God over Satan. Your authority over Satan is directly associated with the wisdom and revelation of the Word of God that is in you. The stronger the Word of God in you, the stronger your authority over the enemy. So immerse yourself in Scripture—the devil needs to know that *you* know that you have been given all authority over him!

Remember that authority is yours whether you feel like you've got it or not. But you must believe you have it in order to exercise it. You might be waiting on God to do something in your life, when He's waiting on you to exercise the authority that He has given to you.

Jesus said, "I tell you the truth, whatever you forbid on earth will be forbidden in heaven, and whatever you permit on earth will be permitted in heaven" (Matthew 18:18, NLT). The Word of God and the Holy Spirit will help you to operate in your authority. Ask for God's leading to quicken your spirit to know specific Scriptures to speak and specific ways to pray. The devil is no match for Christ in you!

*For other helpful categories, see pages 13, 199, 343, 346, 395, 398.*

Proverbs 29:2, NKJV        When the righteous are in authority, the people
                           rejoice; but when a wicked man rules, the people
                           groan.

Matthew 10:1, NCV          Jesus called his twelve followers together and gave
                           them authority to drive out evil spirits and to heal
                           every kind of disease and sickness.

Matthew 12:29, NKJV        How can one enter a strong man's house and
                           plunder his goods, unless he first binds the strong
                           man? And then he will plunder his house.

Matthew 16:19, NKJV        I will give you the keys of the kingdom of heaven,
                           and whatever you bind on earth will be bound in
                           heaven, and whatever you loose on earth will be
                           loosed in heaven.

Mark 11:22-23, NIV         "Have faith in God," Jesus answered. "I tell you
                           the truth, if anyone says to this mountain, 'Go,
                           throw yourself into the sea,' and does not doubt
                           in his heart but believes that what he says will
                           happen, it will be done for him."

Mark 16:17-18, NKJV        These signs will follow those who believe: In My
                           name they will cast out demons; they will speak
                           with new tongues; they will take up serpents; and
                           if they drink anything deadly, it will by no means
                           hurt them; they will lay hands on the sick, and
                           they will recover.

Luke 10:19, NIV            I have given you authority to trample on snakes
                           and scorpions and to overcome all the power of
                           the enemy; nothing will harm you.

Acts 1:8, NIV

You will receive power when the Holy Spirit comes on you; and you will be my witnesses in Jerusalem, and in all Judea and Samaria, and to the ends of the earth.

Ephesians 1:21-22, NCV

God has put Christ over all rulers, authorities, powers, and kings, and every title that can be given, not only in this world but also in the next. God put everything under his power and made him the head over everything for the church.

Ephesians 2:6, NCV

He raised us up with Christ and gave us a seat with him in the heavens. He did this for those in Christ Jesus.

Colossians 2:10, NIV

You have been given fullness in Christ, who is the head over every power and authority.

James 4:7, NIV

Submit yourselves, then, to God. Resist the devil, and he will flee from you.

# BODY PIERCING AND TATTOOS

Many Christians today are getting tattoos and excessive body piercing. Does the Bible give specific instructions when it comes to body piercing and tattoos? On the following pages are Scriptures related to this subject. As you read God's Scriptures and meditate on them, ask Him to speak to your heart concerning your decision. Jesus tells us, "My sheep hear My voice, and I know them, and they follow Me" (John 10:27, NKJV).

God's desire is to set His people apart from worldly cultures and practices. Cut off practices that keep you tied to the old life. "You are a chosen generation, a royal priesthood, a holy nation, His own special people, that you may proclaim the praises of Him who called you out of darkness into His marvelous light" (1 Peter 2:9, NKJV). We are to reflect God's glory in body, mind, and spirit. Remember also that your physical appearance gives an impression of God to people who can't see Him.

If you're wondering if you should get a tattoo or piercing, ask yourself: *Am I glorifying God in this decision? Will my piercing or tattoo cause conflict with my loved ones and my church? Will my piercing or tattoo cause someone who is spiritually weak to stumble and question the Christian faith?*

We often base our moral judgments on opinions and personal preferences rather than on the Word of God. Our focus should be on being an effective witness for Christ and bringing glory to our great and awesome God! Examine your heart. Does it reflect what the Word says and want what God wants?

*For other helpful categories, see pages 13, 193–196, 437, 441.*

| | |
|---|---|
| Leviticus 19:28, NIV | Do not cut your bodies for the dead or put tattoo marks on yourselves. I am the LORD. |
| Deuteronomy 14:1, NKJV | You are the children of the LORD your God; you shall not cut yourselves nor shave the front of your head for the dead. |
| John 10:27, NKJV | My sheep hear My voice, and I know them, and they follow Me. |
| John 17:16-17, NKJV | They are not of the world, just as I am not of the world. Sanctify them by Your truth. Your word is truth. |
| 1 Corinthians 10:31, NIV | Whether you eat or drink or whatever you do, do it all for the glory of God. |
| 2 Corinthians 6:14, NCV | You are not the same as those who do not believe. So do not join yourselves to them. Good and bad do not belong together. Light and darkness cannot share together. |
| 2 Corinthians 7:1, NKJV | Having [God's] promises, beloved, let us cleanse ourselves from all filthiness of the flesh and spirit, perfecting holiness in the fear of God. |
| Galatians 1:10, NCV | Do you think I am trying to make people accept me? No, God is the One I am trying to please. Am I trying to please people? If I still wanted to please people, I would not be a servant of Christ. |

| | |
|---|---|
| 2 Timothy 2:15, NKJV | Be diligent to present yourself approved to God, a worker who does not need to be ashamed, rightly dividing the word of truth. |
| Hebrews 12:14, NKJV | Pursue peace with all people, and holiness, without which no one will see the Lord. |
| 1 Peter 1:14-16, NCV | Now that you are obedient children of God do not live as you did in the past. You did not understand, so you did the evil things you wanted. But be holy in all you do, just as God, the One who called you, is holy. It is written in the Scriptures: "You must be holy, because I am holy." |
| 1 Peter 2:9, NKJV | You are a chosen generation, a royal priesthood, a holy nation, His own special people, that you may proclaim the praises of Him who called you out of darkness into His marvelous light. |

# BUSINESS AND WORK—
# BEGINNING A BUSINESS

Building a business is about more than economic viability and profit. It's also about reaching and influencing your world for Christ.

As a Christian business owner, you have a mandate from God to reach the world with the love and healing power of Jesus Christ. There are those who will never go inside a church or seek out a loving and caring God, but they will notice a business owner who acts with kindness and integrity. Jesus tells us, "Let your light so shine before men, that they may see your good works and glorify your Father in heaven" (Matthew 5:16, NKJV).

It takes wisdom to build a successful business. God has given you that tool in His Word. Seeking God's wisdom through the Scriptures will give you faith to take the next step if it is God's direction. This is what Jesus meant when He said that a wise person builds his house upon the rock of God's Word (Matthew 7:24).

God's Word reminds us that God is ultimately in charge of our work. The business you are building can reflect *His* craftsmanship, whether it is directly related to a "ministry" or not. The purpose of your life is to minister to others, using the gifts God has given you. When you remember this goal, you will be free to allow God to build your business for eternal purposes.

*For other helpful categories, see pages 150, 156, 160, 164, 368, 428, 437.*

| | |
|---|---|
| Deuteronomy 8:18, NIV | Remember the LORD your God, for it is he who gives you the ability to produce wealth, and so confirms his covenant, which he swore to your forefathers, as it is today. |
| Joshua 1:8, NKJV | This Book of the Law shall not depart from your mouth, but you shall meditate in it day and night, that you may observe to do according to all that is written in it. For then you will make your way prosperous, and then you will have good success. |
| Psalm 37:4-5, CEV | Do what the LORD wants, and he will give you your heart's desire. Let the LORD lead you and trust him to help. |
| Psalm 62:10, NLT | Don't make your living by extortion or put your hope in stealing. And if your wealth increases, don't make it the center of your life. |
| Psalm 90:17, NIV | May the favor of the Lord our God rest upon us; establish the work of our hands for us—yes, establish the work of our hands. |
| Psalm 127:1, NKJV | Unless the LORD builds the house, they labor in vain who build it; unless the LORD guards the city, the watchman stays awake in vain. |
| Proverbs 24:27, NKJV | Prepare your outside work, make it fit for yourself in the field; and afterward build your house. |
| Malachi 3:10, NCV | "Bring to the storehouse a full tenth of what you earn so there will be food in my house. Test me in |

this," says the LORD All-Powerful. "I will open the windows of heaven for you and pour out all the blessings you need."

Matthew 7:24-25, NKJV

Whoever hears these sayings of Mine, and does them, I will liken him to a wise man who built his house on the rock: and the rain descended, and the floods came, and the winds blew and beat on that house; and it did not fall, for it was founded on the rock.

Luke 14:28-30, NKJV

For which of you, intending to build a tower, does not sit down first and count the cost, whether he has enough to finish it—lest, after he has laid the foundation, and is not able to finish, all who see it begin to mock him, saying, "This man began to build and was not able to finish"?

Ephesians 3:20, NIV

Now to him who is able to do immeasurably more than all we ask or imagine, according to his power that is at work within us.

Hebrews 13:5, NCV

Keep your lives free from the love of money, and be satisfied with what you have. God has said, "I will never leave you; I will never abandon you."

James 1:5, NIV

If any of you lacks wisdom, he should ask God, who gives generously to all without finding fault, and it will be given to him.

# Business and Work—
# Losing a Business

Whether your business is a few months old or a tradition of generations, if you are closing your doors, you are probably asking, *Is this the right thing to do?* And even, *What did I do wrong? Does this mean I didn't hear God right?*

God's Word reminds us of the difference between our idea of success and failure and God's. Don't measure success the way the world measures success—by the amount of things you possess. Success as measured by God involves obedience and faithfulness. You can be successful by this world's standards and still miss the true purpose for which God created you.

As a business leader or entrepreneur, you had goals in mind for your work. You had a vision for what your company would look like and produce. God gave you gifts to develop that vision, and He is intimately concerned about the details of your work, but He is even more concerned about you.

How have your business ventures—or failures—brought you closer to God? How can you use this time to draw others to Him? Perhaps you believed you were following God in every decision. It's hard to see others thriving financially even though they did not follow God. But God has greater purposes in mind. You may discover them in this life or in eternity.

As you let go of one dream, ask God to give you a new vision for His dream for you. It will be more than you ever imagined. "Trust the LORD with all your heart, and don't depend on your own understanding. Remember the LORD in all you do, and he will give you success" (Proverbs 3:5-6, NCV).

*For other helpful categories, see pages 9, 109, 153, 168, 223, 236, 289, 329, 381.*

Psalm 25:2, NLT

I trust in you, my God! Do not let me be disgraced, or let my enemies rejoice in my defeat.

Psalm 34:5, CEV

Keep your eyes on the Lord! You will shine like the sun and never blush with shame.

Psalm 34:10, NIV

The lions may grow weak and hungry, but those who seek the LORD lack no good thing.

Psalm 46:1-2, NKJV

God is our refuge and strength, a very present help in time of trouble. Therefore we will not fear, even though the earth be removed, and though the mountains be carried into the midst of the sea.

Psalm 84:11-12, NKJV

The LORD God is a sun and shield; the LORD will give grace and glory; no good thing will He withhold from those who walk uprightly. O LORD of hosts, blessed is the man who trusts in You.

Proverbs 4:20-22, NKJV

Give attention to my words; incline your ear to my sayings. Do not let them depart from your eyes; keep them in the midst of your heart; for they are life to those who find them, and health to all their flesh.

Jeremiah 32:27, NKJV

Behold, I am the LORD, the God of all flesh. Is there anything too hard for Me?

Matthew 6:31-32, NLT

Don't worry about all these things, saying, "What will we eat? What will we drink? "What will we wear?" These things dominate the thoughts of unbelievers, but your heavenly Father already knows your needs.

| | |
|---|---|
| John 10:10, NIV | The thief comes only to steal and kill and destroy; I have come that they may have life, and have it to the full. |
| John 16:33, NKJV | These things I have spoken to you, that in Me you may have peace. In the world you will have tribulation; but be of good cheer, I have overcome the world. |
| Romans 8:28, NKJV | We know that all things work together for good to those who love God, to those who are the called according to His purpose. |
| 2 Corinthians 12:9, NKJV | But he said to me, "My grace is sufficient for you, for My strength is made perfect in weakness." |
| 1 Peter 5:7, NKJV | Cast all your cares upon Him; for He cares for you. |

# Business and Work—
# Unemployment and Job Searching

If you are an unemployed worker facing another day, this day can and will be different. Today, you are one day closer to that job!

Look to the promises of God. It is God's will for you, not only to pay your bills on time, but also to prosper to the point of being a blessing to others. Choose to keep this attitude of faith and expectancy.

Ask God to send you to a place where you can serve others and be a light for those who need help, a job that will allow you to use your God-given talents and abilities. Ask Him to open the door that no person can close (Revelation 3:8).

Remember that God knows your needs before you ask Him (Matthew 6:8). Matthew 7:7 says, "Ask, and it will be given to you; seek, and you will find; knock, and it will be opened to you" (NKJV). He said those who are obedient to His Word will eat the good of the land (Isaiah 1:19).

While you are looking and waiting for a door of opportunity to open, find a place where you can offer your talents for a few hours a week. Get involved with helping others when you're in need. Plant seeds of faith in others—and watch God do a miracle for you!

Remember that being anxious will block the blessings of God because fear is the opposite of faith. Faith is what pleases God (Hebrews 11:6). "Be anxious for nothing, but in everything by prayer and supplication with thanksgiving let your requests be made known to God" (Philippians 4:6, NASB).

As you wait and search, watch what is coming out of your mouth! Even if the unemployment rate is high in your area, be careful to keep your words positive. You have God's favor on your life. Speak like it!

*For other helpful categories, see pages 62, 88, 153, 164, 289, 340, 445.*

| | |
|---|---|
| Genesis 6:8, NIV | Noah found favor in the eyes of the LORD. |
| Psalm 119:105, NIV | Your word is a lamp to my feet and a light for my path. |
| Proverbs 3:5-6, NIV | Trust in the LORD with all your heart and lean not on your own understanding; in all your ways acknowledge him, and he will make your paths straight. |
| Isaiah 1:19, NKJV | If you are willing and obedient, you shall eat the good of the land. |
| Jeremiah 29:11-14, NIV | "I know the plans I have for you," declares the LORD, "plans to prosper you and not to harm you, plans to give you hope and a future. Then you will call upon me and come and pray to me, and I will listen to you. You will seek me and find me when you seek me with all your heart. I will be found by you," declares the LORD. |
| Matthew 6:31-33, NCV | Don't worry and say, "What will we eat?" or "What will we drink?" or "What will we wear?" The people who don't know God keep trying to get these things, and your Father in heaven knows you need them. Seek first God's kingdom and what God wants. Then all your other needs will be met as well. |
| Matthew 7:7, NIV | Ask and it will be given to you; seek and you will find; knock and the door will be opened to you. |

Mark 11:24, NKJV

Whatever things you ask when you pray, believe that you receive them, and you will have them.

Romans 2:11, AMP

God shows no partiality [undue favor or unfairness; with Him one man is not different from another].

Romans 8:28, NKJV

We know that all things work together for good to those who love God, to those who are the called according to His purpose.

Philippians 4:6, NIV

Do not be anxious about anything, but in everything, by prayer and petition, with thanksgiving, present your requests to God.

Hebrews 4:15, NIV

We do not have a high priest who is unable to sympathize with our weaknesses, but we have one who has been tempted in every way, just as we are—yet was without sin.

Hebrews 11:6, NKJV

Without faith it is impossible to please Him, for he who comes to God must believe that He is, and that He is a rewarder of those who diligently seek Him.

Revelation 3:8, NIV

I know your deeds. See, I have placed before you an open door that no one can shut. I know that you have little strength, yet you have kept my word and have not denied my name.

# THE CHURCH

When you became a Christian, you became a part of the Church that Jesus referred to: "And I also say to you that you are Peter, and on this rock I will build My church, and the gates of Hades shall not prevail against it" (Matthew 16:18, NKJV).

Your pastor and church family are part of God's ultimate plan in your life to help you discover and fulfill your God-given destiny. It is important to understand that the gifts, talents, and anointing God has placed on your life are not only for you but also for the family of believers God has assigned you to.

That's why it's so important not to keep moving from one church family to another. When a tree is pulled up from its root system, the tree's growth is compromised. When a tree is transplanted and the conditions are right, the new soil and season will support such a move—but only after a period of adjustment. When a tree's roots are allowed to grow in one place, the tree is less likely to topple.

It's the same with a church. There are seasons when God will do something different in your life that requires a transplant. God does not assign you to different churches, however, because of offenses that come from others in the congregation or because of correction from your pastor. Prayerful and patient consideration should take place before you consider such a move.

As the Church, we are "to know the love of Christ which passes knowledge," so that we might reflect "all the fullness of God" (Ephesians 3:19, NKJV). The fullness of God is His light, love, wisdom, holiness, power, and glory. In other words, as a growing part of the Church body, we are reflecting Christ Himself—shining with the glory and radiance of God (John 17:23)!

*For other helpful categories, see pages 13, 59, 65, 136, 193, 196, 329, 378.*

Psalm 133:1, NKJV    Behold, how good and how pleasant it is for brethren to dwell together in unity!

Matthew 16:18, NKJV    I also say to you that you are Peter, and on this rock I will build My church, and the gates of Hades shall not prevail against it.

John 17:22-23, NIV    I have given them the glory that you gave me, that they may be one as we are one: I in them and you in me. May they be brought to complete unity to let the world know that you sent me and have loved them even as you have loved me.

Acts 2:46-47, NKJV    So continuing daily with one accord in the temple, and breaking bread from house to house, they ate their food with gladness and simplicity of heart, praising God and having favor with all the people. And the Lord added to the church daily those who were being saved.

Acts 12:5, NKJV    Peter was therefore kept in prison, but constant prayer was offered to God for him by the church.

1 Corinthians 1:10, NLT    I appeal to you, dear brothers and sisters, by the authority of our Lord Jesus Christ, to live in harmony with each other. Let there be no divisions in the church. Rather, be of one mind, united in thought and purpose.

1 Corinthians 7:17, NIV    Each one should retain the place in life that the Lord assigned to him and to which God has called him. This is the rule I lay down in all the churches.

| | |
|---|---|
| 1 Corinthians 10:32, NIV | Do not cause anyone to stumble, whether Jews, Greeks or the church of God. |
| 1 Corinthians 12:5, NKJV | There are differences of ministries, but the same Lord. |
| 1 Corinthians 12:28, NKJV | God has appointed these in the church: first apostles, second prophets, third teachers, after that miracles, then gifts of healings, helps, administrations, varieties of tongues. |
| Ephesians 1:22, NKJV | He put all things under his feet, and gave Him to be head over all things to the church. |
| Ephesians 2:21, NLT | We are carefully joined together in him, becoming a holy temple for the Lord. |
| Ephesians 3:10, NCV | His purpose was that through the church all the rulers and powers in the heavenly world will now know God's wisdom, which has so many forms. |
| Ephesians 3:19, NKJV | To know the love of Christ which passes knowledge; that you may be filled with all the fullness of God. |
| Ephesians 4:1-6, NIV | As a prisoner for the Lord, then, I urge you to live a life worthy of the calling you have received. Be completely humble and gentle; be patient, bearing with one another in love. Make every effort to keep the unity of the Spirit through the bond of peace. There is one body and one Spirit—just as you were called to one hope when you were called—one Lord, one faith, one baptism; one |

God and Father of all, who is over all and through all and in all.

Ephesians 4:16, NIV — From him the whole body, joined and held together by every supporting ligament, grows and builds itself up in love, as each part does its work.

Colossians 1:18, NLT — Christ is also the head of the church, which is his body. He is the beginning, supreme over all who rise from the dead. So he is first in everything.

1 Timothy 3:5, NCV — If someone does not know how to lead the family, how can that person take care of God's church?

Hebrews 3:6, NLT — Christ, as the Son, is in charge of God's entire house. And we are God's house, if we keep our courage and remain confident in our hope in Christ.

Revelation 2:11, NIV — He who has an ear, let him hear what the Spirit says to the churches. He who overcomes will not be hurt at all by the second death.

# Comfort for Those Who Grieve

God tells us in His Word that Christians do not "grieve like people who have no hope" (1 Thessalonians 4:13, NLT). God has given us the hope and joy of knowing that our loved ones are with Him. This does not mean that we will not miss our loved ones. God's Word tells us that even Jesus wept at the death of His friend Lazarus (John 11:35).

But the comfort and rest that we find for our souls comes through God's Word, which tells us it is better "to be absent from the body and to be present with the Lord" (2 Corinthians 5:8, NKJV). God also promises that "He will wipe away every tear from their eyes, and death shall be no more, neither shall there be mourning, nor crying, nor pain anymore, for the former things have passed away" (Revelation 21:4, ESV).

Don't let your circumstances determine your faith level. Even when you do not understand the circumstances that surround the death of your loved one, "have faith in God" (Mark 11:22, NASB). The spirit of grief is paralyzing without faith in God's purposes.

Because He knows what your pain is like, Christ desires to give you solace amid your grieving. "Peace I leave with you," He promises, "my peace I give to you. Not as the world gives do I give to you. Let not your hearts be troubled, neither let them be afraid" (John 14:27, ESV). This is a real peace from the Holy Spirit, who is able to do a deep and lasting work in your heart.

No matter the circumstances, as you seek God's comfort, with the psalmist you will be able to declare, "My flesh and my heart fail; but God is the strength of my heart and my portion forever" (Psalm 73:26, NKJV).

*For other helpful categories, see pages 180, 223, 226, 230, 311, 411, 434.*

| | |
|---|---|
| Deuteronomy 10:18, NIV | He defends the cause of the fatherless and the widow, and loves the alien, giving him food and clothing. |
| Job 1:22, NIV | In all this, Job did not sin by charging God with wrongdoing. |
| Psalm 27:14, NKJV | Wait on the LORD; be of good courage, and He shall strengthen your heart; wait, I say, on the LORD! |
| Psalm 43:5, NIV | Why are you downcast, O my soul? Why so disturbed within me? Put your hope in God, for I will yet praise him, my Savior and my God. |
| Psalm 68:5, NIV | A father to the fatherless, a defender of widows, is God in his holy dwelling. |
| Psalm 73:26, NKJV | My flesh and my heart fail; but God is the strength of my heart and my portion forever. |
| Psalm 116:15, NIV | Precious in the sight of the LORD is the death of his saints. |
| Psalm 138:3, NLT | As soon as I pray, you answer me; you encourage me by giving me strength. |
| Psalm 147:3, NIV | He heals the brokenhearted and binds up their wounds. |
| Isaiah 41:10, NIV | Do not fear, for I am with you; do not be dismayed, for I am your God. I will strengthen you |

|  | and help you; I will uphold you with my right-eous right hand. |
| Isaiah 57:18, NKJV | I have seen his ways, and will heal him; I will also lead him, and restore comforts to him and to his mourners. |
| Isaiah 66:13, NIV | As a mother comforts her child, so will I comfort you. |
| Matthew 5:4, NIV | Blessed are those who mourn, for they will be comforted. |
| Mark 11:22, NASB | Jesus answered saying to [his disciples], "Have faith in God." |
| John 5:28, NCV | Don't be surprised at this: A time is coming when all who are dead and in their graves will hear his voice. |
| John 14:27, ESV | Peace I leave with you; my peace I give to you. Not as the world gives do I give to you. Let not your hearts be troubled, neither let them be afraid. |
| Romans 8:28, NIV | We know that in all things God works for the good of those who love him, who have been called according to his purpose. |
| Romans 8:38-39, NIV | I am convinced that neither death nor life, neither angels nor demons, neither the present nor the future, nor any powers, neither height nor depth, nor anything else in all creation, will be able to |

separate us from the love of God that is in Christ Jesus our Lord.

| 2 Corinthians 5:8, NKJV | We are confident, yes, well pleased rather to be absent from the body and to be present with the Lord. |

| Ephesians 1:13-14, NIV | Having believed, you were marked in [Christ] with a seal, the promised Holy Spirit, who is a deposit guaranteeing our inheritance until the redemption of those who are God's possession—to the praise of his glory. |

| Philippians 1:21, NIV | For to me, to live is Christ and to die is gain. |

| Philippians 4:19, NKJV | My God shall supply all your need according to His riches in glory by Christ Jesus. |

| 1 Thessalonians 4:13, NLT | Dear brothers and sisters, we want you to know what will happen to the believers who have died so you will not grieve like people who have no hope. |

| 1 Timothy 5:5, NIV | The widow who is really in need and left all alone puts her hope in God and continues night and day to pray and to ask God for help. |

| 1 Peter 5:7, NIV | Cast all your anxiety on him because he cares for you. |

| Revelation 21:4, ESV | He will wipe away every tear from their eyes, and death shall be no more, neither shall there be mourning, nor crying, nor pain anymore, for the former things have passed away. |

# CONFIDENCE

Regardless of what lies before you, you can have confidence based on your relationship with God. The stronger your relationship with your Creator, the more confidence you will have to possess all that He has for you. Knowing who you are in Christ will enable you to see yourself from the right perspective, freeing you to be confident in your identity.

Self-confident people have qualities that everyone admires. Confidence is also an important ingredient for being successful. But for some, having the confidence to make new friends, teach a Sunday school class, or speak in a group setting can be grueling. The good news is that self-confidence can be learned.

When David the shepherd boy heard about the Philistine giant Goliath, he boldly declared, "your servant has killed both the lion and the bear; this uncircumcised Philistine will be like one of them.... The LORD who delivered me from the paw of the lion and the paw of the bear will deliver me from the hand of this Philistine" (1 Samuel 17:36-37, NIV). David rehearsed his past victories and knew that the hand of God was with him.

Just as God was with David, He is with you. What are some of your past successes? Focus on those and stay positive. Low self-confidence can be self-destructive, and it often manifests itself as negativity. Self-confident people believe in themselves and their abilities and they also believe—as David did—in living life to the full.

Scripture also says that the righteous are as bold as a lion (Proverbs 28:1). That kind of boldness comes out of a quiet but firm confidence in God. Elijah prayed and God sent fire from heaven (1 Kings 18). Daniel prayed and was delivered from the lions' den (Daniel 6). Paul prayed and received wisdom from above (2 Peter 3:15).

*You* can pray and expect God to act. "For the LORD will be your confidence, and will keep your foot from being caught" (Proverbs 3:26, NKJV). Confidence in God opens the door for all the promises of God to come to pass in your life.

*For other helpful categories, see pages 9, 11, 13, 65, 132, 199, 329.*

Job 4:6, NCV

You should have confidence because you respect God; you should have hope because you are innocent.

Psalm 71:5, NIV

You have been my hope, O Sovereign LORD, my confidence since my youth.

Psalm 118:8, NKJV

It is better to trust in the LORD than to put confidence in man.

Proverbs 3:26, NKJV

For the LORD will be your confidence, and will keep your foot from being caught.

Proverbs 14:26, NKJV

In the fear of the LORD there is strong confidence.

Proverbs 28:1, NKJV

The wicked flee when no one pursues, but the righteous are bold as a lion.

Isaiah 30:15, NKJV

In returning and rest you shall be saved; in quietness and confidence shall be your strength.

Romans 5:2, NLT

Because of our faith, Christ has brought us into this place of undeserved privilege where we now stand, and we confidently and joyfully look forward to sharing God's glory.

Ephesians 3:12, NIV

In him and through faith in him we may approach God with freedom and confidence.

Philippians 1:6, NIV — Being confident of this, that he who began a good work in you will carry it on to completion until the day of Christ Jesus.

Philippians 3:3, NKJV — We are the circumcision, who worship God in the Spirit, rejoice in Christ Jesus, and have no confidence in the flesh.

Hebrews 10:35, NKJV — Do not cast away your confidence, which has great reward.

1 John 2:28, NIV — Dear children, continue in him, so that when he appears we may be confident and unashamed before him at his coming.

1 John 5:14, NKJV — This is the confidence that we have in Him, that if we ask anything according to His will, He hears us.

# Cutting and Self-Mutilation— If You Are a Cutter

If you cut yourself, burn yourself, or break your own bones, you are in more than physical pain. Cutting is a way of "letting the pain out." Jesus died to set you free from pain.

Here are some practical steps to take as you stand on the Word of God:

1. *Get medical help.* If medical attention is needed, then get that medical attention immediately. A cut is a cut regardless of how it got there.

2. *Don't be afraid to talk about cutting.* Keep trying to find an open door for discussion with someone you trust. It's amazing how helpful it can be to tell someone about your struggles.

3. *Seek counsel.* God often uses trained counselors to bring healing and new life. If you have a friend or relative you trust, ask for that person's help in finding the right counselor for your needs.

4. *Don't be afraid of medication.* God often uses medication to help pull people out of depression or balance their emotions. Medication can be a way to receive God's healing.

5. *Believe that you are loved, even if you don't feel loved.* You are loved no matter what. When Satan's lies taunt you, stand on God's promises about His relationship with you as His beloved child.

God is for you (Romans 8:31). He is reaching out to you with His loving kindness. Will you open your heart to His gentle voice? He will never "leave you nor forsake you" (Hebrews 13:5, NKJV).

*For other helpful categories, see pages 13, 153, 196, 207, 218, 223, 340.*

| | |
|---|---|
| Leviticus 19:28, NKJV | You shall not make any cuttings in your flesh for the dead, nor tattoo any marks on you: I am the LORD. |
| Deuteronomy 14:1, NCV | You are the children of the LORD your God. When someone dies, do not cut yourselves or shave your heads to show your sadness. |
| Psalm 34:18, NCV | The LORD is close to the brokenhearted, and he saves those whose spirits have been crushed. |
| Psalm 55:18, KJV | He delivered my soul in peace from the battle that was against me: for there were many with me. |
| Psalm 62:5, NIV | Find rest, O my soul, in God alone; my hope comes from him. |
| Psalm 69:29, NIV | I am in pain and distress; may your salvation, O God, protect me. |
| Psalm 119:11, NIV | I have hidden your word in my heart that I might not sin against you. |
| Psalm 130:3-4, CEV | If you kept record of our sins, no one could last long. But you forgive us, and so we will worship you. |
| Isaiah 41:10, NLT | Don't be afraid, for I am with you. Don't be discouraged, for I am your God. I will strengthen you and help you. I will hold you up with my victorious right hand. |

Romans 8:31, NCV            If God is for us, no one can defeat us.

Romans 12:2, NLT            Don't copy the behavior and customs of this
                            world, but let God transform you into a new per-
                            son by changing the way you think. Then you
                            will learn to know God's will for you, which is
                            good and pleasing and perfect.

1 Corinthians 6:19-20, CEV  You surely know that your body is a temple where
                            the Holy Spirit lives. The Spirit is in you and is a
                            gift from God. You are no longer your own. God
                            paid a great price for you. So use your body to
                            honor God.

1 Corinthians 10:13, NIV    No temptation has seized you except what is
                            common to man. And God is faithful; he will not
                            let you be tempted beyond what you can bear.
                            But when you are tempted, he will also provide a
                            way out so that you can stand up under it.

Philippians 4:8, CEV        Keep your minds on whatever is true, pure, right,
                            holy, friendly, and proper. Don't ever stop think-
                            ing about what is truly worthwhile and worthy of
                            praise.

2 Timothy 1:7, NKJV         God has not given us a spirit of fear, but of power
                            and of love and of a sound mind.

# CUTTING AND SELF-MUTILATION— IF YOU LOVE SOMEONE WHO IS A CUTTER

If you suspect your child or friend of self-mutilation, you might be overwhelmed and confused. Many of us are not familiar with cutting, but an estimated 2 million Americans regularly injure themselves intentionally and compulsively by cutting their skin, burning themselves, or breaking their own bones. Self-mutilation even occurred thousands of years ago in biblical times (1 Kings 18:24-29).

How do you get to the heart of the issue causing your child or friend to do this? Through relationship. The most important thing to communicate to someone who is a cutter is this: "I'll walk with you through anything. I'll stand in front of you if you're moving to a place where you don't want to be." When you have a trusting relationship, the two of you (often with outside help) can take apart the puzzle and see the logic, progression, thinking, and habits that have moved this cutter to where he or she is.

- Remember that it is not *your* might or *your* power, but it is God's Spirit doing the work in your loved one. Be determined not to trust in your own strength or abilities when you are ministering to a cutter. Instead, depend on God and His work being done in the power of His Spirit. You are very important to God, and He often chooses to work through people—but He is not limited to human effort.
- "Pray without ceasing" for your loved one (1 Thessalonians 5:17, NKJV). Prayer is powerful and it has the ability to turn the situations around for good: "We know that all things work together for good to those who love God, to those who are the called according to His purpose" (Romans 8:28, NKJV).
- Put your trust in the ability of God and His Word to help your loved one (Psalm 37:5).

- Set healthy boundaries for yourself when helping your loved one. Guard yourself from fatigue, weariness, and a sense of hopelessness: "Let us not grow weary while doing good, for in due season we shall reap if we do not lose heart" (Galatians 6:9, NKJV).

The person you love who is a cutter might push you away or deny his or her actions. Pray about whether you are the person to help him or her. Intervene with others if you feel the cutter is in immediate medical danger. But never neglect that relational foundation. It may mean more to your friend than you will ever know.

*For other helpful categories, see pages 174, 199, 343, 346, 398, 411.*

| | |
|---|---|
| Psalm 34:19, NKJV | Many are the afflictions of the righteous, but the LORD delivers him out of them all. |
| Psalm 37:5, NLT | Commit everything you do to the LORD. Trust him, and he will help you. |
| Isaiah 40:28-29, NKJV | Have you not known? Have you not heard? The everlasting God, the LORD, the Creator of the ends of the earth, neither faints nor is weary. He gives power to the weak, and to those who have no might He increases strength. |
| Luke 1:37, NIV | Nothing is impossible with God. |
| Romans 8:28, NKJV | We know that all things work together for good to those who love God, to those who are the called according to His purpose. |
| Galatians 6:9, NKJV | Let us not grow weary while doing good, for in due season we shall reap if we do not lose heart. |
| Philippians 4:5, NIV | The Lord is near. |
| 1 Thessalonians 5:17, NKJV | Pray without ceasing. |
| James 5:15, NKJV | The prayer of faith will save the sick, and the Lord will raise him up. And if he has committed sins, he will be forgiven. |

# DATING—GUIDELINES FOR DATING

In the middle of the intense emotions and questions of a relationship, it can be tempting to forget that God wants the *best* for you in every area of your life. The best in dating relationships begins with guarding your heart (Proverbs 4:23) until it is time for love to be awakened (Song of Solomon 2:7).

Rely on the help of the Holy Spirit to guide you in your dating relationships. The first step in doing this is to be certain that both of you are submitted to God and attuned to His leading.

Does your relationship line up with God's Word? Do godly mentors and friends in your life share any concerns with you about who you are dating? Most importantly, does this person draw you closer to God or push you further away from Him?

As you ask yourself these questions, pray for God to speak to you through your answers. When the time comes for love to be awakened, you will understand how eager God is to give you connection, love, and joy beyond anything you can dream of.

*For other helpful categories, see pages 100, 112, 121, 177, 254, 441.*

Psalm 1:1, CEV

God blesses those people who refuse evil advice and won't follow sinners.

Psalm 119:9, NCV

How can a young person live a pure life? By obeying your word.

Psalm 133:1, NKJV

Behold, how good and how pleasant it is for brethren to dwell together in unity!

Proverbs 4:23, NIV

Above all else, guard your heart, for it is the wellspring of life.

Proverbs 6:25, NIV

Do not lust in your heart after her beauty or let her captivate you with her eyes.

Proverbs 20:3, NIV

It is to a man's honor to avoid strife, but every fool is quick to quarrel.

Proverbs 20:19, NIV

A gossip betrays a confidence; so avoid a man who talks too much.

Proverbs 22:24, NIV

Do not make friends with a hot-tempered man, do not associate with one easily angered.

Song of Solomon 2:7, NCV

Women of Jerusalem, promise me by the gazelles and the deer not to awaken or excite my feelings of love until it is ready.

Romans 13:13, NCV

Let us live in a right way, like people who belong to the day. We should not have wild parties or get drunk. There should be no sexual sins of any kind, no fighting or jealousy.

2 Corinthians 6:14, NIV      Do not be yoked together with unbelievers. For what do righteousness and wickedness have in common? Or what fellowship can light have with darkness?

2 Timothy 2:22, CEV      Run from temptations that capture young people. Always do the right thing. Be faithful, loving, and easy to get along with. Worship with people whose hearts are pure.

# DATING—LIVING TOGETHER
# AND SEXUAL PURITY

It's a popular belief today that living together instead of marrying is sometimes the "right thing to do." After all, many people have been married more than once and it hasn't worked out. Living together takes the pressure off of another marriage. But this belief does not line up with God's Word or His desire for your life.

Our culture would tell us that living a sexually pure life is old-fashioned. In reality, it is a privilege. It is a reflection of God's love for us and His desire to see us live as fully as possible.

God does not instruct you to keep sex within marriage for no reason. He knows that sex outside of marriage brings confusion—confusion that will deceive you and keep you from knowing the truth between real love and lust. Lust can disguise itself as love, making you think that you have found the one whom God intends for you to spend the rest of your life with. Love frees you to be who you really are, ready to receive the good God has for you in another person.

God tells us to "flee sexual immorality. Every sin that a man [or woman] does is outside the body, but he who commits sexual immorality sins against his own body" (1 Corinthians 6:18, NKJV).

If you are in a dating relationship right now, use wisdom about your physical relationship. Be in control of your environment. Don't allow yourself to be put in a compromising situation. Never underestimate your weakness or God's strength.

If you have already had sex outside of marriage, ask God's forgiveness (unless you have already) for sinning against your body. Nothing can change what happened, but God can change *you*, making you pure in His eyes and preparing you for a future loving relationship.

*For other helpful categories, see pages 13, 97, 171, 218, 402, 421.*

| | |
|---|---|
| Psalm 86:11, NLT | Teach me your ways, O LORD, that I may live according to your truth! Grant me purity of heart, so that I may honor you. |
| Matthew 15:19, NIV | Out of the heart come evil thoughts, murder, adultery, sexual immorality, theft, false testimony, slander. |
| 1 Corinthians 5:11, NIV | You must not associate with anyone who calls himself a brother but is sexually immoral or greedy, an idolater or a slanderer, a drunkard or a swindler. With such a man do not even eat. |
| 1 Corinthians 6:9-10, NCV | Surely you know that the people who do wrong will not inherit God's kingdom. Do not be fooled. Those who sin sexually, worship idols, take part in adultery, those who are male prostitutes, or men who have sexual relations with other men, those who steal, are greedy, get drunk, lie about others, or rob—these people will not inherit God's kingdom. |
| 1 Corinthians 6:18, NKJV | Flee sexual immorality. Every sin that a man does is outside the body, but he who commits sexual immorality sins against his own body. |
| Galatians 5:16, NLT | Let the Holy Spirit guide your lives. Then you won't be doing what your sinful nature craves. |
| Galatians 6:1, NIV | If someone is caught in a sin, you who arespiritual should restore him gently. But watch yourself, or you also maybe tempted. |

| | |
|---|---|
| Ephesians 4:30, NLT | Do not bring sorrow to God's Holy Spirit by the way you live. Remember, he has identified you as his own. |
| Ephesians 5:3, NKJV | But fornication and all uncleanness or covetousness, let it not even be named among you, as is fitting for saints. |
| 1 Thessalonians 4:3, MSG | We ask you—urge is more like it—that you keep on doing what we told you to do to please God, not in a dogged religious plod, but in a living, spirited dance. You know the guidelines we laid out for you from the Master Jesus. God wants you to live a pure life. Keep yourselves from sexual promiscuity. |
| 1 Thessalonians 5:22, KJV | Abstain from all appearance of evil. |
| 1 Peter 4:2-3, NCV | Strengthen yourselves so that you will live here on earth doing what God wants, not the evil things people want. In the past you wasted too much time doing what nonbelievers enjoy. You were guilty of sexual sins, evil desires, drunkenness, wild and drunken parties. |
| 1 John 1:9, NKJV | If we confess our sins, He is faithful and just to forgive us our sins and to cleanse us from all unrighteousness. |

# DELIVERANCE

Do you feel that certain thoughts and attitudes have such a grip on your mind that, even though you don't want to think that way, you do? You feel as if your mind is controlling you.

God's Word will deliver you from those strongholds. Renew your mind with His truth (Romans 12:2). Set your mind on victory and not defeat, success and not failure. After all, deliverance, healing, and restoration are God's promise to you! The psalmist tells us, "Many are the afflictions of the righteous, but the LORD [delivers] him out of them all" (Psalm 34:19, KJV). God is our source of power, courage, and wisdom to get us through the sins and troubles that plague us.

If your habits are deeply rooted, you may need the help and strength of someone else as you walk out your deliverance. Ask God to send someone who will encourage you and walk with you during this time.

Remember that Jesus delivered us from the curse of the law by becoming a curse for us—so that we would have freedom and become His children (Galatians 3:13; 4:5). God's Word promises that we will always "triumph in Christ" (2 Corinthians 2:14, NKJV)! Believe it! Speak it! Declare it! It is your legal right!

*For other helpful categories, see pages 13, 65, 147, 199, 343, 346, 398.*

| | |
|---|---|
| Psalm 25:15, NCV | My eyes are always looking to the LORD for help. He will keep me from any traps. |
| Psalm 25:20, NIV | Guard my life and rescue me; let me not be put to shame, for I take refuge in you. |
| Psalm 34:19, KJV | Many are the afflictions of the righteous, but the LORD delivers him out of them all. |
| Psalm 55:18, KJV | He has delivered my soul in peace from the battle that was against me: for there were many with me. |
| Psalm 60:5, NIV | Save us and help us with your right hand, that those you love may be delivered. |
| Psalm 91:3, KJV | Surely he shall deliver you from the snare of the fowler, and from the noisome pestilence. |
| Psalm 107:6, NIV | They cried out to the LORD in their trouble, and he delivered them from their distress. |
| Psalm 107:20, KJV | He sent his word, and healed them, and delivered them from their destructions. |
| Psalm 116:8, NIV | You, O LORD, have delivered my soul from death, my eyes from tears, my feet from stumbling, |
| Psalm 121:1-2, NIV | I lift up my eyes to the hills—where does my help come from? My help comes from the LORD, the Maker of heaven and earth. |
| Proverbs 11:8, NKJV | The righteous is delivered from trouble, and it comes to the wicked instead. |

| Isaiah 41:13, NIV | I am the LORD, your God, who takes hold of your right hand and says to you, Do not fear; I will help you. |
| Jeremiah 15:21, NKJV | I will deliver you from the hand of the wicked, and I will redeem you from the grip of the terrible. |
| John 8:32, NKJV | You shall know the truth, and the truth shall make you free. |
| John 8:36, KJV | If the Son therefore shall make you free, you shall be free indeed. |
| Romans 8:2, NKJV | For the law of the Spirit of life in Christ Jesus has made me free from the law of sin and death. |
| Romans 12:2, NKJV | Do not be conformed to this world, but be transformed by the renewing of your mind, that you may prove what is that good and acceptable and perfect will of God. |
| 2 Corinthians 2:14, NKJV | Thanks be to God who always leads us in triumph in Christ. |
| Galatians 3:13, NKJV | Christ has redeemed us from the curse of the law, having become a curse for us (for it is written, "Cursed is everyone who hangs on a tree"). |
| Colossians 1:13, NKJV | He has delivered us from the power of darkness and conveyed us into the kingdom of the Son of His love, in whom we have redemption through His blood, the forgiveness of sins. |

# DEPRESSION

When you are depressed, victory may seem nearly impossible. All you can see ahead of you is hopelessness.

God knows the struggles of your heart and mind, and He *does* see victory for you. Ask for God's help. Ask for God's joy to take over your mind and spirit.

Receiving God's joy does not mean you gloss over your pain. Godly joy is the biblical antidote for depression. We read in Isaiah that God wants "to console those who mourn in Zion, to give them beauty for ashes, the oil of joy for mourning, the garment of praise for the spirit of heaviness" (Isaiah 61:3, NKJV).

God's joy is real, lasting, and possible.

Even when you don't even feel like leaving the house, take one step toward action. Find help through Bible study, support groups, fellowship among believers, Scripture confessions, forgiveness, counseling, and physicians. You serve a God who "comforts and encourages and refreshes and cheers the depressed and the sinking" (2 Corinthians 7:6, AMP). He knows you even better than you know yourself, and He is cheering you on.

*For other helpful categories, see pages 13, 62, 153, 196, 207, 223, 236, 263, 289, 346, 411, 414, 428.*

| | |
|---|---|
| Psalm 25:17-18, NKJV | The troubles of my heart have enlarged; bring me out of my distresses! Look on my affliction and my pain, and forgive all my sins. |
| Psalm 30:11-12, NIV | You turned my wailing into dancing; you removed my sackcloth and clothed me with joy, that my heart may sing to you and not be silent. O LORD my God, I will give you thanks forever. |
| Psalm 31:7-8, NCV | I will be glad and rejoice in your love, because you saw my suffering; you knew my troubles. You have not handed me over to my enemies but have set me in a safe place. |
| Psalm 31:22, NCV | In my distress, I said, "God cannot see me!" But you heard my prayer when I cried out to you for help. |
| Psalm 34:18, NCV | The LORD is close to the brokenhearted, and he saves those whose spirits have been crushed. |
| Psalm 42:5, NLT | Why am I discouraged? Why is my heart so sad? I will put my hope in God! I will praise him again—my Savior and my God! |
| Psalm 107:2, KJV | Let the redeemed of the LORD say so, whom he has redeemed from the hand of the enemy. |
| Psalm 121:1-2, NIV | I lift up my eyes to the hills—where does my help come from? My help comes from the LORD, the Maker of heaven and earth. |

| | |
|---|---|
| Isaiah 54:10, NCV | "The mountains may disappear, and the hills may come to an end, but my love will never disappear; my promise of peace will not come to an end," says the LORD who shows mercy to you. |
| Isaiah 60:1, NIV | Arise, shine, for your light has come, and the glory of the LORD rises upon you. |
| Micah 7:8, NKJV | Do not rejoice over me, my enemy; when I fall, I will arise; when I sit in darkness, the LORD will be a light to me. |
| Matthew 11:28, NIV | Come to me, all you who are weary and burdened, and I will give you rest. |
| 2 Corinthians 7:6, AMP | God, Who comforts and encourages and refreshes and cheers the depressed and the sinking, comforted and encouraged and refreshed and cheered us. |
| Ephesians 6:12, KJV | We wrestle not against flesh and blood, but against principalities, against powers, against the rulers of the darkness of this world, against spiritual wickedness in high places. |
| 1 John 3:8, KJV | For this purpose the Son of God was manifested, that he might destroy the works of the devil. |

# DESIRE

Psalm 37:4 makes a promise: "[God] shall give you the desires of your heart" (NKJV). Isn't that an amazing promise? Who doesn't want the desires of their heart to be granted?

But what is the prerequisite for receiving such blessing from the Lord? That comes in the first half of the verse: "Delight yourself also in the LORD."

This verse is not promising you anything you want. Rather, it is guaranteeing that if you commit your ways to the Lord in obedient faith, He will give you the very desires that you should have and then He will fulfill them for you.

As you consider this verse, ask God, *Am I delighting in You, Lord? Are my desires lining up with Yours? I want to desire only what You desire.*

One sign of your delight in the Lord is your desire to come into His presence daily. You want to know what He thinks of you, You want Christ to reign in your heart. Just as in any relationship, the more time you spend with God, the more you will get to know what He delights in. Are you joyfully connected to the One who wants to give you the desires of your heart?

*For other helpful categories, see pages 132, 147, 340, 424.*

| | |
|---|---|
| Psalm 10:17, NIV | You hear, O LORD, the desire of the afflicted; you encourage them, and you listen to their cry. |
| Psalm 20:4, NIV | May he give you the desire of your heart and make all your plans succeed. |
| Psalm 21:2, NKJV | You have given him his heart's desire, and have not withheld the request of his lips. |
| Psalm 37:4, NKJV | Delight yourself also in the LORD, and He shall give you the desires of your heart. |
| Psalm 40:8, NIV | I desire to do your will, O my God; your law is within my heart. |
| Psalm 73:25, NKJV | Who have I in heaven but You? And there is none upon earth that I desire besides You. |
| Psalm 84:2, NIV | My soul yearns, even faints, for the courts of the LORD; my heart and my flesh cry out for the living God. |
| Psalm 103:5, NIV | He satisfies your desires with good things so that your youth is renewed like the eagle's. |
| Psalm 145:16, NIV | You open your hand and satisfy the desires of every living thing. |
| Romans 13:14, NIV | Clothe yourselves with the Lord Jesus Christ, and do not think about how to gratify the desires of the sinful nature. |

| | |
|---|---|
| Galatians 5:24, NIV | Those who belong to Christ Jesus have crucified the sinful nature with its passions and desires. |
| 2 Timothy 2:22, NIV | Flee the evil desires of youth, and pursue righteousness, faith, love and peace, along with those who call on the Lord out of a pure heart. |
| 1 Peter 1:14, NIV | As obedient children, do not conform to the evil desires you had when you lived in ignorance. |
| Jude, 16, NIV | These men are grumblers and faultfinders; they follow their own evil desires; they boast about themselves and flatter others for their own advantage. |

# Desiring a Mate

If you are single and desire to be married, remember these two words: *preparation* and *patience*.

When people are looking ahead to a career, they prepare themselves through education and training. When athletes want to join a team, they prepare themselves through practicing their chosen sport. When people want to acquire a skill, such as flying an airplane, they prepare.

In the same way—yet even more importantly—you should be preparing now for your potential marriage. After all, marriage is the second biggest commitment you may ever make (the first being your commitment to Jesus Christ). Preparation meets opportunity.

This preparation includes your body, mind, and spirit as you develop your gifts, build other relationships, and get involved in God's community. You should also prepare yourself by knowing what God's Word has to say about marriage and relationships.

You can use your present stage of life to develop a deeper relationship with the Lord. Stay in His presence so that your ear will be fine-tuned to His voice. You'll want to hear who He has for you!

In the meantime, be determined to wait and "imitate those who through faith and patience inherit the promises" (Hebrews 6:12, NKJV). You can trust that God's plan for your life will be right on time. You can also trust that God is experiencing the lonely moments and questions with you. You are not forgotten. So be encouraged!

*For other helpful categories, see pages 62, 118, 263, 314, 336, 428.*

Genesis 2:18, NIV

The LORD God said, "It is not good for the man to be alone. I will make a helper suitable for him."

Psalm 20:4, NIV

May he give you the desire of your heart and make all your plans succeed.

Psalm 21:2, NIV

You have granted him the desire of his heart and have not withheld the request of his lips.

Psalm 25:4-5, NIV

Show me your ways, O LORD, teach me your paths; guide me in your truth and teach me, for you are God my Savior, and my hope is in you all day long.

Psalm 84:4, NIV

Blessed are those who dwell in your house; they are ever praising you.

Proverbs 4:7, NIV

Wisdom is supreme; therefore get wisdom. Though it cost all you have, get understanding.

Proverbs 4:11, NIV

I guide you in the way of wisdom and lead you along straight paths.

Ecclesiastes 7:8, NKJV

The end of a thing is better than its beginning, the patient in spirit is better than the proud in spirit.

Matthew 6:33, NKJV

Seek first the kingdom of God and His righteousness, and all these things shall be added to you.

1 Corinthians 7:2, ESV — Because of the temptation to sexual immorality each man should have his own wife and each woman her own husband.

2 Corinthians 6:14, NIV — Do not be yoked together with unbelievers. For what do righteousness and wickedness have in common? Or what fellowship can light have with darkness?

# DIRECTION

"Should I take this job or go back to school?"

"Should we move closer to family or stay where we are?"

"Should we pursue adoption or try to content ourselves with childlessness?"

We all have many questions in life—specific, personal questions that often are very important to us. How are we going to answer them?

We could rely on our own common sense and "gut feelings." And those can be helpful. But if we want to make decisions that are truly God honoring, then we need to lean not on our own understanding (Proverbs 3:5) and to seek to know *His* will. We need to inquire of the Lord.

How can you know God's direction? Here are some principles that help:

- Seek God with all your heart through prayer, for this positions you to discern God's direction for your life.
- Read God's Word and listen for His guiding voice. Then obey.
- Know that if you take a wrong turn in life, God is willing and able to bring you back on the right path.
- Seek counsel from one or two godly people. Ask them to be in prayer for wisdom for you.
- Finally, believe that God has a good plan for your life. "For I know the plans I have for you," declares the LORD, "plans to prosper you and not to harm you, plans to give you hope and a future" (Jeremiah 29:11, NIV).

*For other helpful categories, see pages 109, 132, 333, 336, 340, 437.*

Job 36:11, NKJV — If you obey and serve Him, they shall spend their days in prosperity, and their years in pleasures.

Psalm 1:1, NIV — Blessed is the man who does not walk in the counsel of the wicked or stand in the way of sinners or sit in the seat of mockers.

Psalm 16:11, NKJV — You will show me the path of life; in Your presence is fullness of joy, at Your right hand are pleasures forevermore.

Psalm 32:8, NIV — I will instruct you and teach you in the way you should go; I will counsel you and watch over you.

Psalm 37:23, NKJV — The steps of a good man are ordered by the LORD, and He delights in his way.

Psalm 111:10, NIV — The fear of the LORD is the beginning of wisdom; all who follow his precepts have good understanding. To him belongs eternal praise.

Psalm 119:35 NLT — Make me walk along the path of your commands, for that is where my happiness is found.

Psalm 119:105, NIV — Your word is a lamp to my feet and a light for my path.

Psalm 143:8, NCV — Show me what I should do, because my prayers go up to you.

Proverbs 3:5-6, NIV — Trust in the LORD with all your heart and lean not on your own understanding; in all your ways acknowledge him, and he will make your paths straight.

Proverbs 4:11, NIV

I guide you in the way of wisdom and lead you along straight paths.

Daniel 2:22, NIV

He reveals deep and hidden things, he knows what lies in darkness and light dwells with him.

Habakkuk 2:2, NKJV

Then the LORD answered me and said: "Write the vision and make it plain on tablets, that he may run who reads it."

Luke 12:2, NCV

Everything that is hidden will be shown, and everything that is secret will be made known.

John 10:27, NIV

My sheep listen to my voice; I know them, and they follow me.

John 16:13, NIV

When he, the Spirit of truth, comes, he will guide you into all truth. He will not speak on his own; he will speak only what he hears, and he will tell you what is yet to come.

1 Corinthians 2:9-10, NIV

It is written: "No eye has seen, no ear has heard, no mind has conceived what God has prepared for those who love him"—but God has revealed it to us by his Spirit. The Spirit searches all things, even the deep things of God.

# DISCOURAGEMENT
# AND DISAPPOINTMENT

One of the most powerful things you can do when you are discouraged is to speak God's Word out loud. Make it personal to you without changing its truth: "I know that God causes all things to work together for my good because I love Him and have been called according to His purpose" (adaptation of Romans 8:28, NLT). "What is impossible with men is possible with God" (Luke 18:27, NIV). "You are full of compassion and mercy" (adaptation of James 5:11, NIV).

Use God's Word to draw close to Him even when you don't have any words to say yourself. Even when you are angry, disappointed, and confused. Your circumstances may be changing—or not changing enough—but God's truth is the same. His truth will build your faith in times of discouragement.

God's Word will also remind you to draw on the *joy* of the Lord. When David was discouraged, he let his faith supply him with a resource of comfort and strength (1 Samuel 30:6). When you don't see something in the natural that you've been hoping for, remember this truth and take joy in the God of your salvation:

Though the fig tree may not blossom,
Nor fruit be on the vines;
Though the labor of the olive may fail,
And the fields yield no food;
Though the flock may be cut off from the fold,
And there be no herd in the stalls—
Yet I will rejoice in the Lord,
I will joy in the God of my salvation. (Habakkuk 3:17-18, NKJV)

*For other helpful categories, see pages 62, 132, 153, 199, 207, 411, 424.*

| | |
|---|---|
| 1 Samuel 30:6, NIV | David was greatly distressed because the men were talking of stoning him; each one was bitter in spirit because of his sons and daughters. But David found strength in the LORD his God. |
| Isaiah 35:3-4, CEV | Here is a message for all who are weak, trembling, and worried: "Cheer up! Don't be afraid. Your God is coming to punish your enemies. God will take revenge on them and rescue you." |
| Mark 9:23, NIV | Everything is possible for him who believes. |
| Luke 18:27, NIV | What is impossible with men is possible with God. |
| John 16:33, NKJV | In the world you will have tribulation; but be of good cheer, I have overcome the world. |
| Romans 5:5, NLT | And this hope will not lead to disappointment. For we know how dearly God loves us, because he has given us the Holy Spirit to fill our hearts with his love. |
| Romans 8:26, NIV | The Spirit helps us in our weakness. We do not know what we ought to pray for, but the Spirit himself intercedes for us with groans that words cannot express. |
| Romans 8:28, NLT | We know that God causes everything to work together for the good of those who love God and are called according to his purpose for them. |
| Romans 8:31, NIV | If God is for us, who can be against us? |

2 Corinthians 12:9, NKJV    My grace is sufficient for you, for My strength is made perfect in weakness. Therefore most gladly I will rather boast in my infirmities, that the power of Christ may rest upon me.

James 5:11, NIV    We consider blessed those who have persevered. You have heard of Job's perseverance and have seen what the Lord finally brought about. The Lord is full of compassion and mercy.

1 John 4:4, NIV    You, dear children, are from God and have overcome them, because the one who is in you is greater than the one who is in the world.

# DIVORCE—
# WHAT GOD SAYS ABOUT DIVORCE

Divorce is one of many significant things that our culture takes lightly. We gossip about the latest celebrity marriages and break-ups and wonder what they "did wrong." But God doesn't take divorce lightly. Marriage is a blessing and a privilege and we all need to guard our marriages against the pain of divorce.

The first thing to remember is that marriage is a covenant (Malachi 2:14). The Scriptures define a covenant as a solemn and binding relationship that is meant to last a lifetime. The root concept of a covenant is a commitment unto death.

Some in Jesus's day were advocating for easy divorce. But Jesus put the emphasis on the permanency that God had intended for marriage since Creation: "Moses, because of the hardness of your hearts, permitted you to divorce your wives, but from the beginning it was not so" (Matthew 19:8, NKJV). In Matthew 5:31-32, Jesus cites a just cause for the deeply regrettable course of getting a divorce.

Study the Word concerning God's viewpoint on this topic. If you are married, never let go of your responsibility before God regarding your marriage commitment. In this, you will please God as you show our culture a better way.

*For other helpful categories, see pages 144, 199, 269, 274, 277.*

| | |
|---|---|
| Malachi 2:14, NKJV | The LORD has been witness between you and the wife of your youth, with whom you have dealt treacherously; yet she is your companion and your wife by covenant. |
| Malachi 2:16, NIV | "I hate divorce," says the LORD God of Israel, "and I hate a man's covering himself with violence as well as with his garment," says the LORD Almighty. So guard yourself in your spirit, and do not break faith. |
| Matthew 5:31-32, NIV | It has been said, "Anyone who divorces his wife must give her a certificate of divorce." But I tell you that anyone who divorces his wife, except for marital unfaithfulness, causes her to become an adulteress, and anyone who marries the divorced woman commits adultery. |
| Matthew 19:8, NKJV | He said to them, "Moses, because of the hardness of your hearts, permitted you to divorce your wives, but from the beginning it was not so." |
| Matthew 19:9, NIV | I tell you that anyone who divorces his wife, except for marital unfaithfulness, and marries another woman commits adultery. |
| Mark 10:11-12, NIV | He answered, "Anyone who divorces his wife and marries another woman commits adultery against her. And if she divorces her husband and marries another man, she commits adultery." |
| 1 Corinthians 7:10-11, NIV | To the married I give this command (not I, but the Lord): A wife must not separate from her |

husband. But if she does, she must remain un-married or else be reconciled to her husband. And a husband must not divorce his wife.

1 Corinthians 7:12-13, NIV    To the rest I say this (I, not the Lord): If any brother has a wife who is not a believer and she is willing to live with him, he must not divorce her. And if a woman has a husband who is not a be-liever and he is willing to live with her, she must not divorce him.

1 Corinthians 7:27, NIV    Are you married? Do not seek a divorce. Are you unmarried? Do not look for a wife.

1 John 2:9, NIV    Anyone who claims to be in the light but hates his brother is still in the darkness.

# Divorce—If You Are Going Through a Divorce or Separation

If you are in the middle of a divorce or separation from your spouse, you might feel totally out of control. *How could this happen?* you wonder. *This is the kind of thing that happens to other people.*

Here are some steps you can take to regain control of your life as you deepen your trust in God:

First, decide to sow seeds of peace in the midst of turmoil. Though it's tempting to do otherwise, keep yourself from judging your ex-spouse or speaking ill of him or her in casual conversation.

Second, pray for God's will. He is capable of changing hearts (Proverbs 21:1). Keep in mind that He can turn the heart of your divorced or divorcing spouse back toward you.

Third, "if those who are not believers decide to leave, let them leave. When this happens, the Christian man or woman is free. But God called us to live in peace" (1 Corinthians 7:15, NCV).

Even in the midst of tremendous turmoil, you can know the peace that passes understanding. Jesus promises, "Peace I leave with you, My peace I give to you; not as the world gives do I give to you. Let not your heart be troubled, neither let it be afraid" (John 14:27, NKJV).

*For other helpful categories, see pages 13, 44, 132, 140, 144, 147, 153, 333.*

Psalm 34:18, NIV

The LORD is close to the brokenhearted and saves those who are crushed in spirit.

Proverbs 21:1, NIV

The king's heart is in the hand of the LORD; he directs it like a watercourse wherever he pleases.

Matthew 11:29, NKJV

Take My yoke upon you and learn from Me, for I am gentle and lowly in heart, and you will find rest for your souls.

John 14:27, NKJV

Peace I leave with you, My peace I give to you; not as the world gives do I give to you. Let not your heart be troubled, neither let it be afraid.

Romans 12:18, NKJV

If it is possible, as much as depends on you, live peaceably with all men.

1 Corinthians 7:15, NCV

But if those who are not believers decide to leave, let them leave. When this happens, the Christian man or woman is free. But God called us to live in peace.

Philippians 4:6-7, NIV

Do not be anxious about anything, but in everything, by prayer and petition, with thanksgiving, present your requests to God. And the peace of God, which transcends all understanding, will guard your hearts and your minds in Christ Jesus.

Philippians 4:19, NIV

My God will meet all your needs according to his glorious riches in Christ Jesus.

# DIVORCE—HEALING AFTER DIVORCE

Divorce can make you feel as if you've been struck on all sides at once. Yet you serve a God of restoration. He restores people because it is a part of His nature and a part of His plan.

If you are divorced—whether once or many times—you are probably dealing with a lot of pain. And quite possibly, a lot of guilt and confusion. What does God think of you? Where do you go from here in your relationship with Him?

Divorce is a kind of death—the death of a relationship, a love, a dream to grow old with someone. But you *can* begin again after the devastation of divorce. God can and will use you again. So allow yourself the time to heal. Remember that God is unchanging (Malachi 3:6). He is always compassionate, always loving, always forgiving. Never doubt that He still cares for you. Jesus forgives and heals the grief of divorce just like He does anything else.

Finally, though it might seem contradictory, keep praising God in the midst of your pain. Praise helps wash away the debris of divorce left in your mind, heart, and relationships. As you worship God, your heart will grow in wisdom and strength no matter what you've just been through.

*For other helpful categories, see pages 9, 11, 13, 88, 174, 207, 223, 368, 381.*

| | |
|---|---|
| 2 Chronicles 30:9, NIV | The LORD your God is gracious and compassionate. He will not turn his face from you if you return to him. |
| Psalm 25:5, NLT | Lead me by your truth and teach me, for you are the God who saves me. All day long I put my hope in you. |
| Psalm 42:5, NIV | Why are you downcast, O my soul? Why so disturbed within me? Put your hope in God. |
| Psalm 68:5, NIV | A father to the fatherless, a defender of widows, is God in his holy dwelling. |
| Psalm 73:26, NIV | My flesh and my heart may fail, but God is the strength of my heart and my portion forever. |
| Psalm 147:3, NLT | He heals the brokenhearted and bandages their wounds. |
| Matthew 5:9, CEV | God blesses those people who make peace. They will be called his children! |
| Luke 6:37, CEV | Don't judge others, and God won't judge you. Don't be hard on others, and God won't be hard on you. Forgive others, and God will forgive you. |
| 2 Corinthians 12:9-10, NIV | But he said to me, "My grace is sufficient for you, for my power is made perfect in weakness." Therefore I will boast all the more gladly about my weaknesses so that Christ's power may rest on me. That is why, for Christ's sake, I delight in weaknesses, in insults, in hardships, in |

persecutions, in difficulties. For when I am weak, then I am strong.

Philippians 4:19, NIV — My God will meet all your needs according to his glorious riches in Christ Jesus.

Hebrews 3:15, NIV — Do not harden your hearts.

Hebrews 11:6, NIV — And without faith it is impossible to please God, because anyone who comes to him must believe that he exists and that he rewards those who earnestly seek him.

Hebrews 13:8, NIV — Jesus Christ is the same yesterday and today and forever.

James 1:5, NIV — If any of you lacks wisdom, he should ask God, who gives generously to all without finding fault, and it will be given to him.

Revelation 21:5, NKJV — Behold, I make all things new.

# Eating Disorders

If you struggle with anorexia, bulimia, obesity, or other unhealthy eating habits, you know how powerful eating disorders can be. You want to have control over what you eat and what your body looks like, but instead, food has control over you.

Will power—either to stop or start eating—isn't enough. Your mind and body are struggling. But with *God's* power, you are strong. You can be in control of your eating again when you give control first to God. After all, God is the only One who gives "bread that sustains [the] heart" (Psalm 104:15, NIV).

What does it look like to receive God's sustenance? It looks like asking someone for help—a friend or counselor or doctor. It looks like confessing to God that your habits have become disordered and you need His help. It looks like praying for faith and hope, even when you feel faithless and hopeless. And it means realizing that though you are not perfect, God loves you extravagantly.

No matter what your body looks like, you are created in God's image (Genesis 1:27). You might want to shape your body a certain way, but God wants to shape *you*: "You are in my hands like the clay in the potter's hands" (Jeremiah 18:6, NCV). You are beautiful in God's eyes as He crafts you to perfection.

*For other helpful categories, see pages 13, 196, 207, 212, 218, 223, 431.*

| | |
|---|---|
| Genesis 1:27, NIV | God created man in his own image, in the image of God he created him; male and female he created them. |
| Psalm 62:8, NKJV | Trust in Him at all times, you people; pour out your heart before Him; God is a refuge for us. |
| Psalm 138:3, NKJV | In the day when I cried out, You answered me, and made me bold with strength in my soul. |
| Ecclesiastes 4:12, NKJV | A threefold cord is not quickly broken. |
| Isaiah 40:29, NKJV | He gives power to the weak, and to those who have no might He increases strength. |
| Jeremiah 18:6, NCV | You are in my [God's] hands like the clay in the potter's hands. |
| Matthew 6:31-33, NIV | Do not worry, saying, "What shall we eat?" or "What shall we drink?" or "What shall we wear?" For the pagans run after all these things, and your heavenly Father knows that you need them. But seek first his kingdom and his righteousness, and all these things will be given to you as well. |
| Matthew 26:41, NIV | Watch and pray so that you will not fall into temptation. The spirit is willing, but the body is weak. |
| Romans 15:13, NIV | May the God of hope fill you with all joy and peace as you trust in him, so that you may overflow with hope by the power of the Holy Spirit. |

1 Corinthians 6:19-20, NIV — Do you not know that your body is a temple of the Holy Spirit, who is in you, whom you have received from God? You are not your own; you were bought at a price. Therefore honor God with your body.

1 Corinthians 10:13, NIV — No temptation has seized you except what is common to man. And God is faithful; he will not let you be tempted beyond what you can bear. But when you are tempted, he will also provide a way out so that you can stand up under it.

Galatians 2:20, NIV — I have been crucified with Christ and I no longer live, but Christ lives in me. The life I live in the body, I live by faith in the Son of God, who loved me and gave himself for me.

Philippians 4:13, NKJV — I can do all things through Christ who strengthens me.

1 Timothy 4:8, NIV — Physical training is of some value, but godliness has value for all things, holding promise for both the present life and the life to come.

2 Timothy 1:7, NKJV — God has not given us a spirit of fear, but of power and of love and of a sound mind.

# FAITH

It is through faith that we first come to know Jesus and receive forgiveness of our sins. This is called *saving faith*.

But what about the rest of our lives? Do we still need faith?

The answer is yes! Every day! Faith is how we live out our relationship with God. As Hebrews tells us, "Faith is the substance of things hoped for, the evidence of things not seen" (Hebrews 11:1, NKJV).

Think of it this way: God has given you two sets of eyes—natural eyes and spiritual eyes. Faith is seeing with your spiritual eyes. When you move in the direction of what your spiritual eyes see, you're moving in faith. In other words, an exercise of faith is something you do or say without depending on your natural senses.

Faith, then, is not merely sitting around and *thinking* something. It is *doing* something. We should be able to say with the apostle James, "I will show you my faith by my works" (James 2:18, NKJV).

So, how do we get this kind of bold, active faith? Through God's Word. "Faith comes by hearing, and hearing by the word of God" (Romans 10:17, NKJV). Such a faith is based not on human wisdom but on the power of God (1 Corinthians 2:5).

Start moving in the direction of what you are seeing with your spiritual eyes. Start believing and seeing your life through faith. Begin, by faith, to apply God's Word over that area in your life. You can be confident that when you pray God's Word over your life or someone else's life, the Word will have its effect (Isaiah 55:11).

*For other helpful categories, see pages 59, 88, 153, 196, 314.*

| | |
|---|---|
| Isaiah 7:9, NIV | If you do not stand firm in your faith, you will not stand at all. |
| Matthew 8:26, NIV | He replied, "You of little faith, why are you so afraid?" Then he got up and rebuked the winds and the waves, and it was completely calm. |
| Matthew 9:22, NIV | Jesus turned and saw her. "Take heart, daughter," he said, "your faith has healed you." And the woman was healed from that moment. |
| Matthew 9:29, NIV | He touched their eyes and said, "According to your faith will it be done to you." |
| Matthew 21:21, NIV | Jesus replied, "I tell you the truth, if you have faith and do not doubt, not only can you do what was done to the fig tree, but also you can say to this mountain, 'Go, throw yourself into the sea,' and it will be done." |
| Romans 1:17, NCV | But those who are right with God will live by faith. |
| Romans 10:8, NKJV | But what does it say? "The word is near you, in your mouth and in your heart" (that is, the word of faith which we preach). |
| Romans 10:17, NKJV | Faith comes by hearing, and hearing by the word of God. |
| Romans 12:3, NKJV | God has dealt to each one a measure of faith. |
| 1 Corinthians 2:5, NKJV | Your faith should not be in the wisdom of men but in the power of God. |

| | |
|---|---|
| 1 Corinthians 16:13, NKJV | Watch, stand fast in the faith, be brave, be strong. |
| 2 Corinthians 5:7, KJV | We walk by faith, not by sight. |
| Galatians 2:20, NIV | I have been crucified with Christ and I no longer live, but Christ lives in me. The life I live in the body, I live by faith in the Son of God, who loved me and gave himself for me. |
| Galatians 3:9, NCV | So all who believe as Abraham believed are blessed just as Abraham was. |
| Galatians 3:11, NIV | Clearly no one is justified before God by the law, because, "The righteous will live by faith." |
| Galatians 3:26, KJV | You are all the children of God by faith in Christ Jesus. |
| Galatians 5:6, NIV | In Christ Jesus neither circumcision nor uncircumcision has any value. The only thing that counts is faith expressing itself through love. |
| Ephesians 2:8, NKJV | For by grace you have been saved through faith, and that not of yourselves; it is the gift of God. |
| Ephesians 6:16, NKJV | Above all, taking the shield of faith with which you will be able to quench all the fiery darts of the wicked one. |
| Hebrews 10:23, KJV | Let us hold fast the profession of our faith without wavering; for he is faithful that promised. |

Hebrews 10:38, KJV — The just shall live by faith: but if any man draw back, my soul shall have no pleasure in him.

Hebrews 11:1, NKJV — Faith is the substance of things hoped for, the evidence of things not seen.

Hebrews 11:6, NIV — Without faith it is impossible to please God, because anyone who comes to him must believe that he exists and that he rewards those who earnestly seek him.

James 2:18, NKJV — Someone will say, "You have faith, and I have works." Show me your faith without your works, and I will show you my faith by my works.

# Faith—If You
# Have Turned Away from Faith

If you have turned away from your faith, God longs to embrace you again. Paul tells us, "There is now no condemnation for those who are in Christ Jesus" (Romans 8:1, NIV). Paul's words are true for you whether you have made one mistake or have been drifting from God for years. When you turn to God for forgiveness, you are free from guilt, free from shame. Free to make lasting changes with God's help.

Satan wants you to believe that you are too sinful for God to welcome you back. God wants you to believe that He will always forgive you. Satan is "the father of lies." When he lies, he "speaks his native language" (John 8:44, NIV). If you believe his words, you are believing a liar who cares only about keeping you from true life.

*Repent* means to turn around and go the other direction. What changes do you need to make in your life to turn around completely and face God again? The Lord says to you, "If you change your heart and return to me, I will take you back" (Jeremiah 15:19, NCV).

Jesus said, "Remain in me, and I will remain in you. For a branch cannot produce fruit if it is severed from the vine, and you cannot be fruitful unless you remain in me" (John 15:4, NLT). Now you have a new opportunity to rely on His strength. So don't waste time dwelling on what you have done. Take hold of God's truth for all the life-giving possibilities for you in the future.

*For other helpful categories, see pages 13, 80, 144, 398, 421.*

Jeremiah 15:19, NCV
So this is what the LORD says: "If you change your heart and return to me, I will take you back. Then you may serve me. And if you speak things that have worth, not useless words, then you may speak for me. Let the people of Judah turn to you, but you must not change and be like them."

Hosea 6:1, NKJV
Come, and let us return to the LORD; for He has torn, but He will heal us; He has stricken, but He will bind us up.

Matthew 3:8, NIV
Produce fruit in keeping with repentance.

Matthew 5:6, NIV
Blessed are those who hunger and thirst for right-eousness, for they will be filled.

Luke 15:20, NIV
So he got up and went to his father. But while he was still a long way off, his father saw him and was filled with compassion for him; he ran to his son, threw his arms around him and kissed him.

John 15:4, NLT
Remain in me, and I will remain in you. For a branch cannot produce fruit if it is severed from the vine, and you cannot be fruitful unless you remain in me.

Acts 11:23, NIV
When he arrived and saw the evidence of the grace of God, he was glad and encouraged them all to remain true to the Lord with all their hearts.

Romans 2:4, NIV
Do you show contempt for the riches of his kind-ness, tolerance and patience, not realizing that God's kindness leads you toward repentance?

| | |
|---|---|
| Romans 5:8, NIV | God demonstrates his own love for us in this: While we were still sinners, Christ died for us. |
| Romans 8:1, NIV | There is now no condemnation for those who are in Christ Jesus. |
| Romans 8:35, NIV | Who shall separate us from the love of Christ? Shall trouble or hardship or persecution or famine or nakedness or danger or sword? |
| Romans 8:38-39, NIV | I am convinced that neither death nor life, neither angels nor demons, neither the present nor the future, nor any powers, neither height nor depth, nor anything else in all creation, will be able to separate us from the love of God that is in Christ Jesus our Lord. |
| Ephesians 3:16-19, NIV | I pray that out of his glorious riches he may strengthen you with power through his Spirit in your inner being, so that Christ may dwell in your hearts through faith. And I pray that you, being rooted and established in love, may have power, together with all the saints, to grasp how wide and long and high and deep is the love of Christ, and to know this love that surpasses knowledge—that you may be filled to the measure of all the fullness of God. |
| Philippians 1:6, NIV | Being confident of this, that he who began a good work in you will carry it on to completion until the day of Christ Jesus. |

| | |
|---|---|
| 2 Peter 3:9, NKJV | The Lord is not slack concerning His promise, as some count slackness, but is longsuffering toward us, not willing that any should perish but that all should come to repentance. |
| 1 John 1:9, NKJV | If we confess our sins, He is faithful and just to forgive us our sins and to cleanse us from all unrighteousness. |
| Revelation 2:4-5, NIV | Yet I hold this against you: You have forsaken your first love. Remember the height from which you have fallen! Repent and do the things you did at first. If you do not repent, I will come to you and remove your lampstand from its place. |

# Faith—Praying for Someone Who Has Turned Away from Faith

Has someone you love fallen away from the Lord? God calls you to not give up on them. Continue to pray Scripture over them—daily. Regardless of what you see in the natural world, be persistent in the spiritual world. It might seem as if nothing is happening, but your prayers and faith can be the bridge that brings your loved one back to God. "So do not throw away this confident trust in the Lord. Remember the great reward it brings you!" (Hebrews 10:35, NLT). Your persistence is an expression of your faith that God answers prayer.

We fight a powerful army whose goal is to defeat the Christian church. Keep in mind, "our struggle is not against flesh and blood, but against the rulers, against the authorities, against the powers of this dark world and against the spiritual forces of evil in the heavenly realms" (Ephesians 6:12, NIV). Understanding that a spiritual battle is raging against your loved one will help you to keep things in right perspective.

The heart of God cries out to those who have turned away from their faith, "Come back…I am full of mercy" (Jeremiah 3:12, NCV). Pray that your loved one will hear and respond to God's call to return to Him. The power of prayer can change a person's heart and move the hand of God. As you pray, you will have a deeper sense that "nothing is impossible with God" (Luke 1:37, NIV).

*For other helpful categories, see pages 147, 314, 346, 398.*

| 1 Samuel 10:26, NIV | Saul also went to his home in Gibeah, accompanied by valiant men whose hearts God had touched. |
| Jeremiah 3:12, NCV | Go and speak this message toward the north: "Come back, unfaithful people of Israel," says the LORD. "I will stop being angry at you, because I am full of mercy," says the LORD. "I will not be angry with you forever." |
| Ezekiel 36:26, NIV | I will give you a new heart and put a new spirit in you; I will remove from you your heart of stone and give you a heart of flesh. |
| Hosea 14:4, NIV | I will heal their waywardness and love them freely, for my anger has turned away from them. |
| Matthew 9:37-38, NKJV | Then he said to His disciples, "The harvest truly is plentiful, but the laborers are few. Therefore pray the Lord of the harvest to send out laborers into His harvest." |
| Luke 1:37, NIV | Nothing is impossible with God. |
| Luke 24:45, NIV | Then he opened their minds so they could understand the Scriptures. |
| 2 Corinthians 4:6, NIV | God, who said, "Let light shine out of darkness," made his light shine in our hearts to give us the light of the knowledge of the glory of God in the face of Christ. |

| | |
|---|---|
| 2 Corinthians 7:9, NIV | Now I am happy, not because you were made sorry, but because your sorrow led you to repentance. For you became sorrowful as God intended and so were not harmed in any way by us. |
| Galatians 6:1, NIV | If someone is caught in a sin, you who are spiritual should restore him gently. But watch yourself, or you also may be tempted. |
| Ephesians 1:18, NIV | I pray also that the eyes of your heart may be enlightened in order that you may know the hope to which he has called you, the riches of his glorious inheritance in the saints. |
| Ephesians 3:16-19, NIV | I pray that out of his glorious riches [God] may strengthen you with power through his Spirit in your inner being, so that Christ may dwell in your hearts through faith. And I pray that you, being rooted and established in love, may have power, together with all the saints, to grasp how wide and long and high and deep is the love of Christ, and to know this love that surpasses knowledge—that you may be filled to the measure of all the fullness of God. |
| Ephesians 3:20-21, NIV | Now to him who is able to do immeasurably more than all we ask or imagine, according to his power that is at work within us, to him be glory in the church and in Christ Jesus throughout all generations, forever and ever! Amen. |

Ephesians 6:12, NIV

For we do not wrestle against flesh and blood, but against principalities, against powers, against the rulers of the darkness of this age, against spiritual hosts of wickedness in the heavenly places.

Hebrews 10:35, NLT

Do not throw away this confident trust in the Lord. Remember the great reward it brings you!

# THE FAITHFULNESS OF GOD

Spouses break their wedding vows. Business partners violate their contracts. Friends and family members go back on their promises.

Let's face it: human beings are all too commonly unfaithful. If we think of God in human terms, we can easily be led to doubt His faithfulness. Especially when we are in need and are clinging to God's promises, we can start to wonder if He will come through for us.

There's no need to be concerned about that! Faithfulness is a built-in part of God's nature. "If we are faithless, he remains faithful; He cannot deny Himself" (2 Timothy 2:13, NKJV).

God is a covenant-keeping God (Exodus 6:5). His promises are not based on people's faithfulness; they are based on His faithful love for His people. He will always fulfill His promises.

Even when you mess up and walk away from God, He pursues you. Time and time again, He extends His loving hand and an abundance of His grace.

So trust in this: No matter how hopeless your situation might seem, God is always faithful to His Word. As you seek Him, He will be faithful to hear your prayer and answer.

The psalmist was right. "Your mercy, O LORD, is in the heavens; Your faithfulness reaches to the clouds" (Psalm 36:5, NKJV)!

*For other helpful categories, see pages 193, 196, 199, 336, 428.*

| | |
|---|---|
| Exodus 6:5, NKJV | I have also heard the groaning of the children of Israel whom the Egyptians keep in bondage, and I have remembered My covenant. |
| Deuteronomy 7:9, NCV | Know that the LORD your God is God, the faithful God. He will keep his agreement of love for a thousand lifetimes for people who love him and obey his commands. |
| Deuteronomy 32:4, NCV | He is like a rock; what he does is perfect, and he is always fair. He is a faithful God who does no wrong, who is right and fair. |
| 2 Samuel 22:26, NIV | To the faithful you show yourself faithful, to the blameless you show yourself blameless. |
| Psalm 25:10, NLT | The LORD leads with unfailing love and faithfulness all who keep his covenant and obey his demands. |
| Psalm 33:4, NIV | The word of the LORD is right and true; he is faithful in all he does. |
| Psalm 36:5, NKJV | Your mercy, O LORD, is in the heavens; Your faithfulness reaches to the clouds. |
| Psalm 89:1, NIV | I will sing of the LORD's great love forever; with my mouth I will make your faithfulness known through all generations. |
| Psalm 89:2, CEV | God's love can always be trusted, and his faithfulness lasts as long as the heavens. |

| | |
|---|---|
| Psalm 89:8, NIV | O LORD God Almighty, who is like you? You are mighty, O LORD, and your faithfulness surrounds you. |
| Psalm 89:14, NIV | Righteousness and justice are the foundation of your throne; love and faithfulness go before you. |
| Psalm 91:4, CEV | He will spread his wings over you and keep you secure. His faithfulness is like a shield or a city wall. |
| Psalm 145:13, NIV | Your kingdom is an everlasting kingdom, and your dominion endures through all generations. The LORD is faithful to all his promises and loving toward all he has made. |
| 1 Corinthians 1:9, NIV | God, who has called you into fellowship with his Son Jesus Christ our Lord, is faithful. |
| 2 Timothy 2:13, NKJV | If we are faithless, he remains faithful; He cannot deny Himself. |

# FASTING

Fasting is a time when your heart cries out to God, when you hunger for more of Him, when you humble yourself before Him. As we read in James, "Draw near to God and He will draw near to you" (James 4:8, NKJV). When you fast, you are intentionally seeking closer union and fellowship with God. Fasting frees you to focus and rely on God for strength, provision, and wisdom. Fasting is a source of power that will release God's supernatural into your life. It will help you to hear the voice of God more clearly.

Here are seven types of fasts that are based on God's Word:

1. The Esther fast: to seek God's favor in the time of crisis (Esther 4:16).
2. The Daniel fast: eating only fruits and vegetables, drinking only water, and abstaining from any chemicals or artificial foods for a certain amount of time to give you understanding of the vision God gave you so that it will come to pass (Daniel 10:2-3).
3. Fasting for one day with the purpose of self-examination and consecration (Leviticus 23:27).
4. Fasting before a battle (Judges 20). When you are facing a major enemy or launching a new business or ministry, it is essential that you put a fast behind it.
5. Fasting to lift God's judgment from another person's life (1 Kings 21:27-29).
6. Fasting to usher in God's healing (Isaiah 58).
7. The dominion fast: Jesus fasted for forty days and forty nights to take back dominion and authority (Matthew 4:1-2).

Fasting will bring you into alignment with God's plans and purposes for your life and your loved ones. Pray and ask God which fast He desires for you. (This list was drawn from Jentezen Franklin, *Fasting Journal* [Lake Mary, FL: Charisma House, 2008].)

*For other helpful categories, see pages 9, 11, 193–196, 218, 239, 257, 333.*

| | |
|---|---|
| Judges 20:26, NIV | The Israelites, all the people, went up to Bethel, and there they sat weeping before the LORD. They fasted that day until evening and presented burnt offerings and fellowship offerings to the LORD. |
| 1 Kings 21:27-29, NKJV | So it was, when Ahab heard those words, that he tore his clothes and put sackcloth on his body, and fasted and lay in sackcloth, and went about mourning. And the word of the LORD came to Elijah the Tishbite, saying, "See how Ahab has humbled himself before Me? Because he has humbled himself before Me, I will not bring the calamity in his days. In the days of his son I will bring the calamity on his house." |
| Esther 4:16, NKJV | Go, gather all the Jews who are present in Shushan, and fast for me; neither eat nor drink for three days, night or day. My maids and I will fast likewise. And so I will go to the king, which is against the law; and if I perish, I perish! |
| Isaiah 58:6, NIV | Is not this the kind of fasting I have chosen: to loose the chains of injustice and untie the cords of the yoke, to set the oppressed free and break every yoke? |
| Daniel 10:2-3, NKJV | In those days I, Daniel, was mourning three full weeks. I ate no pleasant food, no meat or wine came into my mouth, nor did I anoint myself at all, till three whole weeks were fulfilled. |

| | |
|---|---|
| Matthew 4:1-2, NIV | Jesus was led by the Spirit into the desert to be tempted by the devil. After fasting forty days and forty nights, he was hungry. |
| Matthew 6:16-18, NKJV | When you fast, do not be like the hypocrites, with a sad countenance. For they disfigure their faces that they may appear to men to be fasting. Assuredly, I say to you, they have their reward. But you, when you fast, anoint your head and wash your face, so that you do not appear to men to be fasting, but to your Father who is in the secret place; and your Father who sees in secret will reward you openly. |
| Mark 2:18-20, NLT | Once when John's disciples and the Pharisees were fasting, some people came to Jesus and asked, "Why don't your disciples fast like John's disciples and the Pharisees do?" Jesus replied, "Do wedding guests fast while celebrating with the groom? Of course not. They can't fast while the groom is with them. But someday the groom will be taken away from them, and then they will fast." |
| Mark 9:29, NKJV | He said to them, "This kind can come out by nothing but prayer and fasting." |
| Acts 13:2-3, NIV | While they were worshiping the Lord and fasting, the Holy Spirit said, "Set apart for me Barnabas and Saul for the work to which I have called them." So after they had fasted and prayed, they placed their hands on them and sent them off. |

# THE FAVOR OF GOD

Believers in Jesus Christ need not fear that God's wrath lies upon them. Far from it! Because of the sacrifice of God's Son, His wrath has been removed from us—and His favor rests upon us instead.

You cannot earn God's favor. It is a gift to you through Christ (2 Corinthians 6:2). Yet just as Abel gave his best to God out of a pure heart (Genesis 4) and received his favor, so you should seek to keep your heart pure before the Lord and expect His favor. If you expect God's favor and thank Him when you begin to see His kindness, you will see more and more of it.

Remember that God's favor is not just for your own personal enjoyment or satisfaction. You have received God's favor on your life so that you can be an effective witness for Him. As you strive to make Him known to others, He will increase your sphere of influence for His purposes.

You can proceed in your Christian service and devotion in all confidence. As you pray, know that God's favor rests upon His Word and rests upon you.

*For other helpful categories, see pages 11, 329, 424.*

| | |
|---|---|
| Genesis 4:4, NIV | Abel brought fat portions from some of the first-born of his flock. The LORD looked with favor on Abel and his offering. |
| Leviticus 26:9, NIV | I will look on you with favor and make you fruitful and increase your numbers, and I will keep my covenant with you. |
| Job 10:12, NKJV | You have granted me life and favor, and Your care has preserved my spirit. |
| Job 33:26, NIV | He prays to God and finds favor with him, he sees God's face and shouts for joy; he is restored by God to his righteous state. |
| Psalm 5:12, NKJV | You, O LORD, will bless the righteous; with favor you will surround him as with a shield. |
| Psalm 30:7, AMP | By Your favor, O LORD, You have established me as a strong mountain. |
| Psalm 90:17, NIV | May the favor of the Lord our God rest upon us; establish the work of our hands for us—yes, establish the work of our hands. |
| Proverbs 3:3-4, NIV | Let love and faithfulness never leave you; bind them around your neck, write them on the tablet of your heart. Then you will win favor and a good name in the sight of God and man. |
| Proverbs 8:35, NIV | Whoever finds me finds life and receives favor from the LORD. |

Proverbs 11:27, NKJV    He who earnestly seeks good finds favor, but trouble will come to him who seeks evil.

Proverbs 12:2, NKJV    A good man obtains favor from the LORD, but a man of wicked intentions He will condemn.

Proverbs 14:9, NKJV    Fools mock at sin, but among the upright there is favor.

Proverbs 14:35, NKJV    The king's favor is toward a wise servant, but his wrath is against him who causes shame.

Proverbs 16:7, NIV    When a man's ways are pleasing to the LORD, he makes even his enemies live at peace with him.

Proverbs 22:1, NKJV    A good name is to be chosen rather than great riches, loving favor rather than silver and gold.

Isaiah 60:10, NIV    In favor I will show you compassion.

Romans 8:31, NIV    If God is for us, who can be against us?

2 Corinthians 6:2, NIV    For he says, "In the time of my favor I heard you, and in the day of salvation I helped you." I tell you, now is the time of God's favor, now is the day of salvation.

# FEAR

Fears, worries, and anxieties make up one of the greatest battlegrounds of spiritual warfare. Satan loves to control people by getting them entangled in fear. God, on the other hand, wants to set us free from what worries us. The sword of the Spirit—the Word of God—is our weapon to defeat and defend ourselves from all fear (Ephesians 6:17).

Let the truth of God's Word be fuel for your faith. Keep in mind these two keys to overcoming fear:

1. You can—and should—have complete trust in God. He won't let you down.
2. You can replace your fear with faith. After all, fear and faith cannot coexist.

You have the authority of God's Word to overcome every circumstance you may face. If there is any area in your life where you are gripped with fear, lay hold of God's Word in that area. Stay focused on what the Lord says, not what the circumstance is saying.

One psalmist declared, "In God I have put my trust; I will not be afraid. What can man do to me?" (Psalm 56:11, NKJV). What an awesome position to be in!

Are you in that place? Are you trusting and resting in God? You can be. Christ gives you the victory over all fear (Romans 8:15).

*For other helpful categories, see pages 62, 65, 132, 196, 375, 428.*

Deuteronomy 31:8, NKJV — The LORD, He is the One who goes before you. He will be with you, he will not leave you nor forsake you; do not fear nor be dismayed.

Psalm 23:4, NLT — Even when I walk through the darkest valley, I will not be afraid, for you are close beside me. Your rod and your staff protect and comfort me.

Psalm 27:1, NCV — The LORD is my light and the one who saves me. So why should I fear anyone? The LORD protects my life. So why should I be afraid?

Psalm 27:3, NIV — Though an army besiege me, my heart will not fear; though war break out against me, even then will I be confident.

Psalm 34:4, NCV — I asked the LORD for help, and he answered me. He saved me from all that I feared.

Psalm 56:11, NKJV — In God I have put my trust; I will not be afraid. What can man do to me?

Psalm 91:5, NIV — You will not fear the terror of night, nor the arrow that flies by day.

Proverbs 3:25-26, NIV — Have no fear of sudden disaster or of the ruin that overtakes the wicked, for the LORD will be your confidence and will keep your foot from being snared.

Proverbs 29:25, NLT — Fearing people is a dangerous trap, but trusting the LORD means safety.

| | |
|---|---|
| Isaiah 41:10, NKJV | Fear not, for I am with you; be not dismayed, for I am your God. I will strengthen you, yes, I will help you, I will uphold you with My righteous right hand. |
| Romans 8:15, NKJV | You did not receive the spirit of bondage again to fear, but you received the Spirit of adoption by whom we cry out, "Abba, Father." |
| 2 Timothy 1:7, NKJV | God has not given us a spirit of fear, but of power and of love and of a sound mind. |
| Hebrews 2:14-15, NIV | Since the children have flesh and blood, he too shared in their humanity so that by his death he might destroy him who holds the power of death — that is, the devil — and free those who all their lives were held in slavery by their fear of death. |
| Hebrews 13:6, NKJV | The Lord is my helper; I will not fear. What can man do to me? |
| 1 John 4:18, NKJV | There is no fear in love; but perfect love casts out fear, because fear involves torment. But he who fears has not been made perfect in love. |

# Finances—Financial Principles

Being free to live out the desires of your heart and to walk in financial freedom is within your reach! God gave you financial principles so that you could accomplish everything that He has called you to do. Your desire may be to become financially stable, start a business, or have the means to be a blessing to someone in need.

God's provision for you will come through His blessing on your job, your business, or your investments. His promise in Deuteronomy 28:8 is to bless "everything you put your hand to" (NIV).

How do you activate that promise? By understanding and following the principles outlined in God's Word. As you do, these principles will bring you the financial freedom that God desires for all of His people.

1. **Understand that God owns it all.** " 'The silver is mine and the gold is mine,' declares the Lord Almighty" (Haggai 2:8, NIV).

2. **Recognize that financial blessing comes from God.** "But remember the Lord your God, for it is he who gives you the ability to produce wealth, and so confirms his covenant, which he swore to your forefathers, as it is today" (Deuteronomy 8:18, NIV).

3. **Be a good steward over your finances.** "Moreover it is required in stewards that one be found faithful" (1 Corinthians 4:2, NKJV).

4. **Establish a realistic budget.** "But everything should be done in a fitting and orderly way" (1 Corinthians 14:40, NIV).

5. **Pay your obligations.**

   a. **Tithe** (Malachi 3:10)

b. **Giving commitments** (2 Corinthians 9:5)

c. **Taxes** (Matthew 17:24-27)

d. **Debt** (Romans 13:8)

6. **Stay out of bad debt, such as credit card debt and excessive borrowing.** "The rich rules over the poor, and the borrower is servant to the lender" (Proverbs 22:7, NKJV).

7. **Save a portion of your earnings every month.** "The wise have wealth and luxury, but fools spend whatever they get" (Proverbs 21:20, NLT).

8. **Earn money God's way—honestly.** "God hates cheating in the marketplace; he loves it when business is aboveboard" (Proverbs 11:1, MSG).

9. **Make a financial plan and set goals.** "The plans of the diligent lead to profit as surely as haste leads to poverty" (Proverbs 21:5, NIV).

10. **Ask God for wisdom to help you achieve financial success.** "By wisdom a house is built, and through understanding it is established" (Proverbs 24:3, NIV).

It is God's will for you to break free from living payday to payday, to pay off your mortgage, and to have an abundance to give to others as you are so led.

*For other helpful categories, see pages 160, 164, 368.*

| | |
|---|---|
| Genesis 32:12, NIV | I will surely make you prosper and will make your descendants like the sand of the sea, which cannot be counted. |
| Deuteronomy 8:18, NKJV | You shall remember the LORD your God, for it is He who gives you power to get wealth, that He may establish His covenant which He swore to your fathers, as it is this day. |
| 1 Chronicles 4:10, NKJV | Jabez called on the God of Israel saying, "Oh, that You would bless me indeed, and enlarge my territory, that Your hand would be with me, and that You would keep me from evil, that I may not cause pain!" So God granted him what he requested. |
| Psalm 1:1-3, NKJV | Blessed is the man who walks not in the counsel of the ungodly, nor stands in the path of sinners, nor sits in the seat of the scornful; but his delight is in the law of the LORD, and in His law he meditates day and night. He shall be like a tree planted by the rivers of water, that brings forth its fruit in its season, whose leaf also shall not wither; and whatever he does shall prosper. |
| Psalm 68:19, NKJV | Blessed be the Lord, who daily loads us with benefits, the God of our salvation! |
| Psalm 84:4, NKJV | Blessed are those who dwell in Your house, they will still be praising You. |
| Proverbs 3:9-10, NIV | Honor the LORD with your wealth, with the firstfruits of all your crops; then your barns will be |

filled to overflowing, and your vats will brim over with new wine.

Isaiah 1:19, NKJV

If you are willing and obedient, you shall eat the good of the land.

Matthew 6:33, NKJV

Seek first the kingdom of God and His righteousness, and all these things shall be added to you.

Mark 8:36, NKJV

What will it profit a man if he gains the whole world, and loses his own soul?

Luke 6:38, NKJV

Give and it will be given to you: good measure, pressed down, shaken together, and running over will be put into your bosom. For with the same measure that you use, it will be measured back to you.

Luke 11:42, NIV

Woe to you Pharisees, because you give God a tenth of your mint, rue and all other kinds of garden herbs, but you neglect justice and the love of God. You should have practiced the latter without leaving the former undone.

Luke 12:15, NIV

Watch out! Be on your guard against all kinds of greed; a man's life does not consist in the abundance of his possessions.

Luke 16:11, NCV

If you cannot be trusted with worldly riches, then who will trust you with true riches?

3 John, 2, NKJV

Beloved, I pray that you may prosper in all things and be in health, just as your soul prospers.

# Finances—Financial Debt

Did you know there is a fundamental difference between good debt and bad debt?

Good debt is the responsible use of borrowing. It includes financing your home, starting or building your business, or purchasing a needed vehicle.

Bad debt includes unpaid credit card balances, debt from luxury items, gambling, or buying a home beyond one's financial means.

Bad debt is a captivity that prevents us from living boldly or giving generously. And God wants His dearly loved children to be free.

If you have had the attitude that debt is no big deal, consider this verse from the apostle Paul: "Owe nothing to anyone—except for your obligation to love one another" (Romans 13:8, NLT). Set about the hard work of climbing out of debt one step at a time, starting now. Eventually you'll want to own your home and businesses free and clear. Think of the joy you will have negotiating for your new car and being able to pay cash!

As you are paying off your debts, think about how you got in that situation in the first place. Was it because of wanting more than you could afford? Jesus says to you, "Beware, and be on your guard against every form of greed; for not even when one has an abundance does his life consist of his possessions" (Luke 12:15, NASB; see also 1 Timothy 6:6-10).

Or did you get into debt because of poor money management? Learn from the wisdom of others who have been through financial debt. Go on a personal quest to educate yourself about money. Read books by Christians who have built their financial wealth on the Word of God. God has a lot to say about finances in His Word. There are more than eight hundred verses in the Bible that show us how to handle money God's way!

Perhaps you got into debt through no fault of your own—in fact, you worked very hard to stay out of debt but circumstances were out of your control.

Whatever your situation, it is possible to move on. Pray for forgiveness if it is needed. Pray for motivation to keep going and for wisdom to make good decisions. You might feel as if you're in a bottomless pit of bills and expenses, but God will get you out.

*For other helpful categories, see pages 171, 180, 236, 381, 421, 437.*

| | |
|---|---|
| Psalm 37:21-22, NIV | The wicked borrow and do not repay, but the righteous give generously. |
| Proverbs 11:15, CEV | It's a dangerous thing to guarantee payment for someone's debts. Don't do it! |
| Proverbs 13:22, CEV | If you obey God, you will have something to leave your grandchildren. If you don't obey God, those who live right will get what you leave. |
| Proverbs 22:7, NIV | The rich rule over the poor, and the borrower is servant to the lender. |
| Mark 12:17, NIV | Give to Caesar what is Caesar's and to God what is God's. |
| Luke 12:15, NASB | Beware, and be on your guard against every form of greed; for not even when one has an abundance does his life consist of his possessions. |
| Luke 14:28, NCV | If you want to build a tower, you first sit down and decide how much it will cost, to see if you have enough money to finish the job. |
| John 14:15, NIV | If you love me, you will obey what I command. |
| Romans 13:7, NIV | Give everyone what you owe him: If you owe taxes, pay taxes; if revenue, then revenue; if respect, then respect; if honor, then honor. |
| Romans 13:8, NLT | Owe nothing to anyone—except for your obligation to love one another. If you love your neighbor, you will fulfill the requirements of God's law. |

| | |
|---|---|
| 1 Timothy 6:6-9, NASB | Godliness actually is a means of great gain when accompanied by contentment. For we have brought nothing into the world, so we cannot take anything out of it either. If we have food and covering, with these we shall be content. But those who want to get rich fall into temptation and a snare and many foolish and harmful desires which plunge men into ruin and destruction. |
| 1 Timothy 6:10, NASB | The love of money is a root of all sorts of evil, and some by longing for it have wandered away from the faith and pierced themselves with many griefs. |
| Hebrews 10:26, NLT | Dear friends, if we deliberately continue sinning after we have received knowledge of the truth, there is no longer any sacrifice that will cover these sins. |
| James 1:5, NIV | If any of you lacks wisdom, he should ask God, who gives generously to all without finding fault, and it will be given to him. |
| James 1:14, NCV | People are tempted when their own evil desire leads them away and traps them. |

# FINANCES—
# FINANCIAL GIVING TO THE LORD

Giving to the Lord's work is not primarily about "have to"; it's about "want to." "God loves a cheerful giver" (2 Corinthians 9:7, NIV). When we give to the Lord, we put into motion a spiritual principle found in Luke 6:38: "Give and it will be given to you: good measure, pressed down, shaken together, and running over will be put into your bosom. For with the same measure that you use, it will be measured back to you" (NKJV).

Financial giving enables you to experience the joy of participating in God's great work in this world. Along the way, it builds your faith in Him and frees you from the grip of fear about money. Giving is evidence that you have conquered greed.

God gave His people the Israelites a rule about offering a tithe (tenth) of their income to the Lord (Deuteronomy 14:22-29). And He took it personally when they withheld their money. "Will a man rob God? Yet you have robbed Me!" (Malachi 3:8, NKJV).

Jesus reinforced the importance of following the tithing laws as part of a faithful relationship with God (Luke 11:42). The New Testament goes on to provide many helpful guidelines about giving. We should give regularly (1 Corinthians 16:2), persistently (2 Corinthians 8:11), cheerfully (2 Corinthians 9:7), privately (Matthew 6:1-4), and in proportion to our financial means (2 Corinthians 8:12).

If you're having trouble letting your money go to the work of the Lord, read what the Word says about giving and God's faithfulness: "He who sows sparingly will also reap sparingly, and he who sows bountifully will also reap bountifully" (2 Corinthians 9:6, NKJV). Why miss out on the blessing that can be yours?

*For other helpful categories, see pages 156, 321, 368.*

| | |
|---|---|
| Deuteronomy 14:22, NIV | Be sure to set aside a tenth of all that your fields produce each year. |
| Proverbs 3:9-10, NIV | Honor the LORD with your wealth, with the first-fruits of all your crops; then your barns will be filled to overflowing, and your vats will brim over with new wine. |
| Proverbs 11:25, NIV | A generous man will prosper; he who refreshes others will himself be refreshed. |
| Proverbs 19:17, NCV | Being kind to the poor is like lending to the Lord; he will reward you for what you have done. |
| Malachi 3:8, NKJV | Will a man rob God? Yet you have robbed Me! But you say, "In what way have we robbed You?" In tithes and offerings. |
| Malachi 3:10, NIV | "Bring the whole tithe into the storehouse, that there may be food in my house. Test me in this," says the LORD Almighty, "and see if I will not throw open the floodgates of heaven and pour out so much blessing that you will not have room enough for it. |
| Matthew 5:42, NIV | Give to the one who asks you, and do not turn away from the one who wants to borrow from you. |
| Matthew 6:1-4, NIV | Be careful not to do your "acts of righteousness" before men, to be seen by them. If you do, you will have no reward from your Father in heaven. So when you give to the needy, do not announce it with trumpets, as the hypocrites do in the |

synagogues and on the streets, to be honored by men. I tell you the truth, they have received their reward in full. But when you give to the needy, do not let your left hand know what your right hand is doing, so that your giving may be in secret. Then your Father, who sees what is done in secret, will reward you.

| | |
|---|---|
| Matthew 10:8, NIV | Freely you have received, freely give. |

| | |
|---|---|
| Luke 6:38, NIV | Give, and it will be given to you. A good measure, pressed down, shaken together and running over, will be poured into your lap. For with the measure you use, it will be measured to you. |

| | |
|---|---|
| Luke 11:42, NIV | Woe to you Pharisees, because you give God a tenth of your mint, rue and all other kinds of garden herbs, but you neglect justice and the love of God. You should have practiced the latter without leaving the former undone. |

| | |
|---|---|
| Acts 2:44-45, NIV | All the believers were together and had everything in common. Selling their possessions and goods, they gave to anyone as he had need. |

| | |
|---|---|
| 1 Corinthians 16:2, NLT | On the first day of each week, you should each put aside a portion of the money you have earned. |

| | |
|---|---|
| 2 Corinthians 8:7, NIV | Just as you excel in everything—in faith, in speech, in knowledge, in complete earnestness and in your love for us—see that you also excel in this grace of giving. |

| | |
|---|---|
| 2 Corinthians 9:6, NKJV | He who sows sparingly will also reap sparingly, and he who sows bountifully will also reap bountifully. |
| 2 Corinthians 9:7, NIV | Each man should give what he has decided in his heart to give, not reluctantly or under compulsion, for God loves a cheerful giver. |
| Galatians 6:6, NIV | Anyone who receives instruction in the word must share all good things with his instructor. |
| Galatians 6:7, NIV | Do not be deceived: God cannot be mocked. A man reaps what he sows. |
| 1 John 3:17, NKJV | Whoever has this world's goods, and sees his brother in need, and shuts up his heart from him, how does the love of God abide in him? |

# FORECLOSURE

The threat of foreclosure can be one of the most heart-sinking realities of a difficult economy, job loss, or poor financial decisions. It might seem like something that only happens to "other people"—until it happens to you.

As Job said when he lost what was dear to him: "What I feared has come upon me; what I dreaded has happened to me. I have no peace, no quietness; I have no rest, but only turmoil" (Job 3:25-26, NIV).

God promises to "bring you home" (Zephaniah 3:20) to a place of rest (Psalm 23). Even though you feel desperate right now, ask God where and how He is leading you. Ask for forgiveness if your situation is due to your not following Him. Ask for strength and grace to forgive others if your home is in foreclosure because of wrongs others have done to you.

You are not praying to feel better. You are praying because prayer changes things in the heavenly realms. Prayer gives you wisdom to deal with banks and insurance companies. Prayer can make the impossible possible and allow you to keep your house. Prayer gives you insight into who you can ask for help. Most of all, prayer gives you hope even though the future seems overwhelming now.

No matter what got you into this situation, God is with you. And He still longs to bring you to a quiet place of rest in Him.

*For other helpful categories, see pages 115, 118, 156, 381.*

Job 3:25-26, NIV

What I feared has come upon me; what I dreaded has happened to me. I have no peace, no quietness; I have no rest, but only turmoil.

Psalm 16:11, NKJV

You will show me the path of life; in Your presence is fullness of joy, at Your right hand are pleasures forevermore.

Psalm 23:2, NIV

He makes me lie down in green pastures, he leads me beside quiet waters.

Psalm 37:23, NKJV

The steps of a good man are ordered by the LORD, and He delights in his way.

Psalm 43:5, NIV

Why are you downcast, O my soul? Why so disturbed within me? Put your hope in God, for I will yet praise him, my Savior and my God.

Psalm 46:1, NIV

God is our refuge and strength, an ever-present help in trouble.

Psalm 55:17, NLT

Morning, noon, and night I cry out in my distress, and the LORD hears my voice.

Zephaniah 3:20, NIV

"At that time I will gather you; at that time I will bring you home. I will give you honor and praise among all the peoples of the earth when I restore your fortunes before your very eyes," says the LORD.

Matthew 11:28, NIV

Come to me, all you who are weary and burdened, and I will give you rest.

| | |
|---|---|
| John 14:1, NKJV | Let not your heart be troubled; you believe in God, believe also in Me. |
| Romans 12:2, NLT | Don't copy the behavior and customs of this world, but let God transform you into a new person by changing the way you think. Then you will learn to know God's will for you, which is good and pleasing and perfect. |
| James 1:5, NIV | If any of you lacks wisdom, he should ask God, who gives generously to all without finding fault, and it will be given to him. |
| James 3:17, NCV | The wisdom that comes from God is first of all pure, then peaceful, gentle, and easy to please. This wisdom is always ready to help those who are troubled and to do good for others. It is always fair and honest. |

# FORGIVENESS—GOD'S FORGIVENESS

Sometimes, even after trusting in Jesus Christ for salvation, people feel that God cannot really accept them because of something terrible they have done. The guilt is gone but the guilt *feelings* linger. Does that describe you? If so, I encourage you to let the reality of God's truth and Word set you free!

The truth is: Jesus shed His blood, rose from the grave, and proclaimed victory over sin and death. He gave His life so that we wouldn't have to experience eternal separation from God.

"In [Christ] we have redemption through His blood, the forgiveness of sins, according to the riches of His grace" (Ephesians 1:7, NKJV). Forgiveness is based on the shedding of Jesus's blood. He died as the perfect and final sacrifice. Therefore, when God looks at us, He no longer sees our sin; He sees Christ's purity.

That's why Colossians 2:13 can say, "When you were dead in your sins and in the uncircumcision of your sinful nature, God made you alive with Christ. He forgave us all our sins" (NIV). *All* our sins.

And that's why Psalm 103:12 can say, "He has taken our sins away from us as far as the east is from west" (NCV). That's as far away from us as our sins can get!

Do not deny the cross its power. You are forgiven!

*For other helpful categories, see pages 136, 193–196, 257, 343, 421.*

Psalm 32:5, NCV | I confessed my sins to you and didn't hide my guilt. I said, "I will confess my sins to the LORD," and you forgave my guilt.

Psalm 51:2, NCV | Wash away all my guilt and make me clean again.

Psalm 103:12, NCV | He has taken our sins away from us as far as the east is from west.

Isaiah 1:18, NIV | "Come now, let us reason together," says the LORD. "Though your sins are like scarlet, they shall be as white as snow; though they are red as crimson, they shall be like wool."

Jeremiah 33:8, NIV | I will cleanse them from all the sin they have committed against me and will forgive all their sins of rebellion against me.

Matthew 26:28, NKJV | For this is My blood of the new covenant, which is shed for many for the remission of sins.

Luke 7:47, NIV | Therefore, I tell you, her many sins have been for-given—for she loved much. But he who has been forgiven little loves little.

Luke 24:47, NIV | Repentance and forgiveness of sins will be preached in his name to all nations, beginning at Jerusalem.

Acts 2:38, NKJV | Repent, and let every one of you be baptized in the name of Jesus Christ for the remission of sins; and you shall receive the gift of the Holy Spirit.

Acts 13:38, NIV      I want you to know that through Jesus the forgiveness of sins is proclaimed to you.

Romans 4:7, NIV      Blessed are they whose transgressions are forgiven, whose sins are covered.

Romans 8:1, NIV      There is now no condemnation for those who are in Christ Jesus.

Ephesians 1:7, NKJV      In Him we have redemption through His blood, the forgiveness of sins, according to the riches of His grace.

Colossians 2:13, NIV      When you were dead in your sins and in the uncircumcision of your sinful nature, God made you alive with Christ. He forgave us all our sins.

Hebrews 8:12, NIV      I will forgive their wickedness and will remember their sins no more.

1 John 1:9, NKJV      If we confess our sins, He is faithful and just to forgive us our sins and to cleanse us from all unrighteousness.

# FORGIVENESS—FORGIVING OTHERS

Live long enough in this world, and you *will* get hurt by others—sometimes terribly, sometimes repeatedly. The wounds are real. It can feel impossible to forgive the offender. Yet God's Word says we cannot hold on to that bitterness.

When you forgive, it is not to let the other person off the hook for doing something hurtful. It is for *your* benefit. Prolonged unforgiveness will be like a cancer to your spirit and to the other relationships in your life.

You can forgive because forgiveness is not a mustering up of some false feelings of warmness toward the offender. Rather, forgiveness is an act of the will. So stand firm on your *decision* to forgive and not on your feelings.

Offenses can come frequently. Don't allow them to pile up and hold your feelings captive. Your feelings will eventually follow your decision to release the offense.

Pray for the person who has hurt or wronged you. It's hard to stay angry at someone when you're praying God's Word over him or her.

If you're having trouble forgiving, remember that *you* have been totally forgiven by God. He has forgiven you a debt that you could never repay, so you have no grounds for refusing to forgive others (Matthew 18:15-35).

When someone has wronged you, ask God for His help to forgive. You might feel so wounded that it's hard to get past the pain without God's help. He freely offers that help.

*For other helpful categories, see pages 218, 223, 340, 356, 398.*

| | |
|---|---|
| Genesis 50:20, NLT | You intended to harm me, but God intended it all for good. He brought me to this position so I could save the lives of many people. |
| Matthew 6:12, NLT | Forgive us our sins, as we have forgiven those who sin against us. |
| Matthew 6:14-15, NKJV | If you forgive men their trespasses, your heavenly Father will also forgive you. But if you do not forgive men their trespasses, neither will your Father forgive your trespasses. |
| Matthew 18:21-22, NIV | Then Peter came to Jesus and asked, "Lord, how many times shall I forgive my brother when he sins against me? Up to seven times?" Jesus answered, "I tell you, not seven times, but seventy-seven times." |
| Matthew 18:32-35, NIV | The master called the servant in. "You wicked servant," he said, "I canceled all that debt of yours because you begged me to. Shouldn't you have had mercy on your fellow servant just as I had on you?" In anger his master turned him over to the jailers to be tortured, until he should pay back all he owed. This is how my heavenly Father will treat each of you unless you forgive your brother from your heart. |
| Mark 11:25, NIV | When you stand praying, if you hold anything against anyone, forgive him, so that your Father in heaven may forgive you your sins. |

| | |
|---|---|
| Luke 6:37, NIV | Do not judge, and you will not be judged. Do not condemn, and you will not be condemned. Forgive, and you will be forgiven. |
| Galatians 6:1, NIV | Brothers, if someone is caught in a sin, you who are spiritual should restore him gently. But watch yourself, or you also may be tempted. |
| Colossians 3:13, NIV | Bear with each other and forgive whatever grievances you may have against one another. Forgive as the Lord forgave you. |
| 1 John 4:20, NCV | If people say, "I love God," but hate their brothers or sisters, they are liars. Those who do not love their brothers and sisters, whom they have seen, cannot love God, whom they have never seen. |

# FRIENDSHIP

Friends give us companionship and make life more fun. But God's Word reveals that they do even more than that. They draw us closer to God—or they push us away from Him.

The fact is, we become like the people we associate with. As Proverbs 13:20 says, "Spend time with the wise and you will become wise, but the friends of fools will suffer" (NCV). This is why we need to choose our friends with care.

Real friends will not slow you down, spiritually. Instead, they will help you to grow in your relationship with God. By contrast, anyone who is not helping you fulfill your God-given calling is hurting you.

So it's important to surround yourself with good friends. That's what Jesus did. He surrounded Himself with twelve men whom He handpicked to be His friends. Of course, he associated with many people and loved everyone He came in contact with. But He chose a handful of people to trust, confide in, and walk with every day. He told His disciples, "I have called you friends, for everything that I learned from my Father I have made known to you" (John 15:15, NIV).

Jesus's friends were not perfect (they even included Judas, who betrayed Jesus), and neither are ours. But through their relationship, Jesus and the disciples carried out their respective ministries on earth, praying for each other and influencing each other for good.

*For other helpful categories, see pages 257, 352, 441.*

| | |
|---|---|
| Psalm 119:63, CEV | I choose as my friends everyone who worships you and follows your teachings. |
| Proverbs 12:26, NCV | Good people take advice from their friends, but an evil person is easily led to do wrong. |
| Proverbs 13:20, NCV | Spend time with the wise and you will become wise, but the friends of fools will suffer. |
| Proverbs 17:9, NCV | Whoever forgives someone's sin makes a friend, but gossiping about the sin breaks up friendships. |
| Proverbs 17:17, NCV | A friend loves you all the time, and a brother helps in time of trouble. |
| Proverbs 18:24, CEV | Some friends don't help, but a true friend is closer than your own family. |
| Proverbs 27:6, NCV | The slap of a friend can be trusted to help you, but the kisses of an enemy are nothing but lies. |
| Ecclesiastes 4:10, NIV | If one falls down, his friend can help him up. But pity the man who falls and has no one to help him up! |
| John 15:13-14, NIV | Greater love has no one than this, that he lay down his life for his friends. You are my friends if you do what I command. |
| John 15:15, NIV | I no longer call you servants, because a servant does not know his master's business. Instead, I have called you friends, for everything that I |

learned from my Father I have made known to you.

1 Corinthians 10:24, NCV — Do not look out only for yourselves. Look out for the good of others also.

2 Corinthians 6:14, NCV — You are not the same as those who do not believe. So do not join yourselves to them. Good and bad do not belong together. Light and darkness cannot share together.

James 2:23, NIV — "Abraham believed God, and it was credited to him as righteousness," and he was called God's friend.

James 4:4, NIV — You adulterous people, don't you know that friendship with the world is hatred toward God? Anyone who chooses to be a friend of the world becomes an enemy of God.

# The Fruit of the Spirit

There's something about believers whose relationship with God has ripened to a point of spiritual maturity. They have a character, a way of dealing with people and with God that is a joy to witness. What they have, in fact, are the fruit of the Spirit.

These fruit are described in Galatians 5, a chapter of the Bible that provides a blueprint for living by the Spirit. God does not want us to live a life conflicted by our sinful desires. Instead, He wants us to "live freely, animated and motivated by God's Spirit" (verse 16, MSG). "What happens when we live God's way? He brings gifts into our lives, much the same way that fruit appears in an orchard—things like affection for others, exuberance about life, serenity. We develop a willingness to stick with things, a sense of compassion in the heart, and a conviction that a basic holiness permeates things and people. We find ourselves involved in loyal commitments, not needing to force our way in life, able to marshal and direct our energies wisely" (verses 22-23, MSG).

The ninefold fruit of the Spirit—qualities we might label as love, joy, peace, patience, kindness, goodness, faithfulness, gentleness, and self-control—are not to characterize just *some* believers. They are to be produced in the lives of *all* who enjoy new lives in Jesus Christ and walk with the Holy Spirit. Challenge yourself to memorize them and meditate on them. They can be present in *your* life, too.

*For other helpful categories, see pages 239, 421, 441.*

| | |
|---|---|
| Galatians 5:16, MSG | My counsel is this: Live freely, animated and motivated by God's Spirit. |
| Galatians 5:22-23, NIV | The fruit of the Spirit is love, joy, peace, patience, kindness, goodness, faithfulness, gentleness and self-control. Against such things there is no law. |

### *Love*

| | |
|---|---|
| Matthew 5:46, NIV | If you love those who love you, what reward will you get? Are not even the tax collectors doing that? |
| 1 John 2:10, NIV | Whoever loves his brother lives in the light, and there is nothing in him to make him stumble. |

### *Joy*

| | |
|---|---|
| Nehemiah 8:10, NIV | The joy of the LORD is your strength. |
| Psalm 71:23, NIV | My lips will shout for joy when I sing praise to you—I, whom you have redeemed. |

### *Peace*

| | |
|---|---|
| John 14:27, NIV | Peace I leave with you; my peace I give you. I do not give to you as the world gives. Do not let your hearts be troubled and do not be afraid. |
| Philippians 4:6-7, NIV | Do not be anxious about anything, but in everything, by prayer and petition, with thanksgiving, present your requests to God. And the peace of God, which transcends all understanding, will guard your hearts and your minds in Christ Jesus. |

## Patience

Ecclesiastes 7:8, NCV | It is better to finish something than to start it. It is better to be patient than to be proud.

James 5:10, NIV | Brothers, as an example of patience in the face of suffering, take the prophets who spoke in the name of the Lord.

## Kindness

Proverbs 11:17, NIV | A kind man benefits himself, but a cruel man brings trouble on himself.

Ephesians 4:32, NIV | Be kind and compassionate to one another, forgiving each other, just as in Christ God forgave you.

## Goodness

Ephesians 5:9, NCV | Light brings every kind of goodness, right living, and truth.

2 Peter 1:5, NIV | Make every effort to add to your faith goodness; and to goodness, knowledge.

## Faithfulness (Faith)

1 Corinthians 2:5, NKJV | Your faith should not be in the wisdom of men but in the power of God.

Ephesians 3:16-17, NKJV | [I pray] that He would grant you, according to the riches of His glory, to be strengthened with might through His Spirit in the inner man, that Christ may dwell in your hearts through faith.

## Gentleness (Meekness)

Galatians 6:1, NIV

Brothers, if someone is caught in a sin, you who are spiritual should restore him gently. But watch yourself, or you also may be tempted.

Ephesians 4:1-2, NASB

Therefore I, the prisoner of the Lord, implore you to walk in a manner worthy of the calling with which you have been called, with all humility and gentleness, with patience, showing tolerance for one another in love.

## Self-Control

Proverbs 25:28, NIV

Like a city whose walls are broken down is a man who lacks self-control.

1 Thessalonians 5:6, NIV

Let us not be like others, who are asleep, but let us be alert and self-controlled.

# GAMBLING

At first it seems fun and fairly innocent. Walking into a casino filled with bright lights, noise, and activity. Placing a bet on a sporting event you're going to be watching anyway. Trying out the new online gambling options you've heard about.

But then it gets less fun, less innocent. You have trouble controlling your gambling. You start wagering money you can't really afford to lose. You become more secretive and your loved ones grow more concerned.

You're addicted to gambling. And the feeling that the addiction is stronger than you are scares you.

If that describes you, take heart because there is power available to free you.

First, there's power in standing with other believers (Deuteronomy 32:30). So surround yourself with people who will help you bridge the gap to a healthy lifestyle. If possible, connect with others whose faith has already helped them to walk successfully though the addiction of gambling.

Second, there's power in the Spirit. In battling your addiction, you're engaged in spiritual warfare (Ephesians 6:12). The Holy Spirit is capable of helping you distance yourself from the influences that hold you captive.

Finally, there's power in the Word. Learn and pray Bible truths that will give you confidence in God's power over your addiction—Bible truths like these:

- "The things which are impossible with men are possible with God" (Luke 18:27, NKJV).
- "I can do everything through him who gives me strength" (Philippians 4:13, NIV).

No addiction is stronger than the truth of God's Word.

*For other helpful categories, see pages 13, 31, 103, 177, 199, 346.*

Deuteronomy 32:30, KJV     How should one chase a thousand, and two put ten thousand to flight, except their Rock had sold them, and the LORD had shut them up?

Psalm 28:7, NCV     The LORD is my strength and shield. I trust him, and he helps me. I am very happy, and I praise him with my song.

Psalm 37:3, NCV     Trust the LORD and do good. Live in the land and feed on truth.

Psalm 37:4, NIV     Delight yourself in the LORD and he will give you the desires of your heart.

Psalm 55:16-18, NCV     I will call to God for help, and the LORD will save me. Morning, noon, and night I am troubled and upset, but he will listen to me. Many are against me, but he keeps me safe in battle.

Psalm 62:5, NIV     Find rest, O my soul, in God alone; my hope comes from him.

Ecclesiastes 5:10, NIV     Whoever loves money never has money enough; whoever loves wealth is never satisfied with his income. This too is meaningless.

Micah 7:8, NIV     Do not gloat over me, my enemy! Though I have fallen, I will rise.

Luke 16:13, NIV     No servant can serve two masters. Either he will hate the one and love the other, or he will be devoted to the one and despise the other. You cannot serve both God and Money.

Luke 18:7, NIV

Will not God bring about justice for his chosen ones, who cry out to him day and night? Will he keep putting them off?

Luke 18:27, NKJV

The things which are impossible with men are possible with God.

Romans 15:13, NIV

May the God of hope fill you with all joy and peace as you trust in him, so that you may overflow with hope by the power of the Holy Spirit.

Ephesians 6:12, NIV

Our struggle is not against flesh and blood, but against the rulers, against the authorities, against the powers of this dark world and against the spiritual forces of evil in the heavenly realms.

Philippians 4:13, NIV

I can do everything through him who gives me strength.

1 Timothy 6:10, NIV

The love of money is a root of all kinds of evil. Some people, eager for money, have wandered from the faith and pierced themselves with many griefs.

1 Peter 5:9, NCV

Refuse to give in to [the devil], by standing strong in your faith. You know that your Christian family all over the world is having the same kinds of suffering.

2 Peter 2:19, NIV

A man is a slave to whatever has mastered him.

# GAY COMMUNITY—
# IF YOU ARE GAY

If you are in a gay relationship, you are probably familiar with the Scripture verses about homosexuality. Perhaps people have quoted them to you or you read them yourself. You might even believe that it is against God's Word to be gay, but you don't know how to change.

Many people who have sexual feelings toward others of the same sex pray again and again, *God, if You can deliver me, why do I still have these feelings?*

If you feel trapped in a gay lifestyle, there is hope. The writer of Lamentations prays, "Restore us to yourself, O LORD, that we may return" (Lamentations 5:21, NIV). The psalmist asks God, "Create in me a clean heart, O God, and renew a steadfast spirit within me" (Psalm 51:10, NKJV). Joel reminds us that deliverance is near (2:32).

Remember through these Scriptures and others that God *can* deliver you. It might not look like you hope or want. The process of leaving behind sinful desires or not acting on them can be lonely. Even in that loneliness and confusion, God is with you. His grace is not only extended to you but it is also sufficient for you (2 Corinthians 12:9). He is capable of increasing your faith and shaping your desires to match His heart.

*For other helpful categories, see pages 13, 103, 147, 177, 196, 218, 336.*

| | |
|---|---|
| Genesis 19:5-7, NIV | They called to Lot, "Where are the men who came to you tonight? Bring them out to us so that we can have sex with them." Lot went outside to meet them and shut the door behind him and said, "No, my friends. Don't do this wicked thing." |
| Leviticus 18:22, NIV | Do not lie with a man as one lies with a woman; that is detestable. |
| Deuteronomy 22:5, NIV | A woman must not wear men's clothing, nor a man wear women's clothing, for the LORD your God detests anyone who does this. |
| Psalm 93:5, NLT | Your royal laws cannot be changed. Your reign, O LORD, is holy forever and ever. |
| Psalm 119:11, NIV | I have hidden your word in my heart that I might not sin against you. |
| Psalm 139:23-24, NIV | Search me, O God, and know my heart: test me and know my anxious thoughts. See if there is any offensive way in me, and lead me in the way everlasting. |
| Proverbs 5:21, NIV | A man's ways are in full view of the LORD, and he examines all his paths. |
| Isaiah 55:8, NKJV | "For My thoughts are not your thoughts, nor are your ways My ways," says the LORD. |
| Joel 2:32, KJV | It shall come to pass, that whosoever shall call on the name of the LORD shall be delivered. |

| | |
|---|---|
| Romans 1:26-27, NIV | Because of this, God gave them over to shameful lusts. Even their women exchanged natural relations for unnatural ones. In the same way the men also abandoned natural relations with women and were inflamed with lust for one another. Men committed indecent acts with other men, and received in themselves the due penalty for their perversion. |
| Romans 12:1-2, NIV | I urge you, brothers, in view of God's mercy, to offer your bodies as living sacrifices, holy and pleasing to God—this is your spiritual act of worship. Do not conform any longer to the pattern of this world, but be transformed by the renewing of your mind. Then you will be able to test and approve what God's will is—his good, pleasing and perfect will. |
| 1 Corinthians 6:9-10, NIV | Do you not know that the wicked will not inherit the kingdom of God? Do not be deceived: Neither the sexually immoral nor idolaters nor adulterers nor male prostitutes nor homosexual offenders nor thieves nor the greedy nor drunkards nor slanderers nor swindlers will inherit the kingdom of God. |
| 1 Corinthians 10:13, NKJV | No temptation has overtaken you except such as is common to man; but God is faithful, who will not allow you to be tempted beyond what you are able, but with the temptation will also make the way of escape, that you may be able to bear it. |
| 1 Corinthians 14:33, KJV | God is not the author of confusion, but of peace. |

| 1 Corinthians 15:2, NIV | By this gospel you are saved, if you hold firmly to the word I preached to you. Otherwise, you have believed in vain. |
| 2 Timothy 2:19, NIV | Nevertheless, God's solid foundation stands firm, sealed with this inscription: "The Lord knows those who are his," and, "Everyone who confesses the name of the Lord must turn away from wickedness." |
| 2 Timothy 4:3-4, NIV | The time will come when men will not put up with sound doctrine. Instead, to suit their own desires, they will gather around them a great number of teachers to say what their itching ears want to hear. They will turn their ears away from the truth and turn aside to myths. |
| 1 John 1:9, NKJV | If we confess our sins, He is faithful and just to forgive us our sins and to cleanse us from all unrighteousness. |

# Gay Community—If a Friend or Family Member Is Gay

People often go to one extreme or the other in their attitude toward people in the gay community. Either they are unquestioningly accepting of the gay lifestyle or they are cruelly critical of people in the gay and lesbian community. But God's Word calls us, as followers of Christ, to an attitude that is more subtle—and more loving.

The Scriptures are clear that homosexual activity is wrong. This position is not popular in our society today. But the fact that God's Word is not popular is no reason to discard it. God's Word does not change when the moral conscience of society changes.

For this reason, you cannot condone your friend's involvement in the gay community. At the same time, though, you cannot forget that a heart of compassion was extended to you when you were in sin. Romans reminds us, "God demonstrates His own love toward us, in that while we were still sinners, Christ died for us" (Romans 5:8, NKJV). You have no justification for setting yourself above gay people to judge them. We are all guilty before God apart from salvation in Christ.

So even as you hold fast to truth, you do not need to condemn your friend. In fact, we are commanded to love the one held in the grip of any type of sin. It is God's kindness that leads people to repentance (Romans 2:4), and He calls us to love others in the same kind way (1 Corinthians 13:4).

If you find it hard not to be condemning toward gay people *or* if you find it hard to take a stand against same-sex activity, pray about your attitude. Prayer changes our heart and helps us to understand and accept God's perspective.

*For other helpful categories, see pages 103, 174, 346, 352.*

| | |
|---|---|
| Proverbs 5:21, NIV | A man's ways are in full view of the LORD, and he examines all his paths. |
| Matthew 18:19, NIV | I tell you that if two of you on earth agree about anything you ask for, it will be done for you by my Father in heaven. |
| Romans 5:8, NKJV | God demonstrates His own love toward us, in that while we were still sinners, Christ died for us. |
| 1 Corinthians 13:4, NKJV | Love suffers long and is kind. |
| 2 Corinthians 4:4, NIV | The god of this age has blinded the minds of unbelievers, so that they cannot see the light of the gospel of the glory of Christ, who is the image of God. |
| 2 Corinthians 10:4, NKJV | The weapons of our warfare are not carnal but mighty in God for pulling down strongholds. |
| 2 Timothy 3:16-17, NKJV | All Scripture is given by inspiration of God, and is profitable for doctrine, for reproof, for correction, for instruction in righteousness, that the man of God may be complete, thoroughly equipped for every good work. |
| 2 Timothy 4:3-4, NIV | The time will come when men will not put up with sound doctrine. Instead, to suit their own desires, they will gather around them a great number of teachers to say what their itching ears want to hear. They will turn their ears away from the truth and turn aside to myths. |

# GOD

So often we hear people talk about God from a perspective gained through life experiences, not as a reflection of His true character and nature as revealed through His Word.

Consider these Scriptures describing the history and character of God: In the beginning was God (Genesis 1:1). He was and always will be (Isaiah 57:15) the eternal, omnipresent One (Psalm 139:7-12). He is a loving God (1 John 4:8). He is all-knowing (1 John 3:20), and you were created in His image (Genesis 1:27) to have fellowship with Him.

Also consider these Hebrew names of God, which reveal His immeasurable love:

*Adonai*—The LORD My Great LORD (Isaiah 40:3-5)

*Elohim*—God the Eternal Creator (Genesis 1:28)

*El Shaddai*—God Almighty or God All-Sufficient One (Genesis 17:1-3)

*Immanuel*—The God Who Is With Us (Isaiah 7:14)

*Jehovah/Yahweh*—I AM WHO I AM (Exodus 3:14)

*Jehovah-rohi*—The LORD My Shepherd (Psalm 23)

*Jehovah-rapha*—The LORD Who Heals (Exodus 15:25-26)

*Jehovah-tsidkenu*—The LORD Our Righteousness (Jeremiah 23:6)

*Jehovah-jireh*—The LORD will Provide (Genesis 22:14)

Meditate on these names, the names on pages 11-12, and the following verses about who God is. The Bible promises when you draw near to God He will "draw near to you" (James 4:8, NKJV). As you study how God describes Himself, names Himself, and acts in the Bible, you will unlock more and more of the thousands of promises He has made to you! Ask Him for a personal revelation of His divine character and nature and He will give it to you.

*For other helpful categories, see pages 194–196, 239, 257.*

## *A True Picture of Who God Is*

- The Lord Will Provide (Genesis 22:1-14)
- The Great I AM (Exodus 3:14)
- The Self-Existent One (Exodus 3:14-15)
- The Lord Our Banner (Exodus 17:15)
- The Lord is a merciful God (Deuteronomy 4:31).
- "The Lord our God, the Lord is one" (Deuteronomy 6:4-5, NIV).
- "The Lord your God is God of gods and Lord of lords, the great God, mighty and awesome" (Deuteronomy 10:17, NIV).
- The Lord is Peace (Judges 6:24).
- The Lord is great and majestic (Psalm 8:1).
- The All-Sufficient One (Psalm 18:1-3)
- The Lord is "our God for ever and ever" (Psalm 48:14, NIV).
- "The Lord God is a sun and shield" (Psalm 84:11, NIV).
- The Lord heals all our diseases (Psalm 103:3).
- "The Lord is gracious and righteous; our God is full of compassion" (Psalm 116:5, NIV).
- The Lord is a God of "glorious splendor" and majesty (Psalm 145:5, NIV).
- "The Lord is gracious and compassionate, slow to anger and rich in love" (Psalm 145:8, NIV).
- "The Lord is good to all; he has compassion on all he has made" (Psalm 145:9, NIV).
- "The Lord is faithful to all his promises and loving toward all he has made" (Psalm 145:13, NIV).
- "The Lord is righteous in all his ways" (Psalm 145:17, NIV).
- "The Lord is near to all who call on him…in truth" (Psalm 145:18, NIV).
- The Lord "fulfills the desires of those who fear him" (Psalm 145:19, NIV).
- "The Lord watches over all who love him" (Psalm 145:20, NIV).
- "The Lord sets prisoners free" (Psalm 146:7, NIV).

- "The LORD gives sight to the blind, the LORD lifts up those who are bowed down, the LORD loves the righteous" (Psalm 146:8, NIV).
- "The LORD watches over the alien and sustains the fatherless and the widow" (Psalm 146:9, NIV).
- The Lord builds up his people (Psalm 147:2).
- The Lord grants peace to our borders (Psalm 147:14).
- Immanuel—God is with us (Isaiah 7:14).
- The Lord is our Righteousness (Jeremiah 23:6).
- "The LORD Is There" (Ezekiel 48:35, NIV).
- God is love (1 John 4:8).
- The Lord is our Shepherd (Revelation 7:17).

# GOD'S LOVE

God's Word gives a true picture of who He is: a loving and caring Father. Deuteronomy tells us that God cares for us "as a father cares for his child" (Deuteronomy 1:31, NLT). First John says, "How great is the love the Father has lavished on us, that we should be called children of God!" (3:1, NIV). This original model for fatherhood shows God's primary characteristic to be love for His children.

You may have a distorted picture of God because of the weaknesses of your earthly father or your "spiritual fathers." You may know the words "God is love" (1 John 4:8, NIV) but have trouble believing them because of the pain and struggles you have walked through.

Understanding God's love comes from an understanding of His Word. When words do not seem convincing, consider how God proves His love to you through His faithfulness to forgive, heal, deliver, and restore. In the face of despair, one psalmist declared: "I remember the days of old; I meditate on all that you have done.... Let me hear in the morning of your steadfast love" (Psalm 143:5, 8, ESV).

So meditate on words and deeds in Scripture that show God's love. Psalm 145 gives us a beautiful picture of the manifested love of God: "The LORD is gracious and compassionate, slow to anger and rich in love. The LORD is good to all; he has compassion on all he has made" (verses 8-9, NIV).

Remember that no matter how you *feel*, the truth of God's love remains the same. It is part of His character—it is who He is and always will be.

*For other helpful categories, see pages 109, 193–195, 171, 329.*

Deuteronomy 1:31, NLT — And you saw how the LORD your God cared for you all along the way as you traveled through the wilderness, just as a father cares for his child. Now he has brought you to this place.

Deuteronomy 7:9, NIV — Know therefore that the LORD your God is God; he is the faithful God, keeping his covenant of love to a thousand generations of those who love him and keep his commands.

Psalm 37:28, NIV — The LORD loves the just and will not forsake his faithful ones.

Psalm 143:5, 8, ESV — I remember the days of old; I meditate on all that you have done.... Let me hear in the morning of your steadfast love.

Psalm 145:8-9, NIV — The LORD is gracious and compassionate, slow to anger and rich in love. The LORD is good to all; he has compassion on all he has made.

Psalm 145:17, NIV — The LORD is righteous in all his ways and loving toward all he has made.

Proverbs 8:17, NIV — I love those who love me, and those who seek me find me.

Jeremiah 31:3, NIV — The LORD appeared to us in the past, saying: "I have loved you with an everlasting love; I have drawn you with loving-kindness."

John 3:16, NIV

For God so loved the world that he gave his one and only Son, that whoever believes in him shall not perish but have eternal life.

Romans 5:5, NIV

And hope does not disappoint us, because God has poured out his love into our hearts by the Holy Spirit, whom he has given us.

Ephesians 2:4-5, NLT

God is so rich in mercy, and he loved us so much, that even though we were dead because of our sins, he gave us life when he raised Christ from the dead.

1 John 3:1, NIV

How great is the love the Father has lavished on us, that we should be called children of God!

1 John 4:8-11, NIV

Whoever does not love does not know God, because God is love. This is how God showed his love among us: He sent his one and only Son into the world that we might live through him. This is love: not that we loved God, but that he loved us and sent his Son as an atoning sacrifice for our sins. Dear friends, since God so loved us, we also ought to love one another.

1 John 4:19, NKJV

We love Him because He first loved us.

# GOD'S WORD

God's Word is true even when your circumstances do not line up with what you had hoped would happen. It's true when you've prayed, believed, stood, and spoken it over your life or a loved one's and still have not seen the manifestation of it. It's true because God Himself is the Word (John 1:1). And He is not a God who can lie (Numbers 23:19).

God's Word helps you to see beyond what you see in the natural. Hold onto it. Speak it during the day. Pray it out loud. It is your life and your light.

God's Word has the power to take you from poverty to prosperity, from fear to boldness, and from heartache to healing. Jesus said in Matthew 4:4 that we should live by "every word that comes from the mouth of God" (NIV). The Holy Spirit works in us and through us when we are living out the truth of God's wisdom.

Can you say with the psalmist, "My soul is consumed with longing for your laws at all times" (Psalm 119:20, NIV)? Every need, problem, desire, and situation that will ever come up in your life will find its solution in the Word of God.

*For other helpful categories, see pages 65, 118, 132, 346.*

| Deuteronomy 30:14, NKJV | The word is very near you, in your mouth and in your heart, that you may do it. |
| Joshua 1:8, NKJV | This Book of the Law shall not depart from your mouth, but you shall meditate in it day and night, that you may observe to do according to all that is written in it. For then you will make your way prosperous, and then you will have good success. |
| Psalm 17:4, NKJV | By the word of your lips, I have kept away from the paths of the destroyer. |
| Psalm 107:20, NIV | He sent His word and healed them, and delivered them from their destructions. |
| Psalm 119:89, NKJV | Forever, O LORD, Your word is settled in heaven. |
| Psalm 119:103, NKJV | How sweet are Your words to my taste, sweeter than honey to my mouth! |
| Psalm 119:105, NKJV | Your word is a lamp to my feet and a light to my path. |
| Psalm 119:130, NKJV | The entrance of Your words gives light; it gives understanding to the simple. |
| Psalm 119:133, NIV | Direct my footsteps according to your word; let no sin rule over me. |
| Psalm 119:140, NCV | Your promises are proven, so I, your servant, love them. |

| | |
|---|---|
| Psalm 119:160, NKJV | The entirety of Your word is truth, and every one of Your righteous judgments endures forever. |
| Psalm 138:2, NIV | I will bow down toward your holy temple and will praise your name for your love and your faithfulness, for you have exalted above all things your name and your word. |
| Proverbs 4:4, NIV | Lay hold of my words with all your heart. |
| Proverbs 30:5, NIV | Every word of God is flawless; he is a shield to those who take refuge in him. |
| Ecclesiastes 8:4, NKJV | Where the word of a king is, there is power. |
| Isaiah 40:8, NKJV | The grass withers, the flower fades, but the word of our God stands forever. |
| Isaiah 55:11, NKJV | So shall My word be that goes forth from My mouth; it shall not return to Me void, but it shall accomplish what I please, and it shall prosper in the thing for which I sent it. |
| Jeremiah 1:12, NIV | The LORD said to me, "You have seen correctly, for I am watching to see that my word is fulfilled." |
| Matthew 4:4, NIV | Jesus answered, "It is written: 'Man does not live on bread alone, but on every word that comes from the mouth of God.'" |
| Luke 11:28, NIV | Blessed rather are those who hear the word of God and obey it. |

| | |
|---|---|
| John 1:1, NKJV | In the beginning was the Word, and the Word was with God, and the Word was God. |
| John 1:14, NKJV | The Word became flesh and dwelt among us. |
| Romans 1:16, NIV | I am not ashamed of the gospel, because it is the power of God for the salvation of everyone who believes: first for the Jew, then for the Gentile. |
| Ephesians 6:17-18, NIV | Take the helmet of salvation and the sword of the Spirit, which is the word of God. And pray in the Spirit on all occasions with all kinds of prayers and requests. With this in mind, be alert and always keep on praying for all the saints. |
| Colossians 3:16, NKJV | Let the word of Christ dwell in you richly in all wisdom, teaching and admonishing one another in psalms and hymns and spiritual songs, singing with grace in your hearts to the Lord. |
| 1 Thessalonians 2:13, NIV | We also thank God continually because, when you received the word of God, which you heard from us, you accepted it not as the word of men, but as it actually is, the word of God, which is at work in you who believe. |
| 2 Timothy 3:16-17, NKJV | All Scripture is given by inspiration of God, and is profitable for doctrine, for reproof, for correction, for instruction in righteousness, that the man of God may be complete, thoroughly equipped for every good work. |

| | |
|---|---|
| Hebrews 4:12, NKJV | The word of God is living and powerful, and sharper than any two-edged sword, piercing even to the division of soul and spirit, and of joints and marrow, and is a discerner of the thoughts and intents of the heart. |
| 1 Peter 1:25, NKJV | The word of the LORD endures forever. |

# GOSSIP

Scripture defines someone who gossips as a person who "betrays a confidence" and repeats personal details about another's life (Proverbs 20:19). Paul warns against "gossips and busybodies" who say "things which they ought not" (1 Timothy 5:13, NKJV).

Most of us have had the unfortunate experience of being hurt by gossip. We know that it is a subtle poison that can ruin the best of friendships. Whether someone has confided personal details about you to someone else or talked repeatedly about a mistake you made, gossip is unloving, unnecessary, and does no good for any relationship. "He who covers over an offense promotes love, but whoever repeats the matter separates close friends" (Proverbs 17:9, NIV).

If you have been the injured party of a gossip, remember that the one doing the gossiping is probably doing it because of his or her own insecurity or unhappiness. Resist the urge to retaliate and get revenge. Make a conscious effort to forgive those who have sinned against you. Pray and ask God to expose the truth to those who have heard this gossip.

Christians should not fail to understand how serious gossip is and how it is used by the devil (see the books of Ephesians and James). People who gossip speak words that have the power to discredit or shame another person. Gossips spread false reports that can ruin a good person's reputation (Exodus 23:1). Gossip can be called backbiting, evil speaking, slander, tale bearing, and tattling. Gossip is sin.

If in the past you have gossiped about others, ask God for His forgiveness and for the help of the Holy Spirit to convict you in the future before you even open your mouth. Surrender you tongue to Him!

*For other helpful categories, see pages 174, 177, 421, 441, 445.*

| | |
|---|---|
| Exodus 23:1, NASB | You shall not bear a false report; do not join your hand with a wicked man to be a malicious witness. |
| Psalm 19:14, NKJV | Let the words of my mouth and the meditation of my heart be acceptable in Your sight, O LORD, my strength and my Redeemer. |
| Psalm 50:20, CEV | You sat around gossiping, ruining the reputation of your own relatives. |
| Psalm 101:5, CEV | Anyone who spreads gossip will be silenced, and no one who is conceited will be my friend. |
| Proverbs 11:13, NIV | A gossip betrays a confidence, but a trustworthy man keeps a secret. |
| Proverbs 12:18, NLT | Some people make cutting remarks, but the words of the wise bring healing. |
| Proverbs 16:28, NLT | A troublemaker plants seeds of strife; gossip separates the best of friends. |
| Proverbs 17:9, NIV | He who covers over an offense promotes love, but whoever repeats the matter separates close friends. |
| Proverbs 18:8, AMP | The words of a whisperer or talebearer are as dainty morsels; they go down into the innermost parts of the body. |
| Proverbs 20:19, NIV | A gossip betrays a confidence; so avoid a man who talks too much. |

| | |
|---|---|
| Luke 6:31, NCV | Do to others what you would want them to do to you. |
| Ephesians 4:29, NCV | When you talk, do not say harmful things, but say what people need—words that will help others become stronger. Then what you say will do good to those who listen to you. |
| Ephesians 4:30, NKJV | Do not grieve the Holy Spirit of God, by whom you were sealed for the day of redemption. |
| 1 Timothy 5:13, NKJV | And besides they learn to be idle, wandering about from house to house, and not only idle but also gossips and busybodies, saying things which they ought not. |
| James 4:11, NLT | Don't speak evil against each other, dear brothers and sisters. If you criticize and judge each other, then you are criticizing and judging God's law. But your job is to obey the law, not to judge whether it applies to you. |

# Healing—God's Power to Heal

When you become a child of God, it positions you to be supernaturally healed! If you need healing in your life, find a Scripture to anchor you faith upon. Do all you can in the natural world—the world you can see—then stand on the Word of God to receive His supernatural healing.

Remember that God is a healing God: "I am the LORD who heals you" (Exodus 15:26, NKJV). God heals and restores your...

- heart (Psalm 147:3)
- soul—your mind, will, and emotions (Psalm 30:2)
- physical body (Psalm 41:3)
- finances (Proverbs 3:9-10)
- relationships (James 5:16)
- dreams (Joel 2:25)

Be careful about the words you speak as you seek healing. Proverbs 18:21 says, "Death and life are in the power of the tongue" (NKJV). Believe in God's power and desire to heal you. And above all, praise God for who He is! His name is Jehovah-rapha, the Lord Who Heals (Exodus 15:26; Psalm 103:3).

Even after much prayer and petition, God may not manifest healing the way we need it or desire it. It's more important to seek Him and keep your heart right before Him than it is to understand all the questions that you have of why some are healed and some are not.

*For other helpful categories, see pages 132, 147, 174, 212, 223, 346, 445.*

| | |
|---|---|
| Exodus 15:26, NKJV | If you diligently heed the voice of the LORD your God and do what is right in His sight, give ear to His commandments and keep all His statutes, I will put none of the diseases on you which I have brought on the Egyptians. For I am the LORD who heals you. |
| Exodus 23:25, NKJV | So you shall serve the LORD your God, and He will bless your bread and your water. And I will take sickness away from the midst of you. |
| Psalm 18:39, NIV | You armed me with strength for battle; you made my adversaries bow at my feet. |
| Psalm 30:2, NIV | O LORD my God, I called to you for help and you healed me. |
| Psalm 34:19, NKJV | Many are the afflictions of the righteous, but the LORD delivers him out of them all. |
| Psalm 41:3, NIV | The LORD will sustain him on his sickbed and restore him from his bed of illness. |
| Psalm 55:18, NKJV | He has redeemed my soul in peace from the battle that was against me, for there were many against me. |
| Psalm 86:13, NIV | Great is your love toward me; you have delivered me from the depths of the grave. |
| Psalm 91:10, NKJV | No evil shall befall you, nor shall any plague come near your dwelling. |

| | |
|---|---|
| Psalm 103:3, NCV | He forgives all my sins and heals all my diseases. |
| Psalm 107:2, NKJV | Let the redeemed of the LORD say so, whom He has redeemed from the hand of the enemy. |
| Psalm 107:20, NIV | He sent forth his word and healed them; he rescued them from the grave. |
| Psalm 112:7, NCV | They won't be afraid of bad news; their hearts are steady because they trust the LORD. |
| Psalm 118:17, NIV | I will not die but live, and will proclaim what the LORD has done. |
| Psalm 119:25, NCV | I am about to die. Give me life, as you have promised. |
| Psalm 147:3, NIV | He heals the brokenhearted and binds up their wounds. |
| Proverbs 4:20-22, NKJV | My son, give attention to my words; incline your ear to my sayings. Do not let them depart from your eyes; keep them in the midst of your heart; for they are life to those who find them, and health to all their flesh. |
| Isaiah 38:16, NIV | You restored me to health and let me live. |
| Isaiah 53:5, NKJV | He was wounded for our transgressions, He was bruised for our iniquities; the chastisement for our peace was upon Him, and by His stripes we are healed. |

| Isaiah 57:18, NIV | I have seen his ways, but I will heal him; I will guide him and restore comfort to him. |
| Jeremiah 17:14, NIV | Heal me, O LORD, and I will be healed; save me and I will be saved, for you are the one I praise. |
| Jeremiah 33:6, NIV | I will heal my people and will let them enjoy abundant peace and security. |
| Hosea 14:4, NIV | I will heal their waywardness and love them freely, for my anger has turned away from them. |
| Matthew 8:7, NKJV | And Jesus said to him, "I will come and heal him." |
| Matthew 11:5, NIV | The blind receive sight, the lame walk, those who have leprosy are cured, the deaf hear, the dead are raised, and the good news is preached to the poor. |
| Mark 5:34, NIV | He [Jesus] said to her, "Daughter, your faith has healed you. Go in peace and be freed from your suffering." |
| Luke 1:37, NIV | Nothing is impossible with God. |
| John 8:36, NKJV | If the Son makes you free, you shall be free indeed. |
| Acts 3:16, NIV | By faith in the name of Jesus, this man whom you see and know was made strong. It is Jesus' name and the faith that comes through him that has given this complete healing to him, as you can all see. |

Galatians 3:13, NIV

Christ redeemed us from the curse of the law by becoming a curse for us, for it is written: "Cursed is everyone who is hung on a tree."

Hebrews 13:8, NIV

Jesus Christ is the same yesterday and today and forever.

James 5:16, NIV

Confess your sins to each other and pray for each other so that you may be healed. The prayer of a righteous man is powerful and effective.

1 Peter 2:24, NIV

He himself bore our sins in his body on the tree, so that we might die to sins and live for righteousness; by his wounds you have been healed.

1 John 3:8, NIV

The reason the Son of God appeared was to destroy the devil's work.

3 John, 2, NKJV

Beloved, I pray that you may prosper in all things and be in health, just as your soul prospers.

# Healing—Healing
# from Chronic Pain or Illness

If you are facing ongoing physical challenges, you know that emotional and spiritual pain often accompanies physical struggle. Part of the emotional pain comes from a lack of understanding from loved ones, friends, physicians, pastors, and church members due to the fact that chronic pain and illness are often invisible. Many people dealing with a disability or disease grieve what they have lost from their lives, but others have trouble understanding this.

Chronic pain and illness are not a sign that you have done something wrong (John 9:3) or that you have hidden sin in your life (John 5:14). Pain does not mean that your relationship with your heavenly Father is broken or that you haven't "prayed enough."

If you are on the journey of chronic pain and illness, consider joining a support group with others who are walking on similar paths. Resist the feelings of isolation, failure, and shame that can come with a diagnosis. Even when you are in the darkest place, God can and will use you. One of the greatest powers you will receive through your suffering is the ability to reach out to others who are hurting.

We are told that God's strength is made perfect in our weakness (2 Corinthians 12:9). Stay close to Him in prayer, keep His Word hidden in your heart, and continue to believe and speak His Word over your body in spite of the pain, limitations, or disability that you see with your natural eye. In the midst of all the well-meaning voices coming at you, remember the gentle and loving voice of God that says, "No matter what, I am faithful to love you and will never abandon you" (Hebrews 13:5 and Joshua 1:5).

*For other helpful categories, see pages 193, 196, 207, 336, 340, 346, 411, 428, 445.*

Joshua 1:5, NIV — No one will be able to stand up against you all the days of your life. As I was with Moses, so I will be with you; I will never leave you nor forsake you.

Psalm 46:1, NKJV — God is our refuge and strength, a very present help in trouble.

Isaiah 40:31, NLT — Those who trust in the LORD will find new strength. They will soar high on wings like eagles. They will run and not grow weary. They will walk and not faint.

Matthew 19:26, NKJV — With God all things are possible.

John 9:2-3, NKJV — His disciples asked Him, "Rabbi, who sinned, this man or his parents, that he was born blind?" Jesus answered, "Neither this man nor his parents sinned, but that the works of God should be revealed in him."

Romans 4:17, NLT — That is what the Scriptures mean when God told him, "I have made you the father of many nations." This happened because Abraham believed in the God who brings the dead back to life and who creates new things out of nothing.

Romans 12:12, NCV — Be joyful because you have hope. Be patient when trouble comes, and pray at all times.

2 Corinthians 1:3, NIV — Praise be to the God and Father of our Lord Jesus Christ, the Father of compassion and the God of all comfort.

| | |
|---|---|
| 2 Corinthians 12:9, NKJV | He [God] said to me, "My grace is sufficient for you, for My strength is made perfect in weakness." Therefore most gladly I will rather boast in my infirmities, that the power of Christ may rest upon me. |
| Galatians 3:13, NKJV | Christ has redeemed us from the curse of the law, having become a curse for us (for it is written, "Cursed is everyone who hangs on a tree"). |
| Hebrews 4:12, NKJV | The word of God is living and powerful, and sharper than any two-edged sword, piercing even to the division of soul and spirit, and of joints and marrow, and is a discerner of the thoughts and intents of the heart. |
| Hebrews 11:1, KJV | Faith is the substance of things hoped for, the evidence of things not seen. |
| Hebrews 13:5, NKJV | I will never leave you nor forsake you. |
| James 5:14-15, NKJV | Is anyone among you sick? Let him call for the elders of the church, and let them pray over him, anointing him with oil in the name of the Lord. And the prayer of faith will save the sick, and the Lord will raise him up. And if he has committed sins, he will be forgiven. |
| 1 Peter 2:24, NKJV | Who Himself bore our sins in His own body on the tree, that we, having died to sins, might live for righteousness—by whose stripes you were healed. |

# HEALING—MINISTERING TO THOSE IN THE HOSPITAL

Serious illness or injury causes great emotional upheaval, stress, and uncertainty. You have the opportunity to bring comfort through prayer, compassion, a smile, and your presence.

People who are hospitalized are in a strange environment and long for the comforts of home. They are often lonely and experience depression, insomnia, and hopelessness. Fear can cause people to respond quite differently to hospitalization than you would expect. A seemingly strong person can appear frail and weak. That's why it is so important to respond to those in need with great sensitivity and the leading of the Holy Spirit.

Consider reading God's Word out loud to the person you visit. Share the Word of God concerning health and healing, and pray the word of faith over him or her. You may consider getting a CD player or an iPod and continuously playing Scripture for encouragement.

Remember that emotional pain often comes with ongoing physical pain. If the diagnosis is difficult, give the person you are ministering to the freedom to grieve.

The most important thing you can do for people in the hospital is to be present. Let those who are hospitalized know that you remember them, pray for them, and want to be God's strength for them even when they are weak. Your attentiveness will remind them that "the LORD is close to all who call on him" (Psalm 145:18, NLT).

*For other helpful categories, see pages 153, 207, 311, 411, 428.*

| | |
|---|---|
| Exodus 15:26, NIV | I am the LORD, who heals you. |
| Psalm 23:4, NLT | Even when I walk through the darkest valley, I will not be afraid, for you are close beside me. |
| Psalm 29:11, NIV | The LORD gives strength to his people; the LORD blesses his people with peace. |
| Psalm 34:19, NKJV | Many are the afflictions of the righteous, but the LORD delivers him out of them all. |
| Psalm 41:3, NIV | The LORD will sustain him on his sickbed and restore him from his bed of illness. |
| Psalm 86:7, NKJV | In the day of my trouble I will call upon You, for You will answer me. |
| Psalm 145:18, NLT | The LORD is close to all who call on him, yes, to all who call on him in truth. |
| Psalm 147:3, NKJV | He heals the brokenhearted and binds up their wounds. |
| Proverbs 3:5, NKJV | Trust in the LORD with all your heart, and lean not on your own understanding. |
| Matthew 11:28, NASB | Come to Me, all who are weary and heavy-laden, and I will give you rest. |
| John 11:25-26, NKJV | Jesus said to her, "I am the resurrection and the life. He who believes in Me, though he may die, he shall live. And whoever lives and believes in Me shall never die. Do you believe this?" |

2 Corinthians 5:1, NCV

We know that our body—the tent we live in here on earth—will be destroyed. But when that happens, God will have a house for us. It will not be a house made by human hands; instead, it will be a home in heaven that will last forever.

Philippians 4:5, NIV

The Lord is near.

# The Heart

God wants your heart to be totally surrendered to His Word. How does that happen?

Prayer is the most powerful way to change your heart. As you pray for God to shape your life, ask for His mercy to create in you a clean heart (Psalm 51:10). Jeremiah the prophet said that God shapes us like clay in His hand (Jeremiah 18:6). Through the working of His hands, God has the power to transform our lives. It is God's love for us that puts us on His potter's wheel. But it is our deep love and commitment to Him that keeps us there.

Ask God to shape your desires to match His heart, just as David asked God to search and test his heart (Psalm 139:23-24). When you ask God to point out any wrong motives in your life, as David did, God will show you any areas of wrong attitudes or sin. You can repent and be forgiven.

Remember that your eyes, ears, and mouth are the gateways to your soul. So guard what you see, hear, and say. By guarding your heart, you will stay on the right path and your life will be vibrant and fruitful. "Keep and guard your heart with all vigilance and above all that you guard, for out of it flow the springs of life" (Proverbs 4:23, AMP).

When you allow the principles of God's Word to change your heart, you will have amazing strength and power to take your life to a whole new level.

*For other helpful categories, see pages 109, 329, 445.*

| 1 Samuel 12:24, NIV | Be sure to fear the LORD and serve him faithfully with all your heart; consider what great things he has done for you. |
| Psalm 51:10, NKJV | Create in me a clean heart, O God, and renew a steadfast spirit within me. |
| Psalm 51:17, NCV | The sacrifice God wants is a broken spirit. God, you will not reject a heart that is broken and sorry for sin. |
| Psalm 57:7, NIV | My heart is steadfast, O God, my heart is steadfast; I will sing and make music. |
| Psalm 62:8, NIV | Trust in him at all times, O people; pour out your hearts to him, for God is our refuge. |
| Psalm 84:2, NIV | My soul yearns, even faints, for the courts of the LORD; my heart and my flesh cry out for the living God. |
| Psalm 84:5, NKJV | Blessed is the man whose strength is in You, whose heart is set on pilgrimage. |
| Psalm 86:11, NIV | Teach me your way, O LORD, and I will walk in your truth; give me an undivided heart, that I may fear your name. |
| Psalm 105:3, NIV | Glory in his holy name; let the hearts of those who seek the LORD rejoice. |
| Psalm 119:11, NIV | I have hidden your word in my heart that I might not sin against you. |

| | |
|---|---|
| Psalm 119:36, NIV | Turn my heart toward your statutes and not toward selfish gain. |
| Psalm 139:23-24, NKJV | Search me, O God, and know my heart; try me, and know my anxieties; and see if there is any wicked way in me, and lead me in the way everlasting. |
| Proverbs 4:23, AMP | Keep and guard your heart with all vigilance and above all that you guard, for out of it flow the springs of life. |
| Proverbs 12:20, NIV | There is deceit in the hearts of those who plot evil, but joy for those who promote peace. |
| Proverbs 13:12, NIV | Hope deferred makes the heart sick, but a longing fulfilled is a tree of life. |
| Proverbs 15:13, NKJV | A merry heart makes a cheerful countenance, but by sorrow of the heart the spirit is broken. |
| Proverbs 15:14, NIV | The discerning heart seeks knowledge, but the mouth of a fool feeds on folly. |
| Proverbs 16:23, NIV | A wise man's heart guides his mouth, and his lips promote instruction. |
| Proverbs 18:12, NIV | Before his downfall a man's heart is proud, but humility comes before honor. |
| Proverbs 19:21, NIV | Many are the plans in a man's heart, but it is the LORD's purpose that prevails. |

| | |
|---|---|
| Proverbs 21:1, NKJV | The king's heart is in the hand of the LORD, like the rivers of water; He turns it wherever He wishes. |
| Proverbs 22:11, NIV | He who loves a pure heart and whose speech is gracious will have the king for his friend. |
| Proverbs 23:17, NIV | Do not let your heart envy sinners, but always be zealous for the fear of the LORD. |
| Proverbs 23:19, NIV | Listen, my son, and be wise, and keep your heart on the right path. |
| Proverbs 24:17, NIV | Do not gloat when your enemy falls; when he stumbles, do not let your heart rejoice. |
| Proverbs 24:32, NIV | I applied my heart to what I observed and learned a lesson from what I saw. |
| Proverbs 27:19, NIV | As water reflects a face, so a man's heart reflects the man. |
| Proverbs 28:14, NIV | Blessed is the man who always fears the LORD, but he who hardens his heart falls into trouble. |
| Ezekiel 36:26, NIV | I will give you a new heart and put a new spirit in you; I will remove from you your heart of stone and give you a heart of flesh. |
| Matthew 12:34, NKJV | Out of the abundance of the heart the mouth speaks. |

| | |
|---|---|
| Matthew 22:37, NKJV | You shall love the LORD your God with all your heart, with all your soul, and with all your mind. |
| Luke 6:45, NKJV | A good man out of the good treasure of his heart brings forth good; and an evil man out of the evil treasure of his heart brings forth evil. For out of the abundance of the heart his mouth speaks. |
| Luke 12:34, NIV | Where your treasure is, there your heart will be also. |
| Ephesians 1:18, NIV | I pray also that the eyes of your heart may be enlightened in order that you may know the hope to which he has called you, the riches of his glorious inheritance in the saints. |
| Ephesians 4:18, NIV | They are darkened in their understanding and separated from the life of God because of the ignorance that is in them due to the hardening of their hearts. |
| Hebrews 3:15, NIV | Today, if you hear his voice, do not harden your hearts as you did in the rebellion. |
| 1 John 3:21, NIV | Dear friends, if our hearts do not condemn us, we have confidence before God. |

# HEARTACHE

In your deepest sorrow, you can know that God also experiences heartache. His heart ached when He was separated from Jesus (Mark 15:34). "Jesus wept" when His friend Lazarus died (John 11:35, KJV).

If separation from a loved one or the devastation of bad news has broken your heart, you can be encouraged today! "God heals the brokenhearted and binds up their wounds" (Psalm 147:3, NASB). God rebuilds and strengthens with "limitless strength." He "puts the fallen on their feet again" (Psalm 147:5, 6, MSG).

Memorizing and saying God's comforting words in the mist of your broken heart will bring you the peace and joy that your soul is longing for.

You turned my wailing into dancing;
you removed my sackcloth and clothed me with joy,
that my heart may sing to you and not be silent.
O LORD my God, I will give you thanks forever. (Psalm 30:11-12, NIV)

As you and God move together toward that moment of joy and healing, believe that He is with you along the way. He identifies with you through His Son, Jesus Christ. Earth has no sorrow that He cannot heal. You *will* be restored again.

*For other helpful categories, see pages 13, 118, 207, 236, 263, 311, 428.*

| | |
|---|---|
| Psalm 25:17-18, NKJV | The troubles of my heart have enlarged; bring me out of my distresses! Look on my affliction and my pain, and forgive all my sins. |
| Psalm 30:11-12, NIV | You turned my wailing into dancing; you removed my sackcloth and clothed me with joy, that my heart may sing to you and not be silent. O LORD my God, I will give you thanks forever. |
| Psalm 34:4, NKJV | I sought the LORD, and He heard me, and delivered me from all my fears. |
| Psalm 42:11, NKJV | Why are you cast down, O my soul? And why are you disquieted within me? Hope in God; for I shall yet praise Him, the help of my countenance and my God. |
| Psalm 71:21, NLT | You will restore me to even greater honor and comfort me once again. |
| Psalm 73:26, NIV | My flesh and my heart may fail, but God is the strength of my heart and my portion forever. |
| Psalm 84:6-7, NIV | As they pass through the Valley of Baca, they make it a place of springs; the autumn rains also cover it with pools. They go from strength to strength, till each appears before God in Zion. |
| Psalm 138:7, NKJV | Though I walk in the midst of trouble, You will revive me; You will stretch out Your hand against the wrath of my enemies, and Your right hand will save me. |

Psalm 147:3, NASB

He heals the brokenhearted and binds up their wounds.

Isaiah 43:2, NIV

When you pass through the waters, I will be with you; and when you pass through the rivers, they will not sweep over you. When you walk through the fire, you will not be burned, the flames will not set you ablaze.

Isaiah 53:4, NKJV

Surely He has borne our griefs and carried our sorrows.

Lamentations 3:56, NKJV

You have heard my voice: "Do not hide Your ear from my sighing, from my cry for help."

Matthew 28:20, NIV

Surely I am with you always, to the very end of the age.

Mark 15:34, NKJV

At the ninth hour Jesus cried out with a loud voice, saying, "Eloi, Eloi, lama sabachthani?" which is translated, *"My God, My God, why have You forsaken Me?"*

# Heaven—What
# Happens When a Christian Dies?

What happens when a Christian dies is not based on current philosophies, traditions, or modern-day religions, but on the Word of God. The Scriptures give us insight and truth that bring great comfort and hope.

To be "absent from the body" is to be "present with the Lord" (2 Corinthians 5:8, NKJV). Nowhere does the Scripture teach that at any time the spirit of a person is unconscious. There is no purgatory, no state of unconsciousness or semi-consciousness, no spiritual coma. You're either here or with Christ. If you're ever in Christ, you're always in Christ: "Having believed, you were marked in him with a seal, the promised Holy Spirit, who is a deposit guaranteeing our inheritance until the redemption of those who are God's possession—to the praise of his glory" (Ephesians 1:13-14, NIV).

It is natural to have questions about life after death. In 1 Thessalonians, Paul writes to the Christian church to increase their understanding about death and to bring them comfort from the hope of seeing their loved ones again. "We want you to know about those Christians who have died so you will not be sad, as others who have no hope" (1 Thessalonians 4:13, NCV). For a Christian, saying good-bye to a loved one is never a final good-bye: "Because we know that God raised the Lord Jesus to life. And just as God raised Jesus, he will also raise us to life. Then he will bring us into his presence together with you" (2 Corinthians 4:14, CEV).

*For other helpful categories, see pages 230, 247.*

Psalm 49:15, NIV

But God will redeem my life from the grave; he will surely take me to himself.

Isaiah 57:2, NIV

Those who walk uprightly enter into peace; they find rest as they lie in death.

Matthew 5:8, NKJV

Blessed are the pure in heart, for they shall see God.

Luke 20:38, NIV

He is not the God of the dead, but of the living, for to him all arc alive.

Luke 23:42-43, NIV

Then he said, "Jesus, remember me when you come into your kingdom." Jesus answered him, "I tell you the truth, today you will be with me in paradise."

John 8:51, NIV

I tell you the truth, if anyone keeps my word, he will never see death.

John 10:28, NIV

I give them eternal life, and they shall never perish; no one can snatch them out of my hand.

John 11:25-26, NIV

Jesus said to her, "I am the resurrection and the life. He who believes in me will live, even though he dies; and whoever lives and believes in me will never die. Do you believe this?"

John 14:2-3, NIV

In my Father's house are many rooms; if it were not so, I would have told you. I am going there to prepare a place for you. And if I go and prepare a place for you, I will come back and take you to be with me that you also may be where I am.

| | |
|---|---|
| 1 Corinthians 2:9, NKJV | Eye has not seen, nor ear heard, nor have entered into the heart of man the things which God has prepared for those who love Him. |
| 2 Corinthians 4:14, CEV | We know that God raised the Lord Jesus to life. And just as God raised Jesus, he will also raise us to life. Then he will bring us into his presence together with you. |
| 2 Corinthians 5:1, NCV | We know that our body—the tent we live in here on earth—will be destroyed. But when that happens, God will have a house for us. It will not be a house made by human hands; instead, it will be a home in heaven that will last forever. |
| 2 Corinthians 5:8, NKJV | We are confident, yes, well pleased rather to be absent from the body and to be present with the Lord. |
| Ephesians 1:13-14, NIV | Having believed, you were marked in him with a seal, the promised Holy Spirit, who is a deposit guaranteeing our inheritance until the redemption of those who are God's possession—to the praise of his glory. |
| Philippians 3:20, NIV | Our citizenship is in heaven. And we eagerly await a Savior from there, the Lord Jesus Christ. |
| 1 Thessalonians 4:13, NCV | Brothers and sisters, we want you to know about those Christians who have died so you will not be sad, as others who have no hope. |

| | |
|---|---|
| 2 Timothy 4:18, NIV | The Lord will rescue me from every evil attack and will bring me safely to his heavenly kingdom. To him be glory for ever and ever. |
| Hebrews 11:10, NKJV | He waited for the city which has foundations, whose builder and maker is God. |
| Hebrews 11:16, NKJV | But now they desire a better, that is, a heavenly country. Therefore God is not ashamed to be called their God, for He has prepared a city for them. |
| Revelation 2:7, NIV | He who has an ear, let him hear what the Spirit says to the churches. To him who overcomes, I will give the right to eat from the tree of life, which is in the paradise of God. |
| Revelation 5:9, NIV | You are worthy to take the scroll and to open its seals, because you were slain, and with your blood you purchased men for God from every tribe and language and people and nation. |
| Revelation 7:9, NKJV | I looked, and behold, a great multitude which no one could number, of all nations, tribes, peoples, and tongues, standing before the throne and before the Lamb, clothed with white robes, with palm branches in their hands. |

# HEAVEN—THE NEW HEAVEN

When you wonder what your eternal future holds, remember the promise Jesus gave to His grieving disciples: "I go to prepare a place for you" (John 14:2, NKJV). The place that Jesus prepares is the New Jerusalem—a place that is meant for *you* as well.

God has chosen the geographical Jerusalem as His city (2 Chronicles 6:6). It is the spiritual capital of the earth. But there is also a spiritual Jerusalem of heaven. God's glory and His light shine (Revelation 21:11) in the New Jerusalem—the City of God in the heavens (Revelation 21:2-3). What a future you have! "The nations of those who are saved shall walk in its light, and the kings of the earth bring their glory and honor into it" (Revelation 21:24, NKJV).

Everyone whose name is written in the Lamb's Book of Life (Revelation 21:27) shall walk in this city of pure gold and shall stand on foundations adorned with every precious stone and gem imaginable (Revelations 21:18-20) As a Christian, you will one day enter the gates (Revelation 21:21) of the New Jerusalem and live forever where there is only truth and no lie (Revelation 21:27).

Let this be a word of encouragement: in times of trouble, you know where you are going. No matter how dark your world becomes, you are destined for the City of Light. The earth is not your home. You are just passing through on your way to the New Jerusalem!

*For another helpful category, see page 226.*

| | |
|---|---|
| 2 Chronicles 6:6, NKJV | I have chosen Jerusalem, that My name may be there. |
| Revelation 21:1-2, NIV | Then I saw a new heaven and a new earth, for the first heaven and the first earth had passed away, and there was no longer any sea. I saw the Holy City, the new Jerusalem, coming down out of heaven from God, prepared as a bride beautifully dressed for her husband. |
| Revelation 21:3, NIV | I heard a loud voice from the throne saying, "Now the dwelling of God is with men, and he will live with them. They will be his people, and God himself will be with them and be their God. He will wipe every tear from their eyes. There will be no more death or mourning or crying or pain, for the old order of things has passed away." |
| Revelation 21:10-11, NIV | And he carried me away in the Spirit to a mountain great and high, and showed me the Holy City, Jerusalem, coming down out of heaven from God. It shone with the glory of God, and its brilliance was like that of a very precious jewel, like a jasper, clear as crystal. |
| Revelation 21:15-17, NIV | The angel who talked with me had a measuring rod of gold to measure the city, its gates and its walls. The city was laid out like a square, as long as it was wide. He measured the city with the rod and found it to be 12,000 stadia in length, and as wide and high as it is long. He measured its wall and it was 144 cubits thick, by man's measurement, which the angel was using. |

Revelation 21:18-20, NIV

The wall was made of jasper, and the city of pure gold, as pure as glass. The foundations of the city walls were decorated with every kind of precious stone. The first foundation was jasper, the second sapphire, the third chalcedony, the fourth emerald, the fifth sardonyx, the sixth carnelian, the seventh chrysolite, the eighth beryl, the ninth topaz, the tenth chrysoprase, the eleventh jacinth, and the twelfth amethyst.

Revelation 21:21, NIV

The twelve gates were twelve pearls, each gate made of a single pearl. The great street of the city was of pure gold, like transparent glass.

Revelation 21:22-23, NIV

I did not see a temple in the city, because the Lord God Almighty and the Lamb are its temple. The city does not need the sun or the moon to shine on it, for the glory of God gives it light, and the Lamb is its lamp.

Revelation 21:24-26, NIV

The nations will walk by its light, and the kings of the earth will bring their splendor into it. On no day will its gates ever be shut, for there will be no night there. The glory and honor of the nations will be brought into it.

Revelation 21:27, NIV

Nothing impure will ever enter it, nor will anyone who does what is shameful or deceitful, but only those whose names are written in the Lamb's book of life.

# HELL

Cartoons and jokes about hell abound, but hell is real. It is a literal place. Jesus said in Matthew 13:41-42 that the angels will cast "all things that offend, and those who practice lawlessness" and "will cast them into the furnace of fire. There will be wailing and gnashing of teeth" (NKJV). Hell is a place of eternal torment (Revelation 20:10).

We need to remember that it is not God's will that any would perish, but that all would come to repentance (2 Peter 3:9). Hell was "prepared for the devil and his angels" (Matthew 25:41, NIV), not for the people of the world. In other words, God does not send people to hell. When people reject God and His Son, Jesus Christ, they condemn themselves to eternal damnation.

The word *hell* in the Bible literally means "the grave." It is a place from which no one can return. That's why it is God's will that you and your loved ones receive His love and forgiveness through His Son, Jesus Christ. God wants all people to come to know the truth and spend eternity with Him (1 Timothy 2:4).

Remember that praying God's Word over a lost or unsaved person is powerful—so powerful that it can change someone's eternal destiny. "The effective, fervent prayer of a righteous man avails much" (James 5:16, NKJV).

*For other helpful categories, see pages 388, 392, 395, 398.*

| | |
|---|---|
| Matthew 13:41-42, NKJV | The Son of Man will send out His angels, and they will gather out of His kingdom all things that offend, and those who practice lawlessness, and will cast them into the furnace of fire. There will be wailing and gnashing of teeth. |
| Matthew 25:41, NIV | Then he will say to those on his left, "Depart from me, you who are cursed, into the eternal fire prepared for the devil and his angels." |
| Matthew 25:46, NKJV | These will go away into everlasting punishment, but the righteous into eternal life. |
| Luke 16:23, NIV | In hell, where he was in torment, he looked up and saw Abraham far away, with Lazarus by his side. |
| 2 Thessalonians 1:9, NIV | They will be punished with everlasting destruction and shut out from the presence of the Lord and from the majesty of his power. |
| 1 Timothy 2:3-4, NKJV | For this is good and acceptable in the sight of God our Savior, who desires all men to be saved and to come to the knowledge of the truth. |
| 2 Peter 2:4, NIV | God did not spare angels when they sinned, but sent them to hell, putting them into gloomy dungeons to be held for judgment. |
| 2 Peter 3:9, NIV | The Lord is not slow in keeping his promise, as some understand slowness. He is patient with you, not wanting anyone to perish, but everyone to come to repentance. |

Revelation 14:11, NIV    The smoke of their torment rises for ever and ever. There is no rest day or night for those who worship the beast and his image, or for anyone who receives the mark of his name.

Revelation 20:10, NIV    The devil, who deceived them, was thrown into the lake of burning sulfur, where the beast and the false prophet had been thrown. They will be tormented day and night for ever and ever.

Revelation 20:15, NIV    If anyone's name was not found written in the book of life, he was thrown into the lake of fire.

Revelation 21:8, NIV     The cowardly, the unbelieving, the vile, the murderers, the sexually immoral, those who practice magic arts, the idolaters and all liars—their place will be in the fiery lake of burning sulfur. This is the second death.

# HELP IN TIME OF NEED

Do you feel harassed, chased down, surrounded by your "enemies" (whether they are people or circumstances)? Do you wonder where God is when you need Him?

King David felt the same way at one time. But after God had delivered him from all his enemies, he reflected on a truth: God was there all the time.

Consider these lines from a song of praise that David sang to God:

- "With your help I can advance against a troop; with my God I can scale a wall."
- "You give me your shield of victory; you stoop down to make me great."
- "You armed me with strength for battle; you made my adversaries bow at my feet." (2 Samuel 22:30, 36, 40, NIV)

Even though David had sinned, he loved God and knew where his help came from. He realized that God does not fail to rescue those who love Him. That's why he could boldly declare, "God is a safe place to hide, ready to help when we need him" (Psalm 46:1, MSG).

We see this help from God most clearly in Jesus—God-in-the-flesh. Jesus became a man so that He could identify with our trials and temptations. He understands the heartaches, pains, and difficulties we face. And "he is able to help" (Hebrews 2:18, ESV).

*For other helpful categories, see pages 62, 289, 314, 340, 428.*

| | |
|---|---|
| 2 Samuel 22:30, NIV | With your help I can advance against a troop; with my God I can scale a wall. |
| 2 Chronicles 7:14, NIV | If my people, who are called by my name, will humble themselves and pray and seek my face and turn from their wicked ways, then will I hear from heaven and will forgive their sin and will heal their land. |
| Psalm 5:2, NIV | Listen to my cry for help, my King and my God, for to you I pray. |
| Psalm 10:14, NKJV | You have seen, for You observe trouble and grief, to repay it by Your hand. The helpless commits himself to You. You are the helper of the fatherless. |
| Psalm 18:6, NIV | In my distress I called to the LORD; I cried to my God for help. From his temple he heard my voice; my cry came before him, into his ears. |
| Psalm 28:7, NIV | The LORD is my strength and my shield, my heart trusts in him, and I am helped. My heart leaps for joy and I will give thanks to him in song. |
| Psalm 46:1, MSG | God is a safe place to hide, ready to help when we need him. |
| Psalm 86:7, NIV | In the day of my trouble I will call to you, for you will answer me. |
| Jeremiah 1:8, NIV | "Do not be afraid of them, for I am with you and will rescue you," declares the LORD. |

| | |
|---|---|
| Jeremiah 1:19, NIV | They will fight against you but will not overcome you, for I am with you and will rescue you," declares the LORD. |
| Nahum 1:7, NKJV | The LORD is good, a stronghold in the day of trouble; and He knows those who trust in Him. |
| Romans 12:12, NIV | Be joyful in hope, patient in affliction, faithful in prayer. |
| 2 Corinthians 1:3-4, NIV | Praise be to the God and Father of our Lord Jesus Christ, the Father of compassion and the God of all comfort, who comforts us in all our troubles, so that we can comfort those in any trouble with the comfort we ourselves have received from God. |
| 2 Timothy 4:18, NIV | The Lord will rescue me from every evil attack and will bring me safely to his heavenly kingdom. To him be glory for ever and ever. |
| Hebrews 2:18, ESV | Because he himself has suffered when tempted, he is able to help those who are being tempted. |
| James 5:13, NIV | Is any one of you in trouble? He should pray. |

# THE HOLY SPIRIT

It is God's will for the Holy Spirit to function fully in our lives. In order for this to happen, we must have an open heart and a consuming desire to know all we can about the nature and role of the Holy Spirit.

We need to look to the Bible to properly understand this most intimate presence of God with us and to understand the gifts and ministries of the Holy Spirit. Here are four truths to hold on to:

1. *The Holy Spirit is the third Person of the Trinity.* He is fully God—equal in every way with the Father and the Son. He is eternal, all-knowing, ever-present. He has a will, and He can speak. He plays a special role in bearing witness to Jesus (John 15:26).

2. *The Holy Spirit lives inside those who have believed in Christ for their salvation and is the deposit guaranteeing our inheritance "until the redemption of those who are God's possession"* (Ephesians 1:13-14, NIV). As the indwelling presence of God in our lives, He works to reproduce God's character within us. We learn the qualities of this godly character when we read about the fruit of the Spirit in Galatians 5:22-23.

3. *The Holy Spirit is also active in the lives of non-Christians.* He convicts people's hearts with God's truth concerning sinful human nature. He asks them to repent and turn to God for forgiveness (John 16:8).

4. *The Holy Spirit helps us in our weakness.* He comes alongside us to lead and guide us into all truth. He helps us to birth what we cannot birth by ourselves (Romans 8:26). He teaches us all things and helps us to remember the Word (John 14:26).

*For other helpful categories, see pages 180, 193, 384.*

| John 14:16-17, NIV | I will ask the Father, and he will give you another Counselor to be with you forever—the Spirit of truth. The world cannot accept him, because it neither sees him nor knows him. But you know him, for he lives with you and will be in you. |
| --- | --- |
| John 14:26, NKJV | The Helper, the Holy Spirit, whom the Father will send in My name, He will teach you all things, and bring to your remembrance all things that I said to you. |
| John 15:26, NIV | When the Counselor comes, whom I will send to you from the Father, the Spirit of truth who goes out from the Father, he will testify about me. |
| John 16:7-8, NIV | I tell you the truth: It is for your good that I am going away. Unless I go away, the Counselor will not come to you; but if I go, I will send him to you. When he comes, he will convict the world of guilt in regard to sin and righteousness and judgment. |
| John 16:13, NIV | When he, the Spirit of truth, comes, he will guide you into all truth. He will not speak on his own; he will speak only what he hears, and he will tell you what is yet to come. |
| Acts 2:4, NIV | All of them were filled with the Holy Spirit and began to speak in other tongues as the Spirit enabled them. |
| Acts 2:38, NIV | Repent and be baptized, every one of you, in the name of Jesus Christ for the forgiveness of your |

sins. And you will receive the gift of the Holy Spirit.

Acts 4:31, NIV — After they prayed, the place where they were meeting was shaken. And they were all filled with the Holy Spirit and spoke the word of God boldly.

Romans 5:5, NKJV — The love of God has been poured out in our hearts by the Holy Spirit who was given to us.

Romans 8:16, NIV — The Spirit himself testifies with our spirit that we are God's children.

Romans 8:26, NIV — The Spirit helps us in our weakness. We do not know what we ought to pray for, but the Spirit himself intercedes for us with groans that words cannot express.

1 Corinthians 2:10-11, NIV — The Spirit searches all things, even the deep things of God. For who among men knows the thoughts of a man except the man's spirit within him? In the same way no one knows the thoughts of God except the Spirit of God.

1 Corinthians 2:12-13, NIV — We have not received the spirit of the world but the Spirit who is from God, that we may understand what God has freely given us. This is what we speak, not in words taught us by human wisdom but in words taught by the Spirit, expressing spiritual truths in spiritual words.

1 Corinthians 2:14, NIV    The man without the Spirit does not accept the things that come from the Spirit of God, for they are foolishness to him, and he cannot understand them, because they are spiritually discerned.

1 Corinthians 12:3, NKJV   Therefore I make known to you that no one speaking by the Spirit of God calls Jesus accursed and no one can say that Jesus is Lord except by the Holy Spirit.

Galatians 5:22-23, NIV     The fruit of the Spirit is love, joy, peace, patience, kindness, goodness, faithfulness, gentleness and self-control. Against such things there is no law.

Ephesians 1:13-14, NIV     Having believed, you were marked in him with a seal, the promised Holy Spirit, who is a deposit guaranteeing our inheritance until the redemption of those who are God's possession — to the praise of his glory.

Ephesians 4:30, NIV        Do not grieve the Holy Spirit of God, with whom you were sealed for the day of redemption.

1 John 3:24, NIV           This is how we know that he lives in us: We know it by the Spirit he gave us.

1 John 4:13, NIV           We know that we live in him and he in us, because he has given us of his Spirit.

# Horoscopes, the Occult, New Age, and Witchcraft

First Samuel 28 tells the story of King Saul seeking out the witch of Endor to give him insight into the future. He got news he didn't want to hear.

Many in our day have the same tendency to pursue supernatural knowledge apart from God and His Word. That's always a mistake!

Going to palm readers or tarot card specialists. Trying out the spells of Wicca. Entertaining neopagan ideas. Dabbling in New Age practices. Consulting a horoscope. These are just some of the ways that many people seek spiritual direction through occult means today.

These supernatural avenues can even be tempting to Christians. Be aware of them—and stay far away from all organizations, movies, books, and practices that do not point to salvation through Jesus Christ and that go against the Word of God.

King Saul would have saved himself a trespass against God's will if he'd listened to the warning God had already given: "These nations which you will dispossess listened to soothsayers and diviners; but as for you, the LORD your God has not appointed such for you" (Deuteronomy 18:14, NKJV). Knowing God's Word will guard you against making the same mistakes Saul did. Often His Word will warn you before you act. Pray and ask for God's help to stay pure of occult influences.

*For other helpful categories, see pages 378, 398, 402.*

| | |
|---|---|
| Exodus 22:18, CEV | Death is the punishment for witchcraft. |
| Leviticus 19:26, NCV | You must not try to tell the future by signs or black magic. |
| Leviticus 20:6, CEV | I will be your enemy if you go to someone who claims to speak with the dead, and I will destroy you from among my people. |
| Deuteronomy 4:19, NLT | When you look up into the sky and see the sun, moon, and stars—all the forces of heaven—don't be seduced into worshiping them. The LORD your God gave them to all the peoples of the earth. |
| Deuteronomy 18:10-11, NLT | Do not let your people practice fortune-telling, or use sorcery, or interpret omens, or engage in witchcraft, or cast spells, or function as mediums or psychics, or call forth the spirits of the dead. |
| Deuteronomy 18:14, NKJV | These nations which you will dispossess listened to soothsayers and diviners; but as for you, the LORD your God has not appointed such for you. |
| 1 Samuel 28:7, NCV | Saul said to his servants, "Find me a woman who is a medium so I may go and ask her what will happen." His servants answered, "There is a medium in Endor." |
| 1 Chronicles 10:13-14, NIV | Saul died because he was unfaithful to the LORD; he did not keep the word of the LORD and even consulted a medium for guidance, and did not inquire of the LORD. So the LORD put him to |

death and turned the kingdom over to David son of Jesse.

Isaiah 8:19, NIV

When men tell you to consult mediums and spiritists, who whisper and mutter, should not a people inquire of their God? Why consult the dead on behalf of the living?

Isaiah 47:13, NCV

You are tired of the advice you have received. So let those who study the sky—those who tell the future by looking at the stars and the new moons—let them save you from what is about to happen to you.

Jeremiah 27:9, NCV

Don't listen to your false prophets, those who use magic to tell the future, those who explain dreams, the mediums, or magicians. They all tell you, "You will not be slaves to the king of Babylon."

Daniel 2:27, NCV

Daniel answered, "No wise man, magician, or fortune-teller can explain to the king the secret he has asked about."

Micah 5:12, NIV

I will destroy your witchcraft and you will no longer cast spells.

Matthew 5:17, NIV

Do not think that I have come to abolish the Law or the Prophets; I have not come to abolish them but to fulfill them.

John 14:6, NIV

I am the way and the truth and the life. No one comes to the Father except through me.

Acts 7:42, NLT

God turned away from them and abandoned them to serve the stars of heaven as their gods! In the book of the prophets it is written, "Was it to me you were bringing sacrifices and offerings during those forty years in the wilderness, Israel?"

1 John 4:1, NIV

Dear friends, do not believe every spirit, but test the spirits to see whether they are from God, because many false prophets have gone out into the world.

# HOSPICE

How do you minister to people who are in the critical and vulnerable time of dying? You can't promise that they're going to get well while they're on this earth. But you can comfort them. You cannot deal in false hope or in deceit. But you can play a vital role in ministering the love and grace of Christ to them.

When God heals, He doesn't always cure a disease. But true healing always means finding peace and wholeness in the person of our Lord and Savior Jesus Christ. Those who are terminally ill need the hope and assurance that only the gospel can bring.

The person who is terminally ill may be grieving over leaving loved ones behind. You can reassure him or her that the Bible says we will see our loved ones again. When David's infant son died, David declared, "I will go to him, but he will not return to me" (2 Samuel 12:23, NIV). David assumed that he would be able to recognize his son in heaven. At the transfiguration, Moses and Elijah were recognizable (Matthew 17:3-4). In Luke 16:19-31, Abraham, Lazarus, and the rich man were all recognizable after death.

Remember that *fear* is often associated with death and dying. The antidote to fear is faith. *Faith in the saving knowledge of Jesus Christ.* Encourage the person in hospice to find strength and peace by going to God with his or her fears. Encourage this person to trust in the true and living God, who knows all things, is in control at all times, and has a perfect plan that He will complete (Philippians 1:6). Death is not the end, but it is the new beginning of an eternal and glorious life that all of God's people will one day share together.

Even as you minister to those in hospice, be aware of what they can teach you about God's presence at the end of life. Often God speaks to those who are near physical death in rich ways and reveals great truths about the new life ahead (Revelation 21:2-4).

*For other helpful categories, see pages 171, 196, 226, 230, 311.*

| | |
|---|---|
| Psalm 18:2, NIV | The LORD is my rock, my fortress and my deliverer; my God is my rock, in whom I take refuge. He is my shield and the horn of my salvation, my stronghold. |
| Psalm 23:4, NLT | Even when I walk through the darkest valley, I will not be afraid, for you are close beside me. Your rod and your staff protect and comfort me. |
| Psalm 116:8-9, NIV | For you, O LORD, have delivered my soul from death, my eyes from tears, my feet from stumbling, that I may walk before the Lord in the land of the living. |
| Psalm 116:15, NKJV | Precious in the sight of the LORD is the death of His saints. |
| Proverbs 14:27, AMP | Reverent and worshipful fear of the Lord is a fountain of life, that one may avoid the snares of death. |
| Ecclesiastes 3:1-2, NIV | There is a time for everything, and a season for every activity under heaven: a time to be born and a time to die. |
| Ecclesiastes 8:8, NIV | No man has power over the wind to contain it; so no one has power over the day of his death. |
| Isaiah 57:2, NIV | Those who walk uprightly enter into peace; they find rest as they lie in death. |

| | |
|---|---|
| Luke 10:27, NKJV | You shall love the LORD your God with all your heart, with all your soul, with all your strength, and with all your mind. |
| John 5:24, NIV | I tell you the truth, whoever hears my word and believes him who sent me has eternal life and will not be condemned; he has crossed over from death to life. |
| John 6:51, NKJV | I am the living bread which came down from heaven. If anyone eats of this bread, he will live forever; and the bread that I shall give is My flesh, which I shall give for the life of the world. |
| John 11:25, NIV | I am the resurrection and the life. He who believes in me will live, even though he dies. |
| 1 Corinthians 15:56-57, NIV | The sting of death is sin, and the power of sin is the law. But thanks be to God! He gives us the victory through our Lord Jesus Christ. |
| 2 Corinthians 4:14, NCV | God raised the Lord Jesus from the dead, and we know that God will also raise us with Jesus. God will bring us together with you, and we will stand before him. |
| 2 Corinthians 5:8, NLT | Yes, we are fully confident, and we would rather be away from these earthly bodies, for then we will be at home with the Lord. |
| Ephesians 1:13-14, NIV | You also were included in Christ when you heard the word of truth, the gospel of your salvation. Having believed, you were marked in him with a |

seal, the promised Holy Spirit, who is a deposit guaranteeing our inheritance until the redemption of those who are God's possession—to the praise of his glory.

Philippians 1:21, NIV

For to me, to live is Christ and to die is gain.

2 Thessalonians 3:16, NIV

Now may the Lord of peace himself give you peace at all times and in every way. The Lord be with all of you.

Hebrews 9:27, NCV

Everyone must die once and then be judged.

Hebrews 13:5, NKJV

I will never leave you nor forsake you.

1 John 4:18, NIV

There is no fear in love. But perfect love drives out fear, because fear has to do with punishment. The one who fears is not made perfect in love.

Revelation 21:2-4, NCV

I saw the holy city, the new Jerusalem, coming down out of heaven from God. It was prepared like a bride dressed for her husband. And I heard a loud voice from the throne, saying, "Now God's presence is with people, and he will live with them, and they will be his people. God himself will be with them and will be their God. He will wipe away every tear from their eyes, and there will be no more death, sadness, crying, or pain, because all the old ways are gone."

# INFERTILITY

The pain of infertility does not go unnoticed or untouched by God. Even through the difficulty of accepting the fact that you are not in control of your situation, God's desire is that you live in His peace—a peace that "surpasses all understanding" (Philippians 4:7).

The Bible is filled with examples of God answering prayers to have a baby in situations that seemed impossible. In her nineties, Sarai (Sarah) bore Isaac (Genesis 21:2). Rebekah (Isaac's wife) bore twins, Esau and Jacob, after twenty years of barrenness (Genesis 25:21). Hannah (wife of Elkanah) bore Samuel after years of desperate prayer (1 Samuel 1:20). Elizabeth (wife of Zacharias) in her old age conceived a son, John the Baptist, Jesus's cousin (Luke 1:57-58).

Perhaps you are so weary of hearing of others having babies that these testimonies are hard to consider. These testimonies were written to build your faith and to remind you that God is aware of you. God *can* work in your body to conceive.

As a couple, stand on the promise that Jesus made in Matthew 18:20, "For where two or three are gathered in my name, there am I with them" (NIV). When you come together in the spirit of unity to have a child—whether through your own body or through another's body—your prayer is powerful. Give your desire to be parents to God and trust in His great love to give you the desires of your heart. Life can still be birthed in your relationship through the prayer of agreement.

*For other helpful categories, see pages 109, 115, 118, 132, 207, 340.*

| | |
|---|---|
| Genesis 21:2, NKJV | Sarah conceived and bore Abraham a son in his old age, at the set time of which God had spoken to him. |
| Genesis 25:21, NIV | Isaac prayed to the LORD on behalf of his wife, because she was barren. The LORD answered his prayer, and his wife Rebekah became pregnant. |
| Genesis 30:22-23, NIV | Then God remembered Rachel; he listened to her and opened her womb. She became pregnant and gave birth to a son and said, "God has taken away my disgrace." |
| 1 Samuel 1:10-11, NIV | In bitterness of soul Hannah wept much and prayed to the LORD. And she made a vow, saying, "O LORD Almighty, if you will only look upon your servant's misery and remember me, and not forget your servant but give her a son, then I will give him to the LORD for all the days of his life." |
| 1 Samuel 1:20, NIV | In the course of time, Hannah conceived and gave birth to a son. She named him Samuel, saying, "Because I asked the LORD for him." |
| Psalm 37:4-5, NKJV | Delight yourself also in the LORD, and He shall give you the desires of your heart. Commit your way to the LORD, trust also in Him, and He shall bring it to pass. |
| Psalm 113:9, NCV | He gives children to the woman who has none and makes her a happy mother. Praise the Lord! |

Psalm 115:14, NIV — May the LORD make you increase, both you and your children.

Psalm 128:3-4, NCV — Your wife will give you many children, like a vine that produces much fruit. Your children will bring you much good, like olive branches that produce many olives. This is how the man who respects the LORD will be blessed.

Isaiah 8:18, NKJV — Here am I and the children whom the LORD has given me!

Isaiah 54:1, NIV — "Sing, O barren woman, you who never bore a child; burst into song, shout for joy, you who were never in labor; because more are the children of the desolate woman than of her who has a husband," says the LORD.

Matthew 18:19-20, NIV — Again, I tell you that if two of you on earth agree about anything you ask for, it will be done for you by my Father in heaven. For where two or three come together in my name, there am I with them.

Luke 1:57-58, NIV — When it was time for Elizabeth to have her baby, she gave birth to a son. Her neighbors and relatives heard that the Lord had shown her great mercy, and they shared her joy.

Philippians 4:6-7, NKJV — Be anxious for nothing, but in everything by prayer and supplication, with thanksgiving, let your requests be made known to God; and the peace of God, which surpasses all understanding, will guard your hearts and minds through Christ Jesus.

# JEALOUSY

You were created as a unique and special person (Psalm 139:14), made in the image of God (Genesis 1:27). God had a plan for you long before the creation of the world (Jeremiah 1:5). So if you find yourself jealous of others, you are believing the lies Satan wants you to hear rather than receiving the truth of God about your worth.

God's plan for you is different than His plan for anyone else. That's a good thing because everyone is called to contribute to the body of Christ in unique ways (Ephesians 4:16).

Celebrate who you are—God does! He has given you gifts that He has not given to others. Rather than dwelling on what you don't have, focus on developing and blessing others with the gifts and talents you *do* have. It will help your Spirit-led self-image to soar as you reflect the character and nature of God.

If you have been the recipient of someone's jealousy over you, pray for that person. Jesus said, "Bless those who curse you, pray for those who are cruel to you" (Luke 6:28, NCV).

The only pure jealousy is God's jealousy. God's jealousy comes out of a righteous nature. God is jealous when Christians spend more time seeking advice from magazines, television, the Internet, and non-Christians than they do from God and His Word. God is jealous when His people put their trust in other things to find contentment, peace, and joy. God is jealous when His children serve their own interest instead of God's.

Jealousy is not a benign emotion. Scripture tells us that "jealousy is as strong as the grave" (Song of Solomon 8:6, NCV) and its fury is worse than cruel wrath or overwhelming anger (Proverbs 27:4). It has the potential to stop the plan and purpose of God in a relationship. Apart from God, jealousy is a sin, and we should always be aware of its potential danger in our lives.

*For other helpful categories, see pages 174, 356, 441, 445.*

| | |
|---|---|
| Proverbs 14:30, NLT | A peaceful heart leads to a healthy body; jealousy is like cancer in the bones. |
| Proverbs 27:4, NIV | Anger is cruel and fury overwhelming, but who can stand before jealousy? |
| Song of Solomon 8:6, NCV | Put me like a seal on your heart, like a seal on your arm. Love is as strong as death; jealousy is as strong as the grave. Love bursts into flames and burns like a hot fire. |
| Luke 6:28, NCV | Bless those who curse you, pray for those who are cruel to you. |
| Luke 6:45, NKJV | A good man out of the good treasure of his heart brings forth good; and an evil man out of the evil treasure of his heart brings forth evil. For out of the abundance of the heart his mouth speaks. |
| 1 Corinthians 13:4, NLT | Love is patient and kind. Love is not jealous or boastful or proud. |
| Galatians 5:19-21, NKJV | Now the works of the flesh are evident, which are: adultery, fornication, uncleanness, lewdness, idolatry, sorcery, hatred, contentions, *jealousies,* outbursts of wrath, selfish ambitions, dissensions, heresies, envy, murders, drunkenness, revelries, and the like; of which I tell you beforehand, just as I also told you in time past, that those who practice such things will not inherit the kingdom of God. |

Galatians 6:3-5, NIV    If anyone thinks he is something when he is nothing, he deceives himself. Each one should test his own actions. Then he can take pride in himself, without comparing himself to somebody else.

Colossians 3:13, NIV    Bear with each other and forgive whatever grievances you may have against one another. Forgive as the Lord forgave you.

# JESUS

Jesus is the revelation of God, the redeemer of sin, and the light of the world! He is the image of the invisible God, "the firstborn over all creation" (Colossians 1:15, NIV). He is fully God yet fully human—fully God so that His death was no ordinary death and fully human so that He experienced life like one of us.

The New Testament offers more than seven hundred names or titles of Jesus to describe this incomparable man. How can the power of Jesus change your life right now?

Consider these truths:

- Jesus is your Eternal Savior (Acts 4:12)
- Jesus is your Life (Colossians 3:3-4)
- Jesus is your Shepherd (John 10:14)
- Jesus is your Healer (Matthew 14:14)
- Jesus is your Creator (John 1:3)
- Jesus is your Deliverer (Romans 11:26)
- Jesus is your Hope (1 Timothy 1:1)
- Jesus is your Protection (2 Thessalonians 3:3)
- Jesus is your Truth (John 1:14)
- Jesus is your Redeemer (Mark 10:45)
- Jesus is your Peace (Isaiah 9:6)

Jesus can meet every longing or need you have, just as He met the needs of those who walked with Him two thousand years ago. Jesus is the same yesterday and today and forever (Hebrews 13:8). He is with you to strengthen you, protect you, save you, and give you hope. There is no greater love.

*For other helpful categories, see pages 65, 193–196.*

| | |
|---|---|
| Genesis 1:26, NKJV | Then God said, "Let Us make man in Our image, according to Our likeness." |
| Isaiah 9:6, NKJV | For unto us a Child is born, unto us a Son is given; and the government will be upon His shoulder. And His name will be called Wonderful, Counselor, Mighty God, Everlasting Father, Prince of Peace. |
| Matthew 28:18, NIV | Jesus came to them and said, "All authority in heaven and on earth has been given to me." |
| Mark 10:45, NKJV | Even the Son of Man did not come to be served, but to serve, and to give His life a ransom for many. |
| Luke 1:32, NIV | He will be great and will be called the Son of the Most High. The Lord God will give him the throne of his father David. |
| John 1:1-4, NIV | In the beginning was the Word, and the Word was with God, and the Word was God. He was with God in the beginning. Through him all things were made; without him nothing was made that has been made. In him was life, and that life was the light of men. |
| John 1:14, NIV | The Word became flesh and made his dwelling among us. We have seen his glory, the glory of the One and Only, who came from the Father, full of grace and truth. |

| | |
|---|---|
| John 1:49, NKJV | Nathanael answered and said to Him, "Rabbi, You are the Son of God! You are the King of Israel!" |
| John 6:51, NKJV | I am the living bread which came down from heaven. If anyone eats of this bread, he will live forever; and the bread that I shall give is My flesh, which I shall give for the life of the world. |
| John 8:12, NIV | When Jesus spoke again to the people, he said, "I am the light of the world. Whoever follows me will never walk in darkness, but will have the light of life." |
| John 8:58, NKJV | Jesus said to them, "Most assuredly, I say to you, before Abraham was, I AM." |
| John 10:11, NKJV | I am the good shepherd. The good shepherd gives His life for the sheep. |
| John 10:30, NKJV | I and My Father are one. |
| John 14:5, NKJV | Jesus said to him, "I am the way, the truth, and the life. No one comes to the Father except through Me." |
| John 15:1, NIV | I am the true vine, and my Father is the gardener. |
| John 16:28, NIV | I came from the Father and entered the world; now I am leaving the world and going back to the Father. |

| | |
|---|---|
| John 18:37, NIV | "You are a king, then!" said Pilate. Jesus answered, "You are right in saying I am a king. In fact, for this reason I was born, and for this I came into the world, to testify to the truth. Everyone on the side of truth listens to me." |
| Acts 3:15, NIV | You killed the author of life, but God raised him from the dead. We are witnesses of this. |
| Acts 5:31, NIV | God exalted him to his own right hand as Prince and Savior that he might give repentance and forgiveness of sins to Israel. |
| Acts 10:38, NKJV | God anointed Jesus of Nazareth with the Holy Spirit and with power, who went about doing good and healing all who were oppressed by the devil, for God was with Him. |
| Romans 1:3, NCV | The Good News is about God's Son, Jesus Christ our Lord. As a man, he was born from the family of David. But through the Spirit of holiness he was declared to be God's Son with great power by rising from the dead. |
| Romans 11:26, NKJV | The Deliverer will come out of Zion, and He will turn away ungodliness from Jacob. |
| Romans 14:9, NIV | For this very reason, Christ died and returned to life so that he might be the Lord of both the dead and the living. |

| | |
|---|---|
| 2 Corinthians 5:15, NIV | He died for all, that those who live should no longer live for themselves but for him who died for them and was raised again. |
| Ephesians 5:23, NIV | Christ is the head of the church, his body, of which he is the Savior. |
| Philippians 2:8, NIV | And being found in appearance as a man, he humbled himself and became obedient to death—even death on a cross! |
| Colossians 1:15, NIV | He is the image of the invisible God, the firstborn over all creation. |
| Colossians 1:19-20, NIV | God was pleased to have all his fullness dwell in him, and through him to reconcile to himself all things, whether things on earth or things in heaven, by making peace through his blood, shed on the cross. |
| Hebrews 1:3, NIV | The Son is the radiance of God's glory and the exact representation of his being, sustaining all things by his powerful word. After he had provided purification for sins, he sat down at the right hand of the Majesty in heaven. |
| Hebrews 4:14, NKJV | Seeing then that we have a great High Priest who has passed through the heavens, Jesus the Son of God, let us hold fast our confession. |
| 1 Peter 2:4, NIV | You come to him, the living Stone—rejected by men but chosen by God and precious to him. |

| | |
|---|---|
| Revelation 1:8, NIV | "I am the Alpha and the Omega," says the Lord God, "who is, and who was, and who is to come, the Almighty." |
| Revelation 22:13, NKJV | I am the Alpha and the Omega, the Beginning and the End, the First and the Last. |
| Revelation 22:16, NIV | I, Jesus, have sent my angel to give you this testimony for the churches. I am the Root and the Offspring of David, and the bright Morning Star. |

# LONELINESS

We all need solitude at times, but *loneliness* can be painful and dark—and it can happen even when you are not alone!

You might feel lonely for any number of reasons. You've lost a loved one. You feel like you don't fit in with other people. You are in an abusive or difficult relationship or you have a physical or mental handicap.

David was one of many Bible characters who understood loneliness. At one point he hid alone in a cave, feeling hunted, confused, and unsure of the future (Psalm 57). David knew that in times of trouble and loneliness he could turn to God (Psalm 142:1). You can do the same. It is the power of God's presence in prayer that takes the sting out of your loneliness.

You may *know* that God is present in your life, but have you *acknowledged* it? Doing so is crucial to rising above the feelings of loneliness. So get quiet before the Lord and ask Him to satisfy you with His presence.

Then reach out to other people. Helping others with their needs will help you to fill the lonely void in your life and bring joy into a difficult place. Sometimes just by changing your focus, you can gain a new perspective and get your needs met in the process.

Remember, there is hope! Even when you feel alone, God promises, "I will never leave you nor forsake you" (Hebrews 13:5, NKJV).

*For other helpful categories, see pages 223, 311, 428.*

| | |
|---|---|
| Deuteronomy 31:8, NIV | The LORD himself goes before you and will be with you; he will never leave you nor forsake you. Do not be afraid; do not be discouraged. |
| Joshua 1:9, NIV | Have I not commanded you? Be strong and courageous. Do not be terrified; do not be discouraged, for the LORD your God will be with you wherever you go. |
| Psalm 25:16, NCV | Turn to me and have mercy on me, because I am lonely and hurting. |
| Psalm 31:7, NIV | I will be glad and rejoice in your love, for you saw my affliction and knew the anguish of my soul. |
| Psalm 68:6, NCV | God gives the lonely a home. He leads prisoners out with joy, but those who turn against God will live in a dry land. |
| Psalm 94:14, NIV | For the LORD will not reject his people; he will never forsake his inheritance. |
| Psalm 119:50, AMP | This is my comfort and consolation in my affliction: that Your word has revived me and given me life. |
| Psalm 142:1, NIV | I cry aloud to the LORD; I lift up my voice to the LORD for mercy. |
| Matthew 28:20, NLT | Be sure of this: I am with you always, even to the end of the age. |
| John 16:32, NIV | I am not alone, for my Father is with me. |

| | |
|---|---|
| Romans 8:35, NIV | Who shall separate us from the love of Christ? Shall trouble or hardship or persecution or famine or nakedness or danger or sword? |
| Romans 8:38-39, NKJV | For I am persuaded that neither death nor life, nor angels nor principalities nor powers, nor things present nor things to come, nor height nor depth, nor any other created thing, shall be able to separate us from the love of God which is in Christ Jesus our Lord. |
| 2 Corinthians 4:8-9, NIV | We are hard pressed on every side, but not crushed; perplexed, but not in despair; persecuted, but not abandoned; struck down, but not destroyed. |
| 1 Timothy 5:5, NIV | The widow who is really in need and left all alone puts her hope in God and continues night and day to pray and to ask God for help. |
| 2 Timothy 4:16-17, NIV | At my first defense, no one came to my support, but everyone deserted me. May it not be held against them. But the Lord stood at my side and gave me strength. |
| Hebrews 13:5, NKJV | I will never leave you nor forsake you. |
| James 4:8, NKJV | Draw near to God and He will draw near to you. |

# LOST ARTICLES

In our busy lives, it is easy to lose track of things—particularly as we grow older! It's not just keys and sunglasses that go missing. "Where did we put those insurance papers?" "You know, I haven't seen Grandma and Grandpa's wedding picture for years."

Does the Bible have anything to say about lost articles? Should we even bother God with such matters in our prayers?

If something matters to us, it matters to God—because *we* matter to God! He knows every detail of our lives (Psalm 138:4-6). We can go to Him even about things that seem insignificant or trivial. And certainly the testimony about a woman sweeping her house for a lost coin (Luke 15:8-10) is relevant to us today.

"Be anxious for nothing, but in everything by prayer and supplication, with thanksgiving, let your requests be made known to God" (Philippians 4:6, NJKV). If you have lost something, ask God to reveal to you where you can find it. Then, stay in the position of not being anxious and stressed about the item that you lost. This will enable you to hear from the Holy Spirit on how to find what you are looking for. Even if finding the lost object seems a hopeless cause, remember that "nothing is impossible with God" (Luke 1:37, NIV).

*For other helpful categories, see pages 118, 132, 340.*

| | |
|---|---|
| Psalm 138:4-6, MSG | When they hear what you have to say, GOD, all earth's kings will say "Thank you." They'll sing of what you've done: "How great the glory of GOD!" And here's why: GOD, high above, sees far below; no matter the distance, he knows everything about us. |
| Matthew 7:8, NIV | For everyone who asks receives; he who seeks finds; and to him who knocks, the door will be opened. |
| Matthew 21:22, NKJV | Whatever things you ask in prayer, believing, you will receive. |
| Luke 1:37, NIV | Nothing is impossible with God. |
| Luke 8:17, NIV | There is nothing hidden that will not be disclosed, and nothing concealed that will not be known or brought out into the open. |
| Luke 15:8-9, NIV | Suppose a woman has ten silver coins and loses one. Does she not light a lamp, sweep the house and search carefully until she finds it? And when she finds it, she calls her friends and neighbors together and says, "Rejoice with me; I have found my lost coin." |
| John 14:14, NKJV | If you ask anything in My name, I will do it. |
| John 15:7, NKJV | If you abide in Me, and My words abide in you, you will ask what you desire, and it shall be done for you. |

| John 16:24, NKJV | Ask, and you will receive, that your joy may be full. |
| 1 Corinthians 2:10, NIV | God has revealed it to us by his Spirit. The Spirit searches all things, even the deep things of God. |
| Ephesians 3:20, NKJV | Now to Him who is able to do exceedingly abundantly above all that we ask or think, according to the power that works in us. |

# MARRIAGE—
## GUIDELINES FOR MARRIAGE

God designed marriage to be a sacred union involving a man, a woman, and God. That's how it has been since the beginning. After creating Adam, God said, "It is not good for the man to be alone. I will make him a helper suitable for him.… Then the LORD God made a woman from the rib he had taken out of the man, and he brought her to the man" (Genesis 2:18, 22, NIV).

Still today, the most successful marriages are those that reflect godly guidelines for marriage. Consider these biblically based guidelines:

- *Speak kindly to one another.* "Death and life are in the power of the tongue," says Proverbs 18:21 (NKJV). Words spoken in anger can destroy a relationship that took years to build. Encouraging words, on the other hand, can make a good relationship even stronger.

- *Cover over each other's offenses.* A sure way to bring division in a relationship is to continually bring up your spouse's mistakes. Focus instead on constructive solutions to the problem at hand, addressing the issue itself rather than blaming each other (Proverbs 17:9).

- *Pray often.* Pray for your spouse. It will keep your heart tender toward him or her. Also pray together with your spouse. This will remove ill feelings between you, keep you both kingdom-minded, and produce greater intimacy.

- *Value physical intimacy.* Intimacy with your spouse was designed by God. Stay strong in this area. "It's good for a man to have a wife, and for a woman to have a husband. Sexual drives are strong, but marriage is strong enough to contain them and provide for a balanced and fulfilling sexual life in a world of sexual disorder. The marriage bed must be a place of mutuality—the husband seeking to satisfy his wife, the wife seeking to satisfy her husband" (1 Corinthians 7:2-3, MSG).

- *Choose to forgive.* Offenses from your spouse can come often. You have the opportunity to hold onto them or to release them. Even if the act against you was planned and deliberate, purpose in your heart not to nurse or relive the offense, but rather choose to walk in forgiveness.

For other helpful categories, see pages 174, 180, 274, 277, 356.

| | |
|---|---|
| Psalm 127:1, NKJV | Unless the LORD builds the house, they labor in vain who build it; unless the LORD guards the city, the watchman stays awake in vain. |
| Psalm 133:1, NIV | How good and pleasant it is when brothers live together in unity! |
| Psalm 141:3, NCV | Lord, help me control my tongue; help me be careful about what I say. |
| Proverbs 10:12, NCV | Hatred stirs up trouble, but love forgives all wrongs. |
| Proverbs 17:9, NIV | He who covers over an offense promotes love, but whoever repeats the matter separates close friends. |
| Proverbs 18:21, NKJV | Death and life are in the power of the tongue, and those who love it will eat its fruit. |
| Proverbs 20:3, NLT | Avoiding a fight is a mark of honor; only fools insist on quarreling. |
| Matthew 7:24, NIV | Everyone who hears these words of mine and puts them into practice is like a wise man who built his house on the rock. |
| Matthew 19:5-6, NIV | For this reason a man will leave his father and mother and be united to his wife, and the two will become one flesh so they are no longer two, but one. Therefore what God has joined together, let man not separate. |

| | |
|---|---|
| Luke 6:37, NIV | Do not judge, and you will not be judged. Do not condemn, and you will not be condemned. Forgive, and you will be forgiven. |
| John 13:34, NIV | A new command I give you: Love one another. As I have loved you, so you must love one another. |
| Romans 12:10, NIV | Be devoted to one another in brotherly love. Honor one another above yourselves. |
| Romans 13:10, NLT | Love does no wrong to others, so love fulfills the requirements of God's law. |
| 1 Corinthians 7:2, NIV | Since there is so much immorality, each man should have his own wife, and each woman her own husband. |
| 1 Corinthians 7:3, NLT | The husband should fulfill his wife's sexual needs, and the wife should fulfill her husband's needs. |
| 1 Corinthians 13:4, NIV | Love is patient, love is kind. It does not envy, it does not boast, it is not proud. |
| 1 Corinthians 16:14, NIV | Do everything in love. |
| Galatians 5:15, NKJV | If you bite and devour one another, beware lest you be consumed by one another! |
| Galatians 6:9, NKJV | Let us not grow weary while doing good, for in due season we shall reap if we do not lose heart. |
| Ephesians 4:2-3, NIV | Be completely humble and gentle; be patient, bearing with one another in love. Make every |

effort to keep the unity of the Spirit through the bond of peace.

Ephesians 4:15, NLT | Speak the truth in love.

Ephesians 4:26, NIV | In your anger do not sin. Do not let the sun go down while you are still angry.

Ephesians 5:33, NIV | Each one of you also must love his wife as he loves himself, and the wife must respect her husband.

Colossians 3:12, NIV | As God's chosen people, holy and dearly loved, clothe yourselves with compassion, kindness, humility, gentleness and patience.

1 Thessalonians 5:11, NIV | Encourage one another and build each other up, just as in fact you are doing.

Hebrews 13:4, NIV | Marriage should be honored by all, and the marriage bed kept pure, for God will judge the adulterer and all the sexually immoral.

1 Peter 4:8, NIV | Above all, love each other deeply, because love covers over a multitude of sins.

# MARRIAGE—FOR HUSBANDS

You want to be a wise and godly husband. But it's not easy, is it? God will teach you about your role through prayer and the Word.

First of all, know that to be a godly husband you must first be a godly man. And being a godly man begins with loving God above all else, even above your wife and children (Mark 12:30).

Second, remember that you are both a leader and a servant in the home. God has called the man to be the overseer of his wife and family (1 Corinthians 11:3). Yet Christ calls all of His followers to serve others, just as He came to serve (Matthew 20:26-29). So keep in mind that you are a servant first and a leader second. Following Christ's example will strengthen the bonds of your marriage.

Next, love your wife. The way you love your wife should be a reflection of how Jesus loves the church (Ephesians 5:25; Colossians 3:19). God calls you to sacrifice and forgive, just as Christ does.

Last, be a spiritual pillar in your family. Pray for your wife. Wash her with the water of the Word along with spoken words (Ephesians 5:26). And take your family to a good Bible-teaching church. This will be instrumental in the spiritual growth of everyone in your family.

*For other helpful categories, see pages 269, 277, 293, 392.*

Proverbs 18:22, NIV — He who finds a wife finds what is good and receives favor from the LORD.

Proverbs 19:14, NCV — Houses and wealth are inherited from parents, but a wise wife is a gift from the Lord.

Proverbs 31:23, NIV — Her husband is respected at the city gate, where he takes his seat among the elders of the land.

Proverbs 31:28, NIV — Her children arise and call her blessed; her husband also, and he praises her.

Ecclesiastes 9:9, NLT — Live happily with the woman you love through all the meaningless days of life that God has given you under the sun. The wife God gives you is your reward for all your earthly toil.

Matthew 20:28, NCV — The Son of Man did not come to be served. He came to serve others and to give his life as a ransom for many people.

1 Corinthians 7:3, NIV — The husband should fulfill his marital duty to his wife, and likewise the wife to her husband.

1 Corinthians 7:4, NIV — The wife's body does not belong to her alone but also to her husband. In the same way, the husband's body does not belong to him alone but also to his wife.

1 Corinthians 11:3, NIV — I want you to realize that the head of every man is Christ, and the head of the woman is man, and the head of Christ is God.

| | |
|---|---|
| Ephesians 5:25-26, ESV | Husbands, love your wives, as Christ loved the church and gave himself up for her, that he might sanctify her, having cleansed her by the washing of water with the word. |
| Ephesians 5:28, NIV | Husbands ought to love their wives as their own bodies. He who loves his wife loves himself. |
| Ephesians 5:33, NIV | Each one of you also must love his wife as he loves himself. |
| Colossians 3:19, NIV | Husbands, love your wives and do not be harsh with them. |
| 1 Peter 3:7, NKJV | Husbands, likewise, dwell with them with understanding, giving honor to the wife, as to the weaker vessel, and as being heirs together of the grace of life, that your prayers may not be hindered. |

# Marriage—For Wives

Proverbs 31 offers a vivid depiction of a godly wife who has her priorities in order. Her integrity, resourcefulness, and generosity are her beauty marks. Tenacity, humility, and faithfulness lift her to a place of honor and wisdom.

In this portrait, we do not see the godly wife defined by a religion, a career, or her outward appearance. Rather, she is defined by her relationships with her God, her husband, and her family. These provide the platform to display her true beauty and worth.

Living according to God's ideal should be in the forefront of all of our minds. So allow yourself the time it takes to be intimate with your Savior. It will help you to keep your heart in the right place toward your husband.

Remember that prayer is more powerful than trying to convince your husband of something with your own words, or feeling discouraged that he doesn't change when you want him to. As you pray, you may discover ways *you* can change. You will also be more alert to ways that God is at work in your husband's life—in ways that God, not you, orchestrates.

*For other helpful categories, see pages 269, 274, 293, 392.*

| | |
|---|---|
| Proverbs 12:4, NIV | A wife of noble character is her husband's crown, but a disgraceful wife is like decay in his bones. |
| Proverbs 14:1, NIV | The wise woman builds her house, but with her own hands the foolish one tears hers down. |
| Proverbs 21:19, NLT | It's better to live alone in the desert than with a quarrelsome, complaining wife. |
| Proverbs 31:10-12, NIV | A wife of noble character who can find? She is worth far more than rubies. Her husband has full confidence in her and lacks nothing of value. She brings him good, not harm, all the days of her life. |
| Proverbs 31:21, NKJV | She extends her hand to the poor, yes, she reaches out her hands to the needy. |
| Proverbs 31:26, NLT | When she speaks, her words are wise, and she gives instructions with kindness. |
| Isaiah 54:5, NIV | Your Maker is your husband—the LORD Almighty is his name—the Holy One of Israel is your Redeemer; he is called the God of all the earth. |
| Mark 10:12, NIV | If she divorces her husband and marries another man, she commits adultery. |
| 1 Corinthians 7:4, NIV | The wife's body does not belong to her alone but also to her husband. In the same way, the husband's body does not belong to him alone but also to his wife. |

| | |
|---|---|
| 1 Corinthians 7:10, NIV | To the married I give this command (not I, but the Lord): A wife must not separate from her husband. |
| Ephesians 5:22-24, NIV | Wives, submit to your husbands as to the Lord. For the husband is the head of the wife as Christ is the head of the church, his body, of which he is the Savior. Now as the church submits to Christ, so also wives should submit to their husbands in everything. |
| Ephesians 5:33, NLT | The wife must respect her husband. |
| Titus 2:4-5, NCV | Then they can teach the young women to love their husbands, to love their children, to be wise and pure, to be good workers at home, to be kind, and to yield to their husbands. Then no one will be able to criticize the teaching God gave us. |
| 1 Peter 3:1-5, NIV | Wives, in the same way be submissive to your husbands so that, if any of them do not believe the word, they may be won over without words by the behavior of their wives, when they see the purity and reverence of your lives. Your beauty should not come from outward adornment, such as braided hair and the wearing of gold jewelry and fine clothes. Instead, it should be that of your inner self, the unfading beauty of a gentle and quiet spirit, which is of great worth in God's sight. For this is the way the holy women of the past who put their hope in God used to make themselves beautiful. They were submissive to their own husbands. |

# Military—If You Are
# a Soldier Going to War

As you're preparing to serve on foreign soil, serious thoughts fill your mind. You want to be wise, brave, and successful in your mission. And of course, you hope to come through it all unscathed and return home. But at the same time, your loved ones seem dearer than ever, and the thought of leaving them behind is heart-wrenching.

God knows all this, and He cares about you. Here are a couple more thoughts for you to keep in mind:

First, in a natural sense, you are well prepared for your task. You have been through vigorous and grueling training, and this should give you confidence.

Second, you can stand on God's Word and His promises. They will give you the confidence that you will need to stay spiritually, emotionally, and physically strong. For example, consider this verse: "A thousand may fall at your side, ten thousand at your right hand, but it will not come near you" (Psalm 91:7, NIV).

You may be leaving home, but wherever you go, God goes before you: "The LORD your God, who goes before you, He will fight for you" (Deuteronomy 1:30, NKJV). He is also at home with your family, protecting them in ways you cannot.

*For other helpful categories, see pages 88, 311, 375, 411, 426.*

| Deuteronomy 7:23, NIV | The LORD your God will deliver them over to you, throwing them into great confusion until they are destroyed. |
|---|---|
| Deuteronomy 20:4, NIV | The LORD your God is the one who goes with you to fight for you against your enemies to give you victory. |
| 2 Samuel 22:30, NIV | With your help I can advance against a troop; with my God I can scale a wall. |
| Psalm 3:6, NIV | I will not fear the tens of thousands drawn up against me on every side. |
| Psalm 4:8, NIV | I will lie down and sleep in peace, for you alone, O LORD, make me dwell in safety. |
| Psalm 31:15, NIV | My times are in your hands; deliver me from my enemies and from those who pursue me. |
| Psalm 44:3, NIV | It was not by their sword that they won the land, nor did their arm bring them victory; it was your right hand, your arm, and the light of your face, for you loved them. |
| Psalm 44:7, NIV | You give us victory over our enemies, you put our adversaries to shame. |
| Psalm 91:3-4, NIV | Surely he will save you from the fowler's snare and from the deadly pestilence. He will cover you with his feathers, and under his wings you will find refuge; his faithfulness will be your shield and rampart. |

| | |
|---|---|
| Psalm 91:5-6, NIV | You will not fear the terror of night, nor the arrow that flies by day, nor the pestilence that stalks in the darkness, nor the plague that destroys at midday. |
| Psalm 91:7-8, NIV | A thousand may fall at your side, ten thousand at your right hand, but it will not come near you. You will only observe with your eyes and see the punishment of the wicked. |
| Psalm 118:6, AMP | The Lord is on my side; I will not fear. What can man do to me? |
| Psalm 121:8, NIV | The LORD will watch over your coming and going both now and forevermore. |
| Proverbs 3:25-26, NIV | Have no fear of sudden disaster or of the ruin that overtakes the wicked, for the LORD will be your confidence and will keep your foot from being snared. |
| Proverbs 21:31, NIV | The horse is made ready for the day of battle, but victory rests with the LORD. |
| Isaiah 54:17, NKJV | "No weapon formed against you shall prosper, and every tongue which rises against you in judgment, you shall condemn. This is the heritage of the servants of the LORD, and their righteousness is from Me," says the LORD. |
| Isaiah 59:19, NKJV | When the enemy comes in like a flood, the Spirit of the LORD will lift up a standard against him. |

Jeremiah 1:19, NIV

"They will fight against you but will not over-come you, for I am with you and will rescue you," declares the LORD.

John 14:27, NKJV

Peace I leave with you, My peace I give to you; not as the world gives do I give to you. Let not your heart be troubled, neither let it be afraid.

2 Timothy 2:4, NIV

No one serving as a soldier gets involved in civilian affairs—he wants to please his commanding officer.

# Military—If Someone You Love Is Going to War

You're proud of your soldier. But you're also understandably concerned. Will he or she be safe overseas?

It is God's will for you to live a life free from worry. Even when a loved one is in a potentially dangerous place, He wants you to be "anxious for nothing" (Philippians 4:6, NKJV).

Let these guidelines encourage and steady you:

*1. Trust in God.* As long as you remember that Almighty God is in control, you will know that nothing will happen outside of His loving will. Psalm 112 says that the person who fears the Lord "will have no fear of bad news; his heart is steadfast, trusting in the LORD" (verse 7, NIV).

*2. Pray.* Your prayer is "powerful and effective" (James 5:16, NIV). You have the opportunity to pray a hedge of protection around your loved one who is serving in the military (Job 1:10). Praying will also keep your own heart and mind in peace. You can agree with the psalmist who said, "I sought the LORD, and he answered me; he delivered me from all my fears" (Psalm 34:4, NIV).

*3. Believe God's promises.* Speaking words of faith and believing the best in this situation will help you to stay strong for what you have been called to do as a support for someone in the military: "Then they believed his promises and sang his praise" (Psalm 106:12, NIV).

*For other helpful categories, see pages 263, 314, 336, 428.*

| | |
|---|---|
| Psalm 22:5, NCV | They called to you for help and were rescued. They trusted you and were not disappointed. |
| Psalm 34:4, NIV | I sought the LORD, and he answered me; he delivered me from all my fears. |
| Psalm 84:4, NIV | Blessed are those who dwell in your house; they are ever praising you. |
| Psalm 112:7, NIV | He will have no fear of bad news; his heart is steadfast, trusting in the LORD. |
| Mark 11:22, NIV | Have faith in God. |
| John 14:27, NIV | Peace I leave with you; my peace I give you. I do not give to you as the world gives. Do not let your hearts be troubled and do not be afraid. |
| Philippians 4:6-7, NKJV | Be anxious for nothing, but in everything by prayer and supplication, with thanksgiving, let your requests be made known to God; and the peace of God, which surpasses all understanding, will guard your hearts and minds through Christ Jesus. |
| Philippians 4:19, NKJV | My God shall supply all your need according to His riches in glory by Christ Jesus. |
| James 5:16, NIV | The prayer of a righteous man is powerful and effective. |
| 1 Peter 5:7, NIV | Cast all your anxiety on him because he cares for you. |

# NATURAL DISASTERS

Jesus told His followers that in the last days of the earth "there will be earthquakes in various places, and there will be famines and troubles. These are the beginnings of sorrows" (Mark 13:8, NKJV). Paul later wrote, "In the last days perilous times will come" (2 Timothy 3:1, NKJV).

Natural disasters are a sign of the second coming of Jesus—ultimately good news. But those who have experienced earthquakes, tornadoes, floods, and hurricanes know the grief, questions, and concerns that come with the idea of the ground or seas moving out of their boundaries.

There is nothing that will comfort your soul or nourish your spirit like the presence of God that comes from heartfelt prayer. His name is Jehovah Shalom, the God of Peace. God-given peace is not just the absence of a tragedy or a storm, but rest in the middle of the storm or tragedy. "God is our refuge and strength, a very present help in trouble" (Psalm 46:1, NKJV).

If you are waiting to hear news about a missing friend of family member after a natural disaster, you may feel helpless to do anything. Yet even as officials dig through debris or search homes to find survivors, God has given you His Word as a powerful tool to declare over your loved ones. You can provide a "prayer cover" over them: "Pull me from the trap my enemies set for me, for I find protection in you alone" (Psalm 31:4, NLT).

The earth, seas, and skies may seem like steady things in your life, but they, too, are fragile. Only God will stay the same forever. You can rest in that truth even when the world around you is out of your control.

*For other helpful categories, see pages 196, 340, 343, 375, 411, 428.*

| | |
|---|---|
| Job 29:12, NIV | I rescued the poor who cried for help. |
| Psalm 22:5, NCV | They called to you for help and were rescued. They trusted you and were not disappointed. |
| Psalm 31:4, NLT | Pull me from the trap my enemies set for me, for I find protection in you alone. |
| Psalm 34:4, NKJV | I sought the LORD, and He heard me, and delivered me from all my fears. |
| Psalm 40:2, NIV | He lifted me out of the slimy pit, out of the mud and mire; he set my feet on a rock and gave me a firm place to stand. |
| Psalm 46:1-3, NKJV | God is our refuge and strength, a very present help in trouble. Therefore we will not fear, even though the earth be removed, and though the mountains be carried into the midst of the sea; though its waters roar and be troubled, though the mountains shake with its swelling. |
| Psalm 73:26, NIV | My flesh and my heart may fail, but God is the strength of my heart and my portion forever. |
| Psalm 112:7, NIV | He will have no fear of bad news; his heart is steadfast, trusting in the LORD. |
| Proverbs 4:4, NIV | Lay hold of my words with all your heart. |
| Mark 13:8, NKJV | Nation will rise against nation, and kingdom against kingdom. And there will be earthquakes |

in various places, and there will be famines and troubles. These are the beginnings of sorrows.

| | |
|---|---|
| 1 Corinthians 2:5, NKJV | Your faith should not be in the wisdom of men but in the power of God. |
| Ephesians 6:17-18, NIV | Take the helmet of salvation and the sword of the Spirit, which is the word of God. And pray in the Spirit on all occasions with all kinds of prayers and requests. With this in mind, be alert and always keep on praying for all the saints. |
| Philippians 4:6-7, NIV | Do not be anxious about anything, but in everything, by prayer and petition, with thanksgiving, present your requests to God. And the peace of God, which transcends all understanding, will guard your hearts and your minds in Christ Jesus. |
| Hebrews 10:23, KJV | Let us hold fast the profession of our faith without wavering; (for he is faithful that promised). |
| Hebrews 11:1, NIV | Faith is being sure of what we hope for and certain of what we do not see. |

# OVERCOMING

You were born for victory! God made you in His own image for that reason (Genesis 1:26).

And there's more to it than that. God "has delivered us from the power of darkness and conveyed us into the kingdom of the Son of His love" (Colossians 1:13, NKJV). By redemption as well as by creation, you are meant to be a victor. As you understand this, you will be better equipped to overcome the trials of life.

God has given you resources to help you overcome when the enemy is attacking your life. Pick up these weapons and use them:
- the authority of Jesus (Luke 10:19)
- the name of Jesus (Acts 19:13-14)
- the power of the Holy Spirit (John 16:13)
- the power of the Word of God (Hebrews 4:12)
- faith in the blood of Jesus (Romans 3:25)
- praise and worship (Psalm 149:6)

As Paul said, "We are more than conquerors through him who loved us" (Romans 8:37, NIV). This means you are more than a conqueror in your body, your relationships, your finances, your ministry, and your job. Do you see yourself that way?

Pray and ask God for His help to overcome in the situation you are facing.

*For other helpful categories, see pages 65, 132, 340, 343, 346.*

| | |
|---|---|
| Genesis 1:26, NIV | Then God said, "Let us make man in our image, in our likeness, and let them rule over the fish of the sea and the birds of the air, over the livestock, over all the earth, and over all the creatures that move along the ground." |
| Psalm 18:35, NIV | You give me your shield of victory, and your right hand sustains me; you stoop down to make me great. |
| Psalm 41:11, NIV | I know that you are pleased with me, for my enemy does not triumph over me. |
| Psalm 44:7, CEV | You saved us from our hateful enemies, and you put them to shame. |
| Psalm 54:7, NCV | You have saved me from all my troubles, and I have seen my enemies defeated. |
| Psalm 118:15, NIV | Shouts of joy and victory resound in the tents of the righteous: "The LORD's right hand has done mighty things!" |
| Psalm 149:6, NKJV | Let the high praises of God be in their mouth, and a two-edged sword in their hand. |
| Matthew 16:18, NIV | I tell you that you are Peter, and on this rock I will build my church, and the gates of Hades will not overcome it. |
| Mark 9:24, NIV | Immediately the boy's father exclaimed, "I do believe; help me overcome my unbelief!" |

| | |
|---|---|
| Luke 10:19, NKJV | I give you the authority to trample on serpents and scorpions, and over all the power of the enemy, and nothing shall by any means hurt you. |
| John 16:33, NIV | I have told you these things, so that in me you may have peace. In this world you will have trouble. But take heart! I have overcome the world. |
| Acts 1:8, NIV | You will receive power when the Holy Spirit comes on you. |
| Romans 8:37, NIV | In all these things we are more than conquerors through him who loved us. |
| Colossians 1:13, NKJV | He has delivered us from the power of darkness and conveyed us into the kingdom of the Son of His love. |
| 1 John 4:4, NIV | You, dear children, are from God and have overcome them, because the one who is in you is greater than the one who is in the world. |
| 1 John 5:4-5, NIV | Everyone born of God overcomes the world. This is the victory that has overcome the world, even our faith. Who is it that overcomes the world? Only he who believes that Jesus in the Son of God. |
| Revelation 2:7, NIV | He who has an ear, let him hear what the Spirit says to the churches. To him who overcomes, I will give the right to eat from the tree of life, which is in the paradise of God. |

Revelation 3:5, NIV

He who overcomes will, like them, be dressed in white. I will never blot out his name from the book of life, but will acknowledge his name before my Father and his angels.

Revelation 3:21, NIV

To him who overcomes, I will give the right to sit with me on my throne, just as I overcame and sat down with my Father on his throne.

# Parenting—God's Promises for Your Children

"Like arrows in the hand of a warrior, so are the children of one's youth." This image from Psalm 127:4 (NKJV) reflects what a blessing it is to have children. It also reflects the responsibility we have when we are parents.

Precision and focus are required when aiming an arrow. So it is with our children. As parents, we must give our children the spiritual direction, boundaries, and guidelines that they will need in life.

God promises that the children of the righteous "will be mighty in the land; the generation of the upright will be blessed" (Psalm 112:2, NIV). One translation says that your children will be powerful and "successful everywhere" (NLT)!

God's promises for your children can come to pass only *if you know what they are* and you're standing in faith for them. Stand on God's Word, even in the most difficult times of parenting. Through faith, your children will receive the promises of blessing, salvation, authority and power, freedom, spiritual awakening, provision, divine health, long life, influence, wealth and prosperity.

When God gave you children, He gave you the assignment to pray for them no matter what their age. He called you to take hold of the purposes He has for them. So pray God's words over your children daily. Let them know you are praying for God's promises to be fulfilled in their lives. Their heavenly Father longs to do what He promised.

*For other helpful categories, see pages 144, 196, 392.*

| | |
|---|---|
| Psalm 8:2, NIV | From the lips of children and infants you have ordained praise. |
| Psalm 33:11, NIV | The plans of the LORD stand firm forever, the purposes of his heart through all generations. |
| Psalm 37:25, NIV | I was young and now I am old, yet I have never seen the righteous forsaken or their children begging bread. |
| Psalm 72:4, NIV | He will defend the afflicted among the people and save the children of the needy; he will crush the oppressor. |
| Psalm 90:16, NIV | May your deeds be shown to your servants, your splendor to their children. |
| Psalm 102:28, NIV | The children of your servants will live in your presence; their descendants will be established before you. |
| Psalm 103:17, NCV | The LORD's love for those who respect him continues forever and ever, and his goodness continues to their grandchildren. |
| Psalm 112:1-3, NIV | Praise the LORD. Blessed is the man who fears the LORD, who finds great delight in his commands. His children will be mighty in the land; the generation of the upright will be blessed. Wealth and riches are in his house, and his righteousness endures forever. |

Psalm 115:13-14, NIV

He will bless those who fear the LORD—small and great alike. May the LORD make you increase, both you and your children.

Psalm 115:16, NKJV

The heaven, even the heavens, are the LORD's: but the earth he has given to the children of men.

Psalm 127:3-5, NKJV

Children are a heritage from the LORD, the fruit of the womb is a reward. Like arrows in the hand of a warrior, so are the children of one's youth. Happy is the man who has his quiver full of them; they shall not be ashamed, but shall speak with their enemies in the gate.

Psalm 145:4, NIV

One generation will commend your works to another; they will tell of your mighty acts.

Proverbs 14:26, NCV

Those who respect the LORD will have security, and their children will be protected.

Proverbs 20:7, NIV

The righteous man leads a blameless life; blessed are his children after him.

Isaiah 8:18, NKJV

Here am I and the children whom the LORD has given me! We are for signs and wonders in Israel from the LORD of hosts, who dwells in Mount Zion.

Isaiah 44:3, NLT

For I will pour out water to quench your thirst and to irrigate your parched fields. And I will pour out my Spirit on your descendants, and my blessing on your children.

| | |
|---|---|
| Isaiah 49:17, NLT | Soon your descendants will come back, and all who are trying to destroy you will go away. |
| Isaiah 49:25, NIV | I will contend with those who contend with you, and your children I will save. |
| Isaiah 54:13, NKJV | All your children shall be taught by the LORD, and great shall be the peace of your children. |
| Isaiah 59:21, NKJV | "As for Me," says the LORD, "this is My covenant with them: My Spirit who is upon you, and My words which I have put in your mouth, shall not depart from your mouth, nor from the mouth of your descendants, nor from the mouth of your descendants' descendants," says the LORD, "from this time and forevermore." |
| Isaiah 61:9, NCV | Everyone in all nations will know the children of my people, and their children will be known among the nations. Anyone who sees them will know that they are people the LORD has blessed. |
| Jeremiah 31:17, NIV | "There is hope for your future," declares the LORD. "Your children will return to their own land." |
| Jeremiah 32:39, NKJV | I will give them one heart, and one way, that they may fear Me forever, for the good of them and their children after them. |
| Joel 2:28, NKJV | It shall come to pass afterward that I will pour out My Spirit on all flesh; your sons and daughters |

shall prophesy, your old men shall dream dreams, your young men shall see visions.

Acts 2:39, NIV    The promise is for you and your children and for all who are far off—for all whom the Lord our God will call.

Acts 3:25, NIV    You are heirs of the prophets and of the covenant God made with your fathers. He said to Abraham, "Through your offspring all peoples on earth will be blessed."

Acts 16:31, NKJV    Believe on the Lord Jesus Christ, and you will be saved, you and your household.

# PARENTING—RAISING CHILDREN

As parents, your first priority is to introduce your children to a loving Savior. Plant the seed of God's Word in them when their hearts are tender. Pray for them to hunger after His presence and His Word. Teach them that following God's principles will bring lasting happiness.

As children begin to grasp the extent of God's mercy toward them, they will see how deeply God loves them. This is what you, as a parent, can show them as you teach them biblical truth throughout the course of your everyday lives (Deuteronomy 11:18-20).

Spiritual direction for our children also comes from the church. Seek the help and guidance of mature believers in your spiritual community. Having a pastoral covering from the local church is essential in raising spiritually strong children.

And then, of course, there's your own influence on your children. Are you providing a loving, safe environment in which your kids can grow and thrive (Colossians 3:21)? Are you walking faithfully with God yourself? Do they see you pursuing Him? Are you walking in love? Children learn by example as well as by teaching.

You will not be a perfect parent. But you can reflect the loving perfection of your own heavenly Father. Many children find that obeying and trusting God is a natural response to obeying and trusting an earthly parent who loves them unconditionally.

*For other helpful categories, see pages 59, 293, 392.*

Deuteronomy 11:18-21, NCV   Remember my words with your whole being. Write them down and tie them to your hands as a sign; tie them on your foreheads to remind you. Teach them well to your children, talking about them when you sit at home and walk along the road, when you lie down and when you get up. Write them on your doors and gates.

1 Samuel 1:27-29, NIV   I prayed for this child, and the LORD has granted me what I asked of him. So now I give him to the LORD. For his whole life he will be given over to the LORD.

Psalm 127:3-5, NKJV   Children are a heritage from the LORD, the fruit of the womb is a reward. Like arrows in the hand of a warrior, so are the children of one's youth. Happy is the man who has his quiver full of them; they shall not be ashamed, but shall speak with their enemies in the gate.

Proverbs 13:22, NKJV   A good man leaves an inheritance to his children's children, but the wealth of the sinner is stored up for the righteous.

Proverbs 22:6, NIV   Train a child in the way he should go, and when he is old he will not turn from it.

Proverbs 22:15, NIV   Folly is bound up in the heart of a child, but the rod of discipline will drive it far from him.

Proverbs 29:17, NIV   Discipline your son, and he will give you peace; he will bring delight to your soul.

| | |
|---|---|
| Isaiah 54:13, NIV | All your children shall be taught by the LORD, and great shall be the peace of your children. |
| Matthew 18:5-6, NIV | Whoever welcomes a little child like this in my name welcomes me. But if anyone causes one of these little ones who believe in me to sin, it would be better for him to have a large millstone hung around his neck and to be drowned in the depths of the sea. |
| Romans 15:5, NIV | May the God who gives endurance and encouragement give you a spirit of unity among yourselves as you follow Christ Jesus. |
| Colossians 3:21, NCV | Fathers, do not nag your children. If you are too hard to please, they may want to stop trying. |
| Hebrews 4:16, NLT | Let us come boldly to the throne of our gracious God. There we will receive his mercy, and we will find grace to help us when we need it most. |
| James 3:10, NIV | Out of the same mouth come praise and cursing. My brothers, this should not be. |
| 3 John, 4, NIV | I have no greater joy than to hear that my children are walking in the truth. |

# Parenting—Raising Teenagers

It's natural to want your teenager to be spiritually, mentally, emotionally, socially, and physically well. On some days, peer pressure and the tensions of growing into adulthood may seem overwhelming to both of you. But the revelation of God's Word is powerful! Pray God's Word over your teenager so that he or she will have a determination to do what is right in the face of God. Your prayers act as a wind in your child's sails—guiding, protecting, and strengthening.

People thrive in the right environment. Many teenagers face a daily school environment of negativity, conflict, and peer pressure. Even when you need to correct your teen, you can create an environment of love and acceptance by speaking words of life and encouragement. "It is the Spirit who gives life; the flesh profits nothing. The words that I speak to you are spirit, and they are life" (John 6:63, NKJV).

Make it a priority to keep the lines of communication open with your teen, even if the two of you disagree about certain issues. Do things together that are important to him or her. It validates his or her gifts and desires.

Your teen will soon be an adult who will face a world of uncertainty and challenge. Use the following Scriptures to give him or her guidance.

Knowing *you* have faith in your children will help them to confidently and joyfully become all that God has in mind for them to become!

*For other helpful categories, see pages 177, 293, 392, 437.*

| | |
|---|---|
| Psalm 119:9, NIV | How can a young man keep his way pure? By living according to your word. |
| Proverbs 14:23, NCV | Those who work hard make a profit, but those who only talk will be poor. |
| Proverbs 17:17, NLT | A friend is always loyal, and a brother is born to help in time of need. |
| Proverbs 20:1, NCV | Wine and beer make people loud and uncontrolled; it is not wise to get drunk on them. |
| Proverbs 23:23, NCV | Learn the truth and never reject it. Get wisdom, self-control, and understanding. |
| John 6:63, NKJV | The words that I speak to you are spirit, and they are life. |
| John 14:26, NKJV | The Helper, the Holy Spirit, whom the Father will send in My name, He will teach you all things, and bring to your remembrance all things that I said to you. |
| Romans 8:26, NKJV | The Spirit also helps in our weaknesses. For we do not know what we should pray for as we ought, but the Spirit Himself makes intercession for us with groanings which cannot be uttered. |
| Romans 13:2, NLT | Anyone who rebels against authority is rebelling against what God has instituted, and they will be punished. |

| 1 Corinthians 5:11, NIV | You must not associate with anyone who calls himself a brother but is sexually immoral or greedy, an idolater or a slanderer, a drunkard or a swindler. With such a man do not even eat. |

| 1 Corinthians 6:19-20, NIV | Do you not know that your body is a temple of the Holy Spirit, who is in you, whom you have received from God? You are not your own; you were bought at a price. Therefore honor God with your body. |

| Ephesians 4:29, NIV | Do not let any unwholesome talk come out of your mouths, but only what is helpful for building others up according to their needs, that it may benefit those who listen. |

| Ephesians 5:18, CEV | Don't destroy yourself by getting drunk, but let the Spirit fill your life. |

| 2 Timothy 2:22, CEV | Run from temptations that capture young people. Always do the right thing. Be faithful, loving, and easy to get along with. Worship with people whose hearts are pure. |

| James 3:10, NIV | Out of the same mouth come praise and cursing. My brothers, this should not be. |

| 1 Peter 3:8, NCV | All of you should be in agreement, understanding each other, loving each other as family, being kind and humble. |

# PARENTING—PARENTING A CHILD
# WHO HAS AUTISM OR SPECIAL NEEDS

If your child has autism or special needs, remember this: A diagnosis does not thwart God's purpose in your child's life.

Many teachers, therapists, doctors, and books will give you advice. Some of it will be helpful, some of it overwhelming. Friends and other parents will tell you all the things that "could" happen in your child's life, good and bad. You will probably go through a grieving process, possibly many times as your child reaches different stages of life. Like the expectations of most parents, your expectations for his or her life might need to change. One thing doesn't change: *God's* destiny for your son or daughter (Psalm 33:11).

However close or distant you are from the initial fear, tests, confirmation, questions, and decisions, remember that God was, is, and will be with you. He knows your child's heart even better than you do. He knows how your child's mind and body work.

Healing may or may not look like you want it to—you are on a journey of discovery as well. But Scripture reminds us that our loving God's eternal purpose looks just as He wants it to. And nothing in the world can change that.

*For other helpful categories, see pages 293, 314, 411.*

| 1 Chronicles 16:11, NIV | Look to the LORD and his strength; seek his face always. |
| Psalm 33:11, NIV | The plans of the LORD stand firm forever, the purposes of his heart through all generations. |
| Psalm 56:8, NCV | You have recorded my troubles. You have kept a list of my tears. Aren't they in your records? |
| Psalm 139:1-3, NIV | O LORD, you have searched me and you know me. You know when I sit and when I rise; you perceive my thoughts from afar. You discern my going out and my lying down; you are familiar with all my ways. |
| Psalm 139:5, NIV | You hem me in—behind and before; you have laid your hand upon me. |
| Psalm 139:16, NLT | You saw me before I was born. Every day of my life was recorded in your book. Every moment was laid out before a single day had passed. |
| Proverbs 3:5, AMP | Lean on, trust in, and be confident in the Lord with all your heart and mind and do not rely on your own insight or understanding. |
| Proverbs 14:26, NCV | Those who respect the LORD will have security, and their children will be protected. |
| Jeremiah 29:11, NIV | "I know the plans I have for you," declares the LORD, "plans to prosper you and not to harm you, plans to give you hope and a future." |

Malachi 3:6, NKJV

I am the LORD, I do not change; therefore you are not consumed, O sons of Jacob.

Colossians 2:8, NLT

Don't let anyone capture you with empty philosophies and high-sounding nonsense that come from human thinking and from the spiritual powers of this world, rather than from Christ.

Hebrew 13:5, AMP

I will not in any way fail you nor give you up nor leave you without support. [I will] not, [I will] not, [I will] not in any degree leave you helpless nor forsake nor let [you] down (relax My hold on you)! [Assuredly not!]

1 Peter 5:7, NKJV

Casting all your care upon Him, for He cares for you.

# PARENTING—SINGLE PARENTING

If you are a single parent and sometimes feel overwhelmed with all you need to do and be for your children, take heart that God's power is present in your life even when you feel a void from parenting alone (2 Corinthians 12:9).

When the world seems anything but restful, hold tight to this truth: God longs to lead you to a place of rest. We read in Isaiah, "He tends his flock like a shepherd: He gathers the lambs in his arms and carries them close to his heart; he gently leads those that have young" (40:11, NIV).

What does God's rest look like when you don't feel you have the time or space to receive either one? That is when you can cling to the words of Scripture. Pray God's words back to Him: "You will carry my children close to your heart. You will lead me. You will tend to me. Even though I feel weak, your power is perfect in my life."

Memorize phrases of Scripture. Keep them in front of your mind and eyes during the day: "You lead me beside quiet waters" (adapted from Psalm 23:2, NIV). "You restore my soul" (adapted from Psalm 23:3, NIV). "You will quiet me with your love" (adapted from Zephaniah 3:17, NKJV). "You give me wisdom and knowledge" (adapted from Daniel 2:21, NIV).

As you meditate on God's words when circumstances tempt you to feel alone, you will sense His presence more and more. He will bring you to a place of rest and spiritual power from which you can parent your children to know His truth as well.

*For other helpful categories, see pages 13, 118, 156, 293, 311, 314, 411, 428.*

| | |
|---|---|
| Deuteronomy 31:8, NIV | The LORD himself goes before you and will be with you; he will never leave you nor forsake you. Do not be afraid; do not be discouraged. |
| 1 Samuel 30:6, NIV | David was greatly distressed because the men were talking of stoning him; each one was bitter in spirit because of his sons and daughters. But David found strength in the LORD his God. |
| Job 36:11, NKJV | If they obey and serve Him, they shall spend their days in prosperity, and their years in pleasures. |
| Psalm 10:14, NKJV | You have seen, for You observe trouble and grief, to repay it by Your hand. The helpless commits himself to You. You are the helper of the fatherless. |
| Psalm 21:2, NIV | You have granted him the desire of his heart and have not withheld the request of his lips. |
| Psalm 23:2-3, NIV | He makes me lie down in green pastures, he leads me beside quiet waters, he restores my soul. He guides me in paths of righteousness for his name's sake. |
| Psalm 68:5, NIV | A father to the fatherless, a defender of widows, is God in his holy dwelling. |
| Psalm 71:3, NIV | Be my rock of refuge, to which I can always go; give the command to save me, for you are my rock and my fortress. |
| Psalm 91:3, NCV | God will save you from hidden traps and from deadly diseases. |

| | |
|---|---|
| Psalm 91:5, NCV | You will not fear any danger by night or an arrow during the day. |
| Psalm 91:9-11, NLT | If you make the LORD your refuge, if you make the Most High your shelter, no evil will conquer you; no plague will come near your home. For he will order his angels to protect you wherever you go. |
| Isaiah 40:11, NIV | He tends his flock like a shepherd: He gathers the lambs in his arms and carries them close to his heart; he gently leads those that have young. |
| Matthew 6:33, NIV | Seek first his kingdom and his righteousness, and all these things will be given to you as well. |
| John 14:27, NIV | Peace I leave with you; my peace I give you. I do not give to you as the world gives. Do not let your hearts be troubled and do not be afraid. |
| John 16:32, NIV | I am not alone, for my Father is with me. |
| Acts 1:8, NKJV | You shall receive power when the Holy Spirit has come upon you. |
| 1 Corinthians 12:9, NIV | My grace is sufficient for you, for my power is made perfect in weakness. |
| 2 Corinthians 6:18, NCV | I will be your father, and you will be my sons and daughters, says the Lord Almighty. |
| Philippians 4:13, NKJV | I can do all things through Christ who strengthens me. |

2 Timothy 4:16-17, NIV          At my first defense, no one came to my support,
                                but everyone deserted me. May it not be held
                                against them. But the Lord stood at my side and
                                gave me strength.

# PEACE

The world may define peace through drugs or alcohol or a relationship. They may think of it as the absence of conflict. But this is not true or lasting peace.

Jesus said, "Peace I leave with you; my peace I give you. I do not give to you as the world gives. Do not let your hearts be troubled and do not be afraid" (John 14:27, NIV). Peace is an environment in which God's Spirit is at work. When your heart and mind are at peace, you're able to hear God's voice more clearly. You can discern direction for your life and make better decisions. You can treat others as Christ would.

You can be going through a terrible storm and still have the peace of God, because God's peace surpasses all understanding. "Because you belong to Christ Jesus, God will bless you with peace that no one can completely understand. And this peace will control the way you think and feel" (Philippians 4:7, CEV).

No matter what you are going through, stay in God's Word. Fix your mind on Him. Don't let circumstances overwhelm you to the point that they consume or control you. Take the time to refocus on your relationship with the Lord and allow His Word to point you in the direction of a safe and peaceful harbor.

*For other helpful categories, see pages 118, 144, 180, 314, 428.*

| | |
|---|---|
| Numbers 25:12, NIV | Tell him I am making my covenant of peace with him. |
| Job 22:21, NIV | Submit to God and be at peace with him; in this way prosperity will come to you. |
| Psalm 29:11, NIV | The LORD gives strength to his people; the LORD blesses his people with peace. |
| Psalm 34:14, NIV | Turn from evil and do good; seek peace and pursue it. |
| Psalm 37:11, NCV | People who are not proud will inherit the land and will enjoy complete peace. |
| Psalm 62:5, CEV | Only God gives inward peace, and I depend on him. |
| Psalm 85:8, NIV | I will listen to what God the LORD will say; he promises peace to his people, his saints—but let them not return to folly. |
| Psalm 119:165, NCV | Those who love your teachings will find true peace, and nothing will defeat them. |
| Proverbs 3:17, NCV | Wisdom will make your life pleasant and will bring you peace. |
| Proverbs 14:30, NIV | A heart at peace gives life to the body. |
| Proverbs 16:7, NIV | When a man's ways are pleasing to the LORD, he makes even his enemies live at peace with him. |

| | |
|---|---|
| Isaiah 26:3, NCV | You, LORD, give true peace to those who depend on you, because they trust you. |
| Isaiah 32:17, NIV | The fruit of righteousness will be peace; the effect of righteousness will be quietness and confidence forever. |
| Isaiah 32:18, NKJV | My people will dwell in a peaceful habitation, in secure dwellings, and in quiet resting places. |
| Matthew 5:9, NIV | Blessed are the peacemakers, for they will be called sons of God. |
| John 14:27, NIV | Peace I leave with you; my peace I give you. I do not give to you as the world gives. Do not let your hearts be troubled and do not be afraid. |
| Romans 8:6, NCV | If people's thinking is controlled by the sinful self, there is death. But if their thinking is controlled by the Spirit, there is life and peace. |
| Philippians 4:7, NKJV | The peace of God, which surpasses all understanding, will guard your hearts and minds through Christ Jesus. |

# PERSEVERANCE

When you are struggling to continue in a relationship, task, or season of life, ask yourself, *What will the Lord finally bring about?* This simple question can remind you that God *is* doing something right now, even if you can't see it. Consider this verse in James: "As you know, we consider blessed those who have persevered. You have heard of Job's perseverance and have seen what the Lord finally brought about" (James 5:11, NIV).

Job lost all he had through no fault of his own. As he struggled to understand why this was happening to him, it became clear that he was not meant to know the reasons. He would have to face life with the answers and explanations held back. Only then would his faith fully develop.

Is God trying to fully develop your faith? Romans reminds us that "suffering produces perseverance; perseverance, character; and character, hope. And hope does not disappoint us" (5:3-5, NIV). In other words, the suffering that is putting you in a position of perseverance is a prerequisite not to failure but to *hope*. And God's hope is not an empty hope that will bring more waiting, but an eternal hope that will never let you down. Hold on to this hope when earthly hopes fall through. You will be surprised at the faith God grows in you as you wait for Him.

*For other helpful categories, see pages 88, 132, 289, 411.*

Matthew 24:13, NKJV      He who endures to the end shall be saved.

Romans 5:3-4, NIV      We also rejoice in our sufferings, because we know that suffering produces perseverance; perseverance, character; and character, hope.

Galatians 6:9, NIV      Let us not become weary in doing good, for at the proper time we will reap a harvest if we do not give up.

Ephesians 6:13, NIV      Put on the full armor of God, so that when the day of evil comes, you may be able to stand your ground, and after you have done everything, to stand.

2 Thessalonians 1:4, NIV      Therefore, among God's churches we boast about your perseverance and faith in all the persecutions and trials you are enduring.

2 Timothy 2:12, NIV      If we endure, we will also reign with him.

Hebrews 10:23, NIV      Let us hold unswervingly to the hope we profess, for he who promised is faithful.

Hebrews 10:36, NIV      You need to persevere so that when you have done the will of God, you will receive what he has promised.

Hebrews 11:27, NIV      By faith he left Egypt, not fearing the king's anger; he persevered because he saw him who is invisible.

| | |
|---|---|
| Hebrews 12:1-2, NIV | Let us throw off everything that hinders and the sin that so easily entangles, and let us run with perseverance the race marked out for us. Let us fix our eyes on Jesus, the author and perfecter of our faith. |
| James 1:2-4, NIV | Consider it pure joy, my brothers, whenever you face trials of many kinds, because you know that the testing of your faith develops perseverance. Perseverance must finish its work so that you may be mature and complete, not lacking anything. |
| James 1:12, NIV | Blessed is the man who perseveres under trial, because when he has stood the test, he will receive the crown of life that God has promised to those who love him. |
| James 5:11, NIV | As you know, we consider blessed those who have persevered. You have heard of Job's perseverance and have seen what the Lord finally brought about. The Lord is full of compassion and mercy. |
| James 5:13, NLT | Are any of you suffering hardships? You should pray. |
| 2 Peter 1:5-6, NIV | For this very reason, make every effort to add to your faith goodness; and to goodness, knowledge; and to knowledge, self-control; and to self-control, perseverance; and to perseverance, godliness. |

Revelation 2:19, NIV

I know your deeds, your love and faith, your service and perseverance, and that you are now doing more than you did at first.

Revelation 3:11, NIV

I am coming soon. Hold on to what you have, so that no one will take your crown.

# POLITICS

In the midst of campaign promises and heated political battles, it is important to remember that government is *God's* institution! Civil government exists and functions by God's command. In Daniel 2:20-21, we read that God sets up and removes rulers. Proverbs 21:1 says that He turns a ruler's heart. In Romans 13:1, we learn that He ordains civil powers. Clearly, government is not a secular institution but a God-ordained institution.

When a nation's foundation is built on biblical principles, it will have the strength to withstand the political upheaval that is in the world today. Righteous leaders make a country better, stronger, and more secure. That is why Christians should vote based on their conscience and in line with sound biblical doctrine.

Legislation is not the key to solving the moral problems that plague society. God's Word is. When our leaders submit to God's teaching in Scripture, we can rejoice. When our leaders do not follow God's Word, we are still called to respect them and pray for them: "Revere God. Respect the government" (1 Peter 2:17, MSG).

No matter what is happening in your community or country's government, always remember God's promise: "[If] My people who are called by My name humble themselves and pray and seek My face and turn from their wicked ways, then I will hear from heaven, will forgive their sin and will heal their land" (2 Chronicles 7:14, NASB).

*For other helpful categories, see pages 199, 333, 437.*

| | |
|---|---|
| 2 Chronicles 7:14, NASB | If My people who are called by My name humble themselves and pray and seek My face and turn from their wicked ways, then I will hear from heaven, will forgive their sin and will heal their land. |
| Psalm 75:6-7, NIV | No one from the east or the west or from the desert can exalt a man. But it is God who judges: He brings one down, he exalts another. |
| Psalm 127:1, NIV | Unless the LORD builds the house, its builders labor in vain. Unless the LORD watches over the city, the watchmen stand guard in vain. |
| Proverbs 21:1, AMP | The king's heart is in the hand of the Lord, as are the watercourses; He turns it whichever way He wills. |
| Proverbs 29:2, NIV | When the righteous thrive, the people rejoice; when the wicked rule, the people groan. |
| Daniel 2:21, NIV | He changes times and seasons; he sets up kings and deposes them. He gives wisdom to the wise and knowledge to the discerning. |
| Romans 13:1, NIV | Everyone must submit himself to the governing authorities, for there is no authority except that which God has established. The authorities that exist have been established by God. |
| Romans 13:2, NIV | Consequently, he who rebels against the authority is rebelling against what God has instituted, |

and those who do so will bring judgment on themselves.

Romans 13:5, NIV

Therefore, it is necessary to submit to the authorities, not only because of possible punishment but also because of conscience.

Romans 13:6, NIV

This is also why you pay taxes, for the authorities are God's servants, who give their full time to governing.

Romans 13:7, NIV

Give everyone what you owe him: If you owe taxes, pay taxes; if revenue, then revenue; if respect, then respect; if honor, then honor.

1 Timothy 2:1-2, NIV

I urge, then, first of all, that requests, prayers, intercession and thanksgiving be made for everyone—for kings and all those in authority, that we may live peaceful and quiet lives in all godliness and holiness.

Titus 3:1-2, NIV

Remind the people to be subject to rulers and authorities, to be obedient, to be ready to do whatever is good, to slander no one, to be peaceable and considerate, and to show true humility toward all men.

1 Peter 2:13-14, NIV

Submit yourselves for the Lord's sake to every authority instituted among men: whether to the king, as the supreme authority, or to governors, who are sent by him to punish those who do wrong and to commend those who do right.

# THE POOR AND NEEDY

All through God's Word, we see God's heart toward the poor and the needy. It is open, giving, and loving—and we are to reflect that heart. In the book of Deuteronomy, God told the Israelites to help the poor when they arrived in the Promised Land (Deuteronomy 15:7-11). *This was an important part of possessing their land!* God promises to lift the poor and needy out of the ash heap (1 Samuel 2:8). He hears the cry of the needy (Job 34:28) and defends the cause of the poor (Psalm 140:12). You honor God when you help the poor.

Yet many people close their hearts and their hands to the poor and the needy because they think they are poor through some fault of their own. You are to respond to others' needs no matter who or what is responsible for their condition. The Scriptures say in Psalm 41:1: "Blessed is the one who considers the poor! In the day of trouble the LORD delivers him" (ESV).

God accepts your help for others as if you had offered it directly to Him: "He who is kind to the poor lends to the LORD, and he will reward him for what he has done" (Proverbs 19:17, NIV). Financial help is important, but so is verbal and emotional support: "Open your mouth, judge righteously, and plead the cause of the poor and needy" (Proverbs 31:9, NKJV). God's people are guilty of oppressing the poor when they become indifferent toward the needy (see the book of Amos). Indifference today often looks like ignorance because we feel helpless to make any change in the world.

You are not helpless. Pray and ask God to show you how to help others who are struggling. And be prepared for an assignment. Action always follows true compassion!

*For other helpful categories, see pages 164, 196, 236, 343.*

| | |
|---|---|
| Deuteronomy 15:11, NKJV | The poor will never cease from the land; therefore I command you, saying, "You shall open your hand wide to your brother, to your poor and your needy, in your land." |
| 1 Samuel 2:8, NIV | He raises the poor from the dust and lifts the needy from the ash heap; he seats them with princes and has them inherit a throne of honor. |
| Job 34:28, NIV | They caused the cry of the poor to come before him, so that he heard the cry of the needy. |
| Psalm 35:10, NIV | My whole being will exclaim, "Who is like you, O LORD? You rescue the poor from those too strong for them, the poor and needy from those who rob them." |
| Psalm 41:1, ESV | Blessed is the one who considers the poor! In the day of trouble the LORD delivers him |
| Psalm 70:5, NIV | I am poor and needy; come quickly to me, O God. You are my help and my deliverer; O LORD, do not delay. |
| Proverbs 14:31, NCV | Whoever mistreats the poor insults their Maker, but whoever is kind to the needy honors God. |
| Proverbs 19:17, NIV | He who is kind to the poor lends to the LORD, and he will reward him for what he has done. |
| Proverbs 21:13, NLT | Those who shut their ears to the cries of the poor will be ignored in their own time of need. |

| | |
|---|---|
| Proverbs 28:27, NIV | He who gives to the poor will lack nothing, but he who closes his eyes to them receives many curses. |
| Proverbs 31:9, NKJV | Open your mouth, judge righteously, and plead the cause of the poor and needy. |
| Isaiah 41:17, NIV | The poor and needy search for water, but there is none; their tongues are parched with thirst. But I the LORD will answer them; I, the God of Israel, will not forsake them. |
| Jeremiah 22:16, NIV | "He defended the cause of the poor and needy, and so all went well. Is that not what it means to know me?" declares the LORD. |
| Matthew 5:42, NKJV | Give to him who asks you, and from him who wants to borrow from you do not turn away. |
| Matthew 6:2, NKJV | When you do a charitable deed, do not sound a trumpet before you as the hypocrites do in the synagogues and in the streets, that they may have glory from men. Assuredly, I say to you, they have their reward. |
| Luke 14:12-14, ESV | When you give a dinner or a banquet, do not invite your friends or your brothers or your relatives or rich neighbors, lest they also invite you in return and you be repaid. But when you give a feast, invite the poor, the crippled, the lame, the blind, and you will be blessed, because they cannot repay you. For you will be repaid at the resurrection of the just. |

| | |
|---|---|
| Acts 20:35, NIV | In everything I did, I showed you that by this kind of hard work we must help the weak, remembering the words the Lord Jesus himself said: "It is more blessed to give than to receive." |
| 1 Corinthians 13:3, NIV | If I give all I possess to the poor and surrender my body to the flames, but have not love, I gain nothing. |
| Galatians 2:10, NIV | All they asked was that we should continue to remember the poor, the very thing I was eager to do. |
| Hebrews 13:16, ESV | Do not neglect to do good and to share what you have, for such sacrifices are pleasing to God. |
| 1 John 3:17, NIV | If anyone has material possessions and sees his brother in need but has no pity on him, how can the love of God be in him? |

# PORNOGRAPHY

Millions suffer in silence. They can tell no one of their problem. The shame of pornography addiction among Christians and non-Christians has grown to an alarming epidemic. Due to easy access to the Internet, destructive sexual practices are rampant.

The single biggest factor in overcoming porn addiction is to come under the authority of Jesus Christ. You cannot be free in your own power. "For our struggle is not against flesh and blood, but against the rulers, against the powers, against the world forces of this darkness, against the spiritual forces of wickedness in the heavenly places" (Ephesians 6:12, NASB). If you have accepted Jesus's salvation, God will help you overcome temptation.

The sin of pornography is not above God's unconditional love and forgiveness. It does not shock God. Go to Him and confess your sin. When you confess your sins before God, it breaks the power of sin in your life. It's like taking air out of a balloon. The Scriptures tell us to "come boldly to the throne of grace, that we may obtain mercy and find grace to help in time of need" (Hebrews 4:16, NKJV).

Don't let shame and pride become Satan's weapons to keep you trapped. Reach out to someone who can hold you accountable and pray with and for you. Proverbs says, "One's pride will bring him low, but he who is lowly in spirit will obtain honor" (Proverbs 29:23, ESV).

*For other helpful categories, see pages 13, 34, 171, 236, 336, 346, 356, 402, 411.*

| | |
|---|---|
| Psalm 101:3, NIV | I will set before my eyes no vile thing. |
| Psalm 107:6, NIV | They cried out to the LORD in their trouble, and he delivered them from their distress. |
| Psalm 119:9, NIV | How can a young man keep his way pure? By living according to your word. |
| Psalm 119:11, NKJV | Your word I have hidden in my heart, that I might not sin against You. |
| Psalm 143:11, NIV | For your name's sake, O LORD, preserve my life; in your righteousness, bring me out of trouble. |
| Proverbs 11:2, NIV | When pride comes, then comes disgrace, but with humility comes wisdom. |
| Proverbs 29:23, ESV | One's pride will bring him low, but he who is lowly in spirit will obtain honor. |
| Isaiah 59:19, NKJV | When the enemy comes in like a flood, the Spirit of the LORD will lift up a standard against him. |
| Matthew 5:27-28, NIV | You have heard that it was said, "Do not commit adultery." But I tell you that anyone who looks at a woman lustfully has already committed adultery with her in his heart. |
| John 8:36, NKJV | If the Son makes you free, you shall be free indeed. |
| Romans 7:15-20, NIV | I do not understand what I do. For what I want to do I do not do, but what I hate I do. And if I |

do what I do not want to do, I agree that the law is good. As it is, it is no longer I myself who do it, but it is sin living in me. I know that nothing good lives in me, that is, in my sinful nature. For I have the desire to do what is good, but I cannot carry it out. For what I do is not the good I want to do; no, the evil I do not want to do—this I keep on doing. Now if I do what I do not want to do, it is no longer I who do it, but it is sin living in me that does it.

Romans 12:1, NIV — I urge you, brothers, in view of God's mercy, to offer your bodies as living sacrifices, holy and pleasing to God—this is your spiritual act of worship.

Romans 12:2, NIV — Do not conform any longer to the pattern of this world, but be transformed by the renewing of your mind. Then you will be able to test and approve what God's will is—his good, pleasing and perfect will.

Romans 16:18, NIV — Such people are not serving our Lord Christ, but their own appetites. By smooth talk and flattery they deceive the minds of naive people.

Galatians 5:16-17, NIV — So I say, live by the Spirit, and you will not gratify the desires of the sinful nature. For the sinful nature desires what is contrary to the Spirit, and the Spirit what is contrary to the sinful nature. They are in conflict with each other, so that you do not do what you want.

| | |
|---|---|
| Galatians 5:24-25, AMP | Those who belong to Christ Jesus (the Messiah) have crucified the flesh (the godless human nature) with its passions and appetites and desires. If we live by the [Holy] Spirit, let us also walk by the Spirit. [If by the Holy Spirit we have our life in God, let us go forward walking in line, our conduct controlled by the Spirit.] |
| Ephesians 6:12, NASB | Our struggle is not against flesh and blood, but against the rulers, against the powers, against the world forces of this darkness, against the spiritual forces of wickedness in the heavenly places. |
| Hebrews 4:16, NKJV | Let us therefore come boldly to the throne of grace, that we may obtain mercy and find grace to help in time of need. |
| 1 Peter 5:6-7, NIV | Humble yourselves, therefore, under God's mighty hand, that he may lift you up in due time. Cast all your anxiety on him because he cares for you. |
| 1 John 3:8, NIV | The reason the Son of God appeared was to destroy the devil's work. |

# Prayer—A Prayerful Lifestyle

You were created for intimate fellowship with your loving God. Prayer is a direct response to the Holy Spirit's moving and calling in your life. He calls daily; do you hear Him? Do you sense His summons to commune with Him?

Never forget that prayer is "powerful and effective" (James 5:16, NIV). Your prayers make a difference in your life and in the lives of others. Nothing is too big or too small for the Lord. Nothing is too little or too much. He can handle it all.

The Scriptures say to "pray without ceasing" (1 Thessalonians 5:17, NKJV). It is not practical or realistic to stay in one place and pray all day, especially with the busy life that you lead. You can, however, follow God's instruction and have a prayerful attitude at all times, acknowledging God's constant presence with you.

With this in mind, a prayerful attitude does not replace a daily time of prayer and fellowship with God. Take time out of your day to seek Him with your whole heart. Jesus told His followers, "Go into your inner room, close your door and pray to your Father who is in secret, and your Father who sees what is done in secret will reward you" (Matthew 6:6, NASB). Just as you find blessings coming back to you when you set aside money to give to God, so you will find abundant blessings when you set aside time to spend only with Him.

*For other helpful categories, see pages 9, 11, 333, 336, 340, 343, 346.*

| | |
|---|---|
| Deuteronomy 4:29, NIV | But if from there you seek the LORD your God, you will find him if you look for him with all your heart and with all your soul. |
| Deuteronomy 32:30, NIV | How could one man chase a thousand, or two put ten thousand to flight, unless their Rock had sold them, unless the LORD had given them up? |
| 1 Samuel 12:23, NIV | Far be it from me that I should sin against the LORD by failing to pray for you. |
| 2 Chronicles 7:14, NIV | If My people who are called by My name will humble themselves, and pray and seek My face, and turn from their wicked ways, then I will hear from heaven, and will forgive their sin and heal their land. |
| Job 42:10, NIV | After Job had prayed for his friends, the LORD made him prosperous again and gave him twice as much as he had before. |
| Psalm 34:7, MSG | God's angel sets up a circle of protection around us while we pray. |
| Psalm 102:17, NIV | He will respond to the prayer of the destitute; he will not despise their plea. |
| Psalm 105:4, NIV | Look to the LORD and his strength; seek his face always. |
| Psalm 145:18, NIV | The LORD is near to all who call on him, to all who call on him in truth. He fulfills the desires of |

those who fear him; he hears their cry and saves them.

| | |
|---|---|
| Proverbs 8:17, NKJV | I love those who love me, and those who seek me diligently will find me. |
| Jeremiah 29:13, NIV | You will seek me and find me when you seek me with all your heart. |
| Jeremiah 33:3, NKJV | Call to Me, and I will answer you, and show you great and mighty things, which you do not know. |
| Matthew 6:6, NASB | When you pray, go into your inner room, close your door and pray to your Father who is in secret, and your Father who sees what is done in secret will reward you. |
| Matthew 6:33, NKJV | Seek first the kingdom of God and His righteousness, and all these things shall be added to you. |
| Matthew 18:19, NIV | I tell you that if two of you on earth agree about anything you ask for, it will be done for you by my Father in heaven. |
| Luke 18:1, NIV | Jesus told his disciples a parable to show them that they should always pray and not give up. |
| Romans 4:17, NIV | As it is written: "I have made you a father of many nations."He is our father in the sight of God, in whom he believed—the God who gives life to the dead and calls things that are not as though they were. |

| | |
|---|---|
| Romans 8:26, NIV | The Spirit helps us in our weakness. We do not know what we ought to pray for, but the Spirit himself intercedes for us with groans that words cannot express. |
| Romans 12:12, NIV | Be joyful in hope, patient in affliction, faithful in prayer. |
| Philippians 4:6, KJV | In everything by prayer and supplication with thanksgiving let your requests be made known unto God. |
| 1 Thessalonians 5:17, KJV | Pray without ceasing. |
| Hebrews 4:16, KJV | Let us therefore come boldly unto the throne of grace, that we may obtain mercy, and find grace to help in time of need. |
| Hebrews 11:6, KJV | Without faith it is impossible to please Him, for he who comes to God must believe that He is, and that He is a rewarder of those who diligently seek Him. |
| James 5:16, NIV | The prayer of a righteous man is powerful and effective. |
| Jude, 20, NCV | But dear friends, use your most holy faith to build yourselves up, praying in the Holy Spirit. |

# PRAYER—HEARING GOD'S VOICE

God created you to be in constant fellowship with Him (Genesis 3:8; Thessalonians 5:17). You can *expect* to hear His voice when you pray.

How is God's voice heard?

- Through prayer (John 16:24)
- Through fasting (Daniel 10:9)
- Through His Word (2 Timothy 3:16-17)
- Through dreams and visions (Job 33:15)
- In an audible voice (Acts 9:4)
- In a still, small voice in your spirit (1 Kings 19:12)
- Through placing His desires in your heart (Psalm 40:8)
- Through other believers (1 Corinthians 2:7)
- Through prophets (2 Peter 1:21)
- Through situations and circumstances (James 1:2-3)

What are the reasons for not hearing God's voice?

- The same power that separated Adam from God still separates people from God today: the power of sin (Isaiah 59:2).
- You don't want to hear God's voice because you don't want to know Him (John 10:26-27).
- You are under the influence of wrong teachings (2 Timothy 4:3-4).
- Your heart is not pure before Him (Psalm 51:10).

Ask God to help you to quiet the voices that keep you from hearing His. God wants you to know Him more and to distinguish His voice from everything else in your life. As Jesus said, "My sheep hear My voice, and I know them, and they follow Me" (John 10:27, NKJV).

*For other helpful categories, see pages 9, 11, 329, 336, 340, 343, 346.*

ACTIVATING THE PROMISES OF GOD

| Job 33:15, AMP | [One may hear God's voice] in a dream, in a vision of the night, when deep sleep falls on men while slumbering upon the bed. |
| Isaiah 50:5, NIV | The Sovereign LORD has opened my ears, and I have not been rebellious; I have not drawn back. |
| Daniel 10:9, NKJV | Yet I heard the sound of his words; and while I heard the sound of his words I was in a deep sleep on my face, with my face to the ground. |
| John 10:4-5, NKJV | When he brings out his own sheep, he goes before them; and the sheep follow him, for they know his voice. Yet they will by no means follow a stranger, but will flee from him, for they do not know the voice of strangers. |
| John 10:27, NKJV | My sheep hear My voice, and I know them, and they follow Me. |
| John 15:15, NKJV | No longer do I call you servants, for a servant does not know what his master is doing; but I have called you friends, for all things that I heard from My Father I have made known to you. |
| Acts 9:4, NKJV | He fell to the ground, and heard a voice saying to him, "Saul, Saul, why are you persecuting Me?" |
| 2 Timothy 4:3-4, NIV | The time will come when men will not put up with sound doctrine. Instead, to suit their own desires, they will gather around them a great number of teachers to say what their itching ears |

want to hear. They will turn their ears away from the truth and turn aside to myths.

2 Peter 1:21, NKJV     Prophecy never came by the will of man, but holy men of God spoke as they were moved by the Holy Spirit.

Revelation 1:10-11, NKJV     I was in the Spirit on the Lord's Day, and I heard behind me a loud voice, as of a trumpet, saying, "I am the Alpha and the Omega, the First and the Last."

Revelation 3:20, NIV     Here I am! I stand at the door and knock. If anyone hears my voice and opens the door, I will come in and eat with him, and he with me.

# Prayer—Does God Hear Me?

Your thoughts about prayer might fluctuate with your feelings or circumstances. What does not fluctuate is God's promise to hear "the prayer of the righteous" (Proverbs 15:29, NASB). "Call to Me," God says, "and I will answer you, and show you great and mighty things, which you do not know" (Jeremiah 33:3, NKJV).

Is sin standing between you and God? Isaiah tells us, "Your iniquities have made a separation between you and your God, and your sins have hidden his face from you so that he does not hear" (Isaiah 59:2, ESV). If you believe a specific sin is hindering your relationship with God, confess it to Him. God "is faithful and just to forgive us our sins and to cleanse us from all unrighteousness" (1 John 1:9, ESV).

If you have a vague sense of guilt but no real conviction, Satan might be telling you lies about God's not hearing you. Speak this truth: "This is the confidence which we have before Him, that, if we ask anything according to His will, He hears us" (1 John 5:14, NASB). Pray with confidence as you ask to know God's will. And ask in Jesus's name: "Whatever you ask in My name, that will I do, so that the Father may be glorified in the Son" (John 14:13, NKJV).

Sometimes God says "no" or "wait" in answer to your prayers. But He still hears you. He still values the relationship you are building together through speaking and listening to one another. So believe: "Whatever things you ask in prayer, believing, you will receive" (Matthew 21:22, NKJV).

*For other helpful categories, see pages 9, 11, 329, 333, 340, 343, 346.*

| | |
|---|---|
| Deuteronomy 4:7, NIV | What other nation is so great as to have their gods near them the way the LORD our God is near us whenever we pray to him? |
| 2 Chronicles 7:14, NIV | If my people, who are called by my name, will humble themselves and pray and seek my face and turn from their wicked ways, then will I hear from heaven and will forgive their sin and will heal their land. |
| Job 22:27, NIV | You will pray to him, and he will hear you, and you will fulfill your vows. |
| Psalm 4:3, NIV | Know that the LORD has set apart the godly for himself; the LORD will hear when I call to him. |
| Psalm 6:9, NIV | The LORD has heard my cry for mercy; the LORD accepts my prayer. |
| Psalm 34:15-17, NASB | The eyes of the LORD are toward the righteous and His ears are open to their cry. The face of the LORD is against evildoers, to cut off the memory of them from the earth. The righteous cry, and the LORD hears and delivers them out of all their troubles. |
| Psalm 55:17, KJV | Evening, and morning, and at noon, will I pray, and cry aloud: and he shall hear my voice. |
| Psalm 66:18-19, NIV | If I had cherished sin in my heart, the LORD would not have listened. But God has surely listened and heard my voice in prayer. |

| | |
|---|---|
| Psalm 91:15, NIV | He will call upon me, and I will answer him; I will be with him in trouble. |
| Psalm 102:17, NIV | He will respond to the prayer of the destitute; he will not despise their plea. |
| Psalm 138:3, CEV | When I asked for your help, you answered my prayer and gave me courage. |
| Psalm 139:4, NLT | You know what I am going to say even before I say it, LORD. |
| Psalm 145:18, NLT | The LORD is close to all who call on him, yes, to all who call on him in truth. |
| Proverbs 15:8, NIV | The LORD detests the sacrifice of the wicked, but the prayer of the upright pleases him. |
| Isaiah 59:1, NKJV | Behold, the LORD's hand is not shortened, that it cannot save; nor his ear heavy, that it cannot hear. |
| Isaiah 65:24, NKJV | It shall come to pass that before they call, I will answer; and while they are still speaking, I will hear. |
| Jeremiah 29:11-13, NIV | Then you will call upon me and come and pray to me, and I will listen to you. You will seek me and find me when you seek me with all your heart. |
| Jeremiah 33:3, NKJV | Call to Me, and I will answer you, and show you great and mighty things, which you do not know. |

| | |
|---|---|
| Daniel 9:23, NIV | As soon as you began to pray, an answer was given, which I have come to tell you, for you are highly esteemed. Therefore, consider the message and understand the vision. |
| 1 Corinthians 8:3, NIV | The man who loves God is known by God. |
| James 5:16, NIV | Therefore confess your sins to each other and pray for each other so that you may be healed. The prayer of a righteous man is powerful and effective. |
| 1 Peter 3:12, NIV | The eyes of the Lord are on the righteous and his ears are attentive to their prayer, but the face of the Lord is against those who do evil. |
| 1 John 5:14, NASB | This is the confidence which we have before Him, that, if we ask anything according to His will, He hears us. |

# Prayer—Asking

When you ask God for His help, you're inviting Him to show up in your life. How wonderful and pleasing that is to Him!

God could take care of your needs without your asking. But when you petition God for something, you are acknowledging that He alone is God and that you cannot accomplish in your own strength what needs to be accomplished.

As you ask, pray the Word! God gave you His Word so that you would look to Him for the answers to all your needs. When you pray the Word, you pray the will of God. When you pray the will of God, you can overcome the two most common problems in prayer: asking for the wrong things and asking for the wrong reasons (James 4:3).

God has given us many promises in His Word. If we know these promises and know how to activate them in our lives, we will reap the rewards of walking in victory, joy, and eternal peace. But if we do not know His promises, we will not walk in the fullness of all that God has for us and we will suffer great loss.

We read in Isaiah 43:26, "Put Me in remembrance [of My word]" (NKJV). Our strongest plea is to remind God of His own promises. As you speak and declare the promises of God over your life, remember that the Bible says, "So shall My word be that goes forth from My mouth; it shall not return to Me void, but it shall accomplish what I please, and it shall prosper in the thing for which I sent it" (Isaiah 55:11, NKJV).

You can approach God with confidence in your petitions, not by your own merit, but because Jesus has made you acceptable to Him. As Jesus told His disciples, "Ask, and you will receive, that your joy may be full" (John 16:24, ESV). God *wants* you to ask Him for help in the details of your life. Strengthen your relationship with Him by bringing Him your needs.

*For other helpful categories, see pages 9, 11, 329, 333, 336, 343, 346.*

| | |
|---|---|
| Psalm 2:8, NKJV | Ask of Me, and I will give You the nations for Your inheritance, And the ends of the earth for Your possession. |
| Psalm 21:4, NIV | He asked you for life, and you gave it to him— length of days, for ever and ever. |
| Psalm 27:4, NIV | One thing I ask of the LORD, this is what I seek: that I may dwell in the house of the LORD all the days of my life, to gaze upon the beauty of the LORD and to seek him in his temple. |
| Isaiah 43:26, NKJV | Put Me in remembrance; let us contend together; state your case, that you may be acquitted. |
| Matthew 7:7, NKJV | Ask, and it will be given to you; seek, and you will find; knock, and it will be opened to you. |
| Matthew 7:9, NIV | Which of you, if his son asks for bread, will give him a stone? |
| Matthew 21:22, NKJV | Whatever things you ask in prayer, believing, you will receive. |
| John 14:13-14, NKJV | Whatever you ask in My name, that I will do, that the Father may be glorified in the Son. If you ask anything in My name, I will do it. |
| John 15:7, NKJV | If you abide in Me, and My words abide in you, you will ask what you desire, and it shall be done for you. |

| | |
|---|---|
| John 16:24, ESV | Until now you have asked nothing in my name. Ask, and you will receive, that your joy may be full. |
| Ephesians 1:16-17, NCV | I always remember you in my prayers, asking the God of our Lord Jesus Christ, the glorious Father, to give you a spirit of wisdom and revelation so that you will know him better. |
| Ephesians 3:20-21, NKJV | Now to Him who is able to do exceedingly abundantly above all that we ask or think, according to the power that works in us, to Him be glory in the church by Christ Jesus to all generations, forever and ever. Amen. |
| James 1:5-6, NKJV | If any of you lacks wisdom, let him ask of God, who gives to all liberally and without reproach, and it will be given to him. But let him ask in faith, with no doubting, for he who doubts is like a wave of the sea driven and tossed by the wind. |
| James 4:3, NIV | When you ask, you do not receive, because you ask with wrong motives, that you may spend what you get on your pleasures. |
| 1 John 3:22, NKJV | Whatever we ask we receive from Him, because we keep His commandments and do the things that are pleasing in His sight. |
| 1 John 5:14-15, NIV | This is the confidence we have in approaching God: that if we ask anything according to his will, he hears us. And if we know that he hears us—whatever we ask—we know that we have what we asked of him. |

# PRAYER—
# THE BLOOD OF JESUS

The blood of Jesus is the foundation of redemption. "But you know that you were not rescued by such things as silver or gold that don't last forever. You were rescued by the precious blood of Christ, that spotless and innocent lamb" (1 Peter 1:18-19, CEV).

The Bible speaks of the blood of Jesus in two ways: blood shed and blood sprinkled. In the Gospels we read that Jesus took the cup during the Last Supper and said, "This cup is the new covenant in My blood, which is *shed* for you" (Luke 22:20, NKJV). We also read that in Old Testament times, "When Moses had spoken every precept to all the people according to the law, he took the blood of calves and goats, with water, scarlet wool, and hyssop, and *sprinkled* both the book itself and all the people" (Hebrews 9:19, NKJV). This was a foreshadowing of the blood of Jesus that would cover and cleanse your life.

Both shed blood and sprinkled blood in the Bible speak of sacrifice. Jesus, as the final sacrifice, shed His blood for us as an act of salvation, redemption, justification, righteousness, sanctification, reconciliation, deliverance, forgiveness, and overcoming the power of the enemy.

As you pray, the greatest offensive spiritual weapon that you can have in your arsenal is the blood of Jesus! If you need God's healing or protection or deliverance from a demonic attack, or if you're battling any kind of adversity, you have the right—according to Job 1:10—to declare the victory of the blood of Jesus over yourself, your household, your possessions, your business and ministry (the work of your hands), your influence and increase (substance): "Have You not made a hedge around him, around his household, and around all that he has on every side? You have blessed the work of his hands, and his possessions have increased in the land" (Job 1:10, NKJV).

*For other helpful categories, see pages 329, 333, 336, 340, 346.*

Exodus 12:13, NIV

The blood will be a sign for you on the houses where you are; and when I see the blood, I will pass over you. No destructive plague will touch you when I strike Egypt.

Leviticus 17:11, NIV

For the life of a creature is in the blood, and I have given it to you to make atonement for yourselves on the altar; it is the blood that makes atonement for one's life.

Job 1:10, NKJV

Have You not made a hedge around him, around his household, and around all that he has on every side? You have blessed the work of his hands, and his possessions have increased in the land.

Luke 22:20, NKJV

He also took the cup after supper, saying, "This cup is the new covenant in My blood, which is shed for you."

Romans 3:25, CEV

God sent Christ to be our sacrifice. Christ offered his life's blood, so that by faith in him we could come to God. And God did this to show that in the past he was right to be patient and forgive sinners. This also shows that God is right when he accepts people who have faith in Jesus.

Hebrews 9:19, NKJV

When Moses had spoken every precept to all the people according to the law, he took the blood of calves and goats, with water, scarlet wool, and hyssop, and sprinkled both the book itself and all the people.

Hebrews 10:9-10, NKJV    He said, "Behold, I have come to do Your will, O God." He takes away the first that He may establish the second. By that will we have been sanctified through the offering of the body of Jesus Christ once for all.

1 Peter 1:18-19, CEV    You were rescued from the useless way of life that you learned from your ancestors. But you know that you were not rescued by such things as silver or gold that don't last forever. You were rescued by the precious blood of Christ, that spotless and innocent lamb.

Revelation 12:11, NIV    They overcame him by the blood of the Lamb and by the word of their testimony; they did not love their lives so much as to shrink from death.

# Prayer—The Blood of Jesus as a Weapon for Powerful Prayer

The blood of Jesus is not an abstract concept. It is a powerful reminder to Satan that Jesus has paid the final sacrifice for your sins and will protect and deliver you as you pray. The blood of Jesus is a witness of all of the following:

- *Salvation.* You are saved and born again, being rescued from hell, which is eternal damnation (John 3:17 and Acts 4:12).
- *Redemption.* The payment of ransom frees you from the captivity of sin and death (Psalm 107:2 and Ephesians 1:7).
- *Justification.* According to God's requirements, you have been acquitted of guilt and sin (Romans 5:9). Justification is based completely and solely upon Jesus's sacrifice on the cross (1 Peter 2:24) and is received by faith alone (Ephesians 2:8-9). No works are necessary to obtain justification. Otherwise, it would not be a gift (Romans 6:23). Therefore, you are "justified by faith" (Romans 5:1, 9, NKJV).
- *Righteousness.* You are in right standing with God. You are loved and accepted through Christ (Romans 3:25).
- *Sanctification.* To be sanctified is to be set apart for God. Sanctification is a process, not instantaneous, because it is not the work of God alone. The justified person is actively involved in submitting to God's will, resisting sin, seeking holiness, and working to become more godly (Galatians 5:22-23 and Hebrews 10:10).
- *Reconciliation.* Christ reconciled you to God (Romans 5:10). Your relationship to God that was once broken has now been healed (Colossians 1:20-21).
- *Overcoming the power of the enemy.* Through the blood of Jesus, you have been given all authority and power over the enemy (Luke 10:19). The purpose of exercising authority is to remove burdens and destroy yokes of bondage.

- *Deliverance.* You are set free from powers of darkness and are no longer held captive by the enemy (Colossians 1:13).
- *Forgiveness.* You have been forgiven and your sins no longer count against you. You have been declared *not guilty* (Colossians 1:14)!

*For other helpful categories, see pages 9, 11, 329, 333, 336, 340, 346.*

| | |
|---|---|
| Romans 3:25, NLT | God presented Jesus as the sacrifice for sin. People are made right with God when they believe that Jesus sacrificed his life, shedding his blood. This sacrifice shows that God was being fair when he held back and did not punish those who sinned in times past. |
| Romans 5:9-10, NIV | Since we have now been justified by his blood, how much more shall we be saved from God's wrath through him! For if, when we were God's enemies, we were reconciled to him through the death of his Son, much more, having been reconciled, we shall be saved by His life! |
| Romans 6:23, NKJV | The wages of sin is death, but the gift of God is eternal life in Christ Jesus our Lord. |
| Ephesians 1:7, NIV | In him we have redemption through his blood, the forgiveness of sins, in accordance with the riches of God's grace. |
| Colossians 1:13-14, NCV | God has freed us from the power of darkness, and he brought us into the kingdom of his dear Son. The Son paid for our sins, and in him we have forgiveness. |
| Colossians 1:19-21, NIV | For God was pleased to have all his fullness dwell in him, and through him to reconcile to himself all things, whether things on earth or things in heaven, by making peace through his blood, shed on the cross. |

| | |
|---|---|
| Hebrews 10:10, CEV | We are made holy because Christ obeyed God and offered himself once for all. |
| 1 Peter 2:24, NKJV | He Himself bore our sins in His own body on the tree, that we, having died to sins, might live for righteousness—by whose stripes you were healed. |

# PREGNANCY

The season when you are expecting a child is a powerful time of waiting, hope, and questions. Modern medical technology can tell you many things about the child inside you, but ultimately the miracle of new life—and what the future holds—is a mystery. As the author of Ecclesiastes writes, "As you do not know the path of the wind, or how the body is formed in a mother's womb, so you cannot understand the work of God, the Maker of all things" (Ecclesiastes 11:5, NIV).

Even as you are wondering who this child will be and what kind of life he or she will have, God knows every day of that life already. "Before I formed you in the womb I knew you," God told Jeremiah (Jeremiah 1:5, NIV). A psalmist praised God: "You are the one who put me together inside my mother's body, and I praise you because of the wonderful way you created me" (Psalm 139:13-14, CEV).

Pray for your child inside the womb. Speak the promises for your children (pages 294-297) over your womb. Lay hands on the baby as he or she grows. Pray for your child to sense God's love. Ask God to reveal your child's gifts and talents to you at a young age so you can nurture and encourage him or her in those areas. Pray for wisdom in joining God in the plans He has for your little one. May one day your child remember with the psalmist: "From birth I have relied on you; you brought me forth from my mother's womb. I will ever praise you" (Psalm 71:6, NIV).

*For other helpful categories, see pages 15, 293, 298, 411.*

| | |
|---|---|
| Job 31:15, AMP | Did not He Who made me in the womb make [my servant]? And did not One fashion us both in the womb? |
| Psalm 68:19, NIV | Praise be to the Lord, to God our Savior, who daily bears our burdens. |
| Psalm 71:6, NIV | From birth I have relied on you; you brought me forth from my mother's womb. I will ever praise you. |
| Psalm 119:73, NIV | Your hands made me and formed me. |
| Psalm 127:3, NLT | Children are a gift from the LORD; they are a reward for him. |
| Psalm 139:13-14, CEV | You are the one who put me together inside my mother's body, and I praise you because of the wonderful way you created me. Everything you do is marvelous! Of this I have no doubt. |
| Ecclesiastes 11:5, NIV | As you do not know the path of the wind, or how the body is formed in a mother's womb, so you cannot understand the work of God, the Maker of all things. |
| Isaiah 44:2, NIV | This is what the LORD says, he who made you, who formed you in the womb. |
| Jeremiah 1:5, NIV | Before I formed you in the womb I knew you, before you were born I set you apart; I appointed you as a prophet to the nations. |

# PREJUDICE

Prejudice is a belief or judgment toward a group of people. It is rooted in pride, hatred, and misunderstanding.

Prejudice takes many forms. It might look like sexism, ageism, racism, or judgment against those with a disability, those in a certain social class, or simply those who look different. Favoritism is also a form of prejudice: "Be fair with everyone, and don't have any favorites" (1 Timothy 5:21, CEV).

Jesus is the only person who walked the earth who knew no prejudice. He showed a respect to women that was unheard of in His culture (Luke 8:1). He welcomed the poor, the elite, the disabled, the outcast. Most importantly, "On the cross Christ did away with our hatred for each other. He also made peace between us and God by uniting Jews and Gentiles in one body" (Ephesians 2:16, CEV).

If you struggle with prejudice—maybe because of your upbringing or the area where you live—ask for God's forgiveness.

Only Jesus can break down the wall of prejudice in the world today. He already paid the price for our sin by giving His own body. This truth frees us to treat others based on the fact that they were made in the image of God—not based on their physical, social, or economic position. Christ Himself is our peace.

*For other helpful categories, see pages 171, 174, 180, 356, 445.*

| | |
|---|---|
| Luke 6:37, NIV | Do not judge, and you will not be judged. Do not condemn, and you will not be condemned. Forgive, and you will be forgiven. |
| Acts 10:34-35, NIV | Peter began to speak: "I now realize how true it is that God does not show favoritism but accepts men from every nation who fear him and do what is right." |
| Acts 15:8, NIV | God, who knows the heart, showed that he accepted them by giving the Holy Spirit to them, just as he did to us. |
| Acts 17:26, NCV | God began by making one person, and from him came all the different people who live everywhere in the world. God decided exactly when and where they must live. |
| Romans 12:16-17, NIV | Live in harmony with one another. Do not be proud, but be willing to associate with people of low position. Do not be conceited. Do not repay anyone evil for evil. Be careful to do what is right in the eyes of everybody. |
| Romans 15:7, NIV | Accept one another, then, just as Christ accepted you, in order to bring praise to God. |
| Ephesians 2:14, NCV | Christ himself is our peace. He made both Jewish people and those who are not Jews one people. They were separated as if there were a wall between them, but Christ broke down that wall of hate by giving his own body. |

| | |
|---|---|
| Ephesians 2:16, CEV | On the cross Christ did away with our hatred for each other. He also made peace between us and God by uniting Jews and Gentiles in one body. |
| Colossians 3:8, AMP | Now put away and rid yourselves [completely] of all these things: anger, rage, bad feeling toward others, curses and slander, and foulmouthed abuse and shameful utterances from your lips! |
| Titus 3:3-5, NIV | At one time we too were foolish, disobedient, deceived and enslaved by all kinds of passions and pleasures. We lived in malice and envy, being hated and hating one another. But when the kindness and love of God our Savior appeared, he saved us, not because of righteous things we had done, but because of his mercy. |
| James 2:3-4, NCV | You show special attention to the one wearing nice clothes and say, "Please, sit here in this good seat." But you say to the poor person, "Stand over there," or, "Sit on the floor by my feet." What are you doing? You are making some people more important than others, and with evil thoughts you are deciding that one person is better. |
| James 2:9, AMP | If you show servile regard (prejudice, favoritism) for people, you commit sin and are rebuked and convicted by the Law as violators and offenders. |
| 1 John 2:9, NIV | Anyone who claims to be in the light but hates his brother is still in the darkness. |

1 John 4:20, NIV          If anyone says, "I love God," yet hates his brother,
                          he is a liar. For anyone who does not love his
                          brother, whom he has seen, cannot love God,
                          whom he has not seen.

Revelation 5:9, NIV       You are worthy to take the scroll and to open its
                          seals, because you were slain, and with your blood
                          you purchased men for God from every tribe and
                          language and people and nation.

# PRIDE

Pride is a dangerous enemy. It is also an enemy of God. It was pride that removed Satan (the highest created angel) from the presence of a loving God (Ezekiel 28:12-14 and Isaiah 14:12-15). Satan became arrogant in his beauty and status and wanted to sit on a throne above God (Isaiah 14:13-14; Ezekiel 28:15; 1 Timothy 3:6). He began to reason that he was equal to God. Satan is the king of pride.

When you fall into pride's trap, as Satan did, you, too, could be devoured by it. Pride can cause you to lose your marriage, home, relationships, job, car, business, and eternal destiny. It's easy for pride to disguise itself and sneak in on your life if you aren't aware of its entry points. Proverbs 16:18 warns that "pride goes before destruction, and a haughty spirit before a fall" (NIV).

Give yourself a "pride check-up" from time to time. Remember that pride is rooted in self. It shifts the focus to yourself and usually speaks with statements that start with "I" or "I'm":

- I should be first; I've been here the longest.
- I'm not going to apologize; they were at fault.
- I'm not going to church; they are all hypocrites.
- I'm too educated to take that job.
- I've had more education; I should have been promoted.
- I didn't have it, so you don't need it.
- I've never asked anyone for anything, so I'm not helping them.
- I helped them do that. If it wasn't for me, they would not be there.
- I know more than you. I went to school for that.
- I've already heard that speaker.

Pray and ask God to reveal any areas of pride in your life. To safeguard yourself, you might want to ask loved ones to gently confront you if they see you begin to walk in a prideful manner. As God's Word tells us, "God resists the proud, but gives grace to the humble" (James 4:6, NKJV).

*For other helpful categories, see pages 395, 398, 402.*

Psalm 138:6, NCV

Though the Lord is supreme, he takes care of those who are humble, but he stays away from the proud.

Proverbs 6:16-17, NKJV

These six things the LORD hates, Yes, seven are an abomination to Him: A proud look.

Proverbs 11:2, NKJV

When pride comes, then comes shame; but with the humble is wisdom.

Proverbs 13:10, NKJV

By pride comes nothing but strife, but with the well-advised is wisdom.

Proverbs 16:5, AMP

Everyone proud and arrogant in heart is disgusting, hateful, and exceedingly offensive to the Lord; be assured [I pledge it] they will not go unpunished.

Proverbs 16:18, NIV

Pride goes before destruction, a haughty spirit before a fall.

Proverbs 21:4, NIV

Haughty eyes and a proud heart, the lamp of the wicked, are sin!

Proverbs 25:14, NIV

Like clouds and wind without rain is a man who boasts of gifts he does not give.

Proverbs 26:12, NIV

Do you see a man wise in his own eyes? There is more hope for a fool than for him.

Proverbs 27:2, NIV

Let another praise you, and not your own mouth; someone else, and not your own lips.

Habakkuk 2:4, NLT      Look at the proud! They trust in themselves, and their lives are crooked. But the righteous will live by their faithfulness to God.

1 Corinthians 10:12, NKJV      Let him who thinks he stands take heed lest he fall.

James 4:6, NKJV      God resists the proud, but gives grace to the humble.

James 4:10, NIV      Humble yourselves before the Lord, and he will lift you up.

1 John 2:16, NKJV      All that is in the world—the lust of the flesh, the lust of the eyes, and the pride of life—is not of the Father but is of the world.

# Prison—
# If Someone You Love Is in Prison

If someone you love is in prison, you probably feel discouraged, angry, and helpless. Perhaps you have been helping your friend or relative for years but he or she keeps making the same mistakes. You might feel as if this person threw away your efforts because he or she ended up in the same place—again.

Real love is an unconditional commitment to an imperfect person. Choose to show your loved one real love, even if you don't feel like it. Prayer will help you love her with Christ's love. So pray the Scriptures over your loved one. Pray for release from any spiritual, emotional, or relational prison he is in. God promises "to open eyes that are blind, to free captives from prison and to release from the dungeon those who sit in darkness" (Isaiah 42:7, NIV).

Seeing someone you love go through the process of trial, conviction, and sentencing is also a journey of grief. You are letting go of your expectations for your relationship, for holidays, for the future. You miss sharing everyday life with someone you love. You might feel as if you're in prison yourself.

Even when you are apart, even when negative feelings seem to separate you from one another, God can bring you together. Just as God is at work in prison cells to turn pain into something good, so He can be at work in your life during this time.

*For other helpful categories, see pages 118, 174, 180, 428, 445.*

| | |
|---|---|
| Psalm 59:16, NIV | I will sing of your strength, in the morning I will sing of your love; for you are my fortress, my refuge in times of trouble. |
| Psalm 73:26, NIV | My flesh and my heart may fail, but God is the strength of my heart and my portion forever. |
| Psalm 86:7, NIV | In the day of my trouble I will call to you, for you will answer me. |
| Psalm 86:13, NIV | Great is your love toward me. |
| Psalm 119:132, NIV | Turn to me and have mercy on me, as you always do to those who love your name. |
| Matthew 25:36, NIV | I was in prison and you came to visit me. |
| Romans 8:28, NIV | We know that in all things God works for the good of those who love him, who have been called according to his purpose. |
| Romans 8:35, NKJV | Who shall separate us from the love of Christ? Shall tribulation, or distress, or persecution, or famine, or nakedness, or peril, or sword? |
| Romans 15:13, NIV | May the God of hope fill you with all joy and peace as you trust in him, so that you may overflow with hope by the power of the Holy Spirit. |
| 2 Corinthians 5:7, NKJV | We walk by faith, not by sight. |

Galatians 6:1, NIV

Brothers, if someone is caught in a sin, you who are spiritual should restore him gently. But watch yourself, or you also may be tempted.

Hebrews 10:34, NIV

You sympathized with those in prison and joyfully accepted the confiscation of your property, because you knew that you yourselves had better and lasting possessions.

Hebrews 13:3, NIV

Remember those in prison as if you were their fellow prisoners, and those who are mistreated as if you yourselves were suffering.

# Prison—If You Are in Prison

Whether you are in prison for a crime you blatantly committed or because of someone else's sin and influence, the presence of God is with you. Whether you have tried to follow God or knowingly disobeyed Him, the presence of God is with you. "I revealed myself to those who did not ask for me," God says; "I was found by those who did not seek me.... I said, 'Here am I, here am I'" (Isaiah 65:1, NIV).

The presence of God is a literal place where peace, joy, and an abundance of love reside. It is accessible from a cell, in a corner of a yard, or in a room full of people. God's promise to you is that He will never leave you or forsake you.

Prison can be a very lonely place because you feel so unknown. God knows you. He calls you by name: "He calls his own sheep by name and leads them out" (John 10:3, ESV).

As you grow closer to God, ask Him to reveal how you can make the most of the relationships around you. "Encourage one another and build each other up" (1 Thessalonians 5:11, NIV). Encouragement is always a source of strength. You can harness your sadness and use it to uplift and encourage others. You might be surprised at what God will do in and through you as you wait for Him.

*For other helpful categories, see pages 13, 153, 171, 174, 177, 180, 196, 333, 365.*

| | |
|---|---|
| Exodus 33:14, NIV | My Presence shall go with you, and I will give you rest. |
| 2 Kings 20:5, NIV | I have heard your prayer and seen your tears; I will heal you. |
| Psalm 32:7, NLT | You are my hiding place; you protect me from trouble. You surround me with songs of victory. |
| Psalm 59:16, NIV | I will sing of your strength, in the morning I will sing of your love; for you are my fortress, my refuge in times of trouble. |
| Psalm 130:4, NIV | With you there is forgiveness. |
| Psalm 142:6, NCV | Listen to my cry, because I am helpless. Save me from those who are chasing me, because they are too strong for me. |
| Psalm 142:7, NCV | Free me from my prison, and then I will praise your name. Then good people will surround me, because you have taken care of me. |
| Isaiah 65:1, NIV | I revealed myself to those who did not ask for me; I was found by those who did not seek me. To a nation that did not call on my name, I said, "Here am I, here am I." |
| Jeremiah 29:11, NIV | "I know the plans I have for you," declares the LORD, "plans to prosper you and not to harm you, plans to give you hope and a future." |
| John 6:37, NIV | Whoever comes to me I will never drive away. |

| | |
|---|---|
| 2 Corinthians 9:8, NIV | God is able to make all grace abound toward you, that you, always having all sufficiency in all things, may have an abundance for every good work. |
| Philippians 1:6, NIV | Being confident of this, that he who began a good work in you will carry it on to completion until the day of Christ Jesus. |
| Philippians 4:13, NKJV | I can do all things through Christ who strengthens me. |
| 2 Timothy 1:7, NKJV | God has not given us a spirit of fear, but of power and of love and of a sound mind. |
| 2 Timothy 2:16, NIV | Avoid godless chatter, because those who indulge in it will become more and more ungodly. |
| James 5:13, NIV | Are any of you suffering hardships? You should pray. |
| 1 Peter 2:13, NIV | Submit yourselves for the Lord's sake to every authority instituted among men. |
| 1 Peter 2:17, NLT | Respect everyone, and love your Christian brothers and sisters. Fear God, and respect the king. |

# Prison—Wisdom as You Are Released from Prison

Committing a crime may have led you to prison, but God is still on your side! He still wants great life and joy for you ahead. " 'Not by might nor by power, but by My Spirit,' says the LORD of hosts" (Zechariah 4:6, NKJV).

You may feel discouraged, labeled, and at a disadvantage as you face the current job market or return to your family. God wants you to depend on His Spirit as you are released from your debt to society. As you continually surrender your life to Him, it is the work and the power of the Holy Spirit that will enable you to become all that God has in mind for you.

As you live for God, determine not to trust in your own strength or abilities. Purpose in your heart to walk in the knowledge of His Word, which says, "Forget the former things; do not dwell on the past. See, I am doing a new thing!" (Isaiah 43:18-19, NIV). Move forward in the confidence of God's promises to you and His never-ending love for you.

Proverbs 12:2 says that "a good man obtains favor from the LORD" (NKJV). You don't earn that favor, or deserve it, but you can receive it from a loving God who has your best interest at heart—and who never gives up on you.

*For other helpful categories, see pages 153, 156, 336, 381, 428, 441.*

| | |
|---|---|
| Joshua 1:9, NKJV | Have I not commanded you? Be strong and of good courage; do not be afraid, nor be dismayed, for the LORD your God is with you wherever you go. |
| Psalm 84:11, NIV | The LORD God is a sun and shield; the LORD bestows favor and honor; no good thing does he withhold from those whose walk is blameless. |
| Psalm 121:2, NKJV | My help comes from the LORD, who made heaven and earth. |
| Proverbs 3:5-6, NKJV | Trust in the LORD with all your heart, and lean not on your own understanding; in all your ways acknowledge Him, and He shall direct your paths. |
| Proverbs 12:2, NCV | The Lord is pleased with a good person, but he will punish anyone who plans evil. |
| Isaiah 43:18, NIV | Forget the former things; do not dwell on the past. |
| Isaiah 43:19, NIV | See, I am doing a new thing! Now it springs up; do you not perceive it? I am making a way in the desert and streams in the wasteland. |
| Isaiah 48:17, NKJV | I am the LORD your God, who teaches you to profit, who leads you by the way you should go. |
| Zechariah 4:6, NKJV | "Not by might nor by power, but by My Spirit," says the LORD of hosts. |

| | |
|---|---|
| Romans 12:2, NIV | Do not be conformed to this world, but be transformed by the renewing of your mind, that you may prove what is that good and acceptable and perfect will of God. |
| 2 Corinthians 5:7, NKJV | We walk by faith, not by sight. |
| 2 Corinthians 5:15, NIV | He died for all, that those who live should live no longer for themselves, but for Him who died for them and rose again. |
| 2 Corinthians 12:9, NIV | "My grace is sufficient for you, for my power is made perfect in weakness." Therefore I will boast all the more gladly about my weaknesses, so that Christ's power may rest on me. |
| Philippians 3:13, NIV | One thing I do: Forgetting what is behind and straining toward what is ahead. |
| Philippians 4:19, NKJV | My God shall supply all your need according to His riches in glory by Christ Jesus. |
| 2 Peter 1:3-4, NIV | His divine power has given us everything we need for life and godliness through our knowledge of him who called us by his own glory and goodness. Through these he has given us his very great and precious promises, so that through them you may participate in the divine nature and escape the corruption in the world caused by evil desires. |

# PROSPERITY

When we think of prosperity, many of us immediately think about money. But prosperity means more than just finances. God's desire is for you to have wholeness in every area of your life: spirit, soul, body, relationships, and finances.

You prosper when you live according to the Word of God. Joshua 1:8 says, "This Book of the Law shall not depart from your mouth, but you shall meditate in it day and night, that you may observe to do according to all that is written in it. For then you will make your way prosperous, and then you will have good success" (NKJV).

God wants you to prosper! He wants to bless you so that you will be a blessing to others who are in need. That's why He gave you instructions on how to prosper.

In 1 Chronicles 4:10, Jabez prayed, " 'Oh, that you would bless me and enlarge my territory! Let your hand be with me, and keep me from harm so that I will be free from pain.' And God granted his request" (NIV). Jabez asked God to bless him, help him in his work (enlarge his territory), and be with him in all that he did.

As you pray for God's blessings, be sure to keep God in His rightful position in your life. Is He Lord over your life, family, work, and money? Remember that God does not promise to keep you from all hardship. But He does promise ultimate blessing for those who trust Him. His promise to you is "If you are willing and obedient, you shall eat the good of the land" (Isaiah 1:19, NKJV).

Your desire to increase your wealth, achievements, and influence should come from a desire to glorify God. Strengthening your gifts, growing your financial wealth, and being rich in wisdom allows you to help others more, always pointing them to Jesus, who frees you to prosper.

*For other helpful categories, see pages 156, 160, 164, 174, 207, 441.*

| | |
|---|---|
| Deuteronomy 8:18, NKJV | Remember the LORD your God, for it is He who gives you power to get wealth, that He may establish His covenant which He swore to your fathers. |
| Deuteronomy 28:8, NKJV | The LORD will command the blessing on you in your storehouses and in all to which you set your hand, and He will bless you in the land which the LORD your God is giving you. |
| Joshua 1:8, NKJV | This Book of the Law shall not depart from your mouth, but you shall meditate in it day and night, that you may observe to do according to all that is written in it. For then you will make your way prosperous, and then you will have good success. |
| Psalm 35:27, NKJV | Let the LORD be magnified, who has pleasure in the prosperity of His servant. |
| Psalm 68:19, NKJV | Blessed be the Lord, who daily loads us with benefits, the God of our salvation! |
| Psalm 84:11, NKJV | No good thing will He withhold from those who walk uprightly. |
| Psalm 90:17, NIV | May the favor of the LORD our God rest upon us; establish the work of our hands for us—yes, establish the work of our hands. |
| Psalm 92:12, NKJV | The righteous shall flourish like a palm tree, he shall grow like a cedar in Lebanon. |

| Proverbs 8:20-21, NCV | I do what is right and follow the path of justice. I give wealth to those who love me, filling their houses with treasures. |
| --- | --- |
| Proverbs 10:4, NKJV | He who has a slack hand becomes poor, but the hand of the diligent makes rich. |
| Proverbs 17:20, NIV | A man of perverse heart does not prosper; he whose tongue is deceitful falls into trouble. |
| Isaiah 1:19, NKJV | If you are willing and obedient, you shall eat the good of the land. |
| Matthew 6:33, NKJV | Seek first the kingdom of God and His righteousness, and all these things shall be added to you. |
| Luke 6:38, NKJV | Give, and it will be given to you: good measure, pressed down, shaken together, and running over will be put into your bosom. For with the same measure that you use, it will be measured back to you. |
| 2 Corinthians 9:11, NIV | You will be made rich in every way so that you can be generous on every occasion, and through us your generosity will result in thanksgiving to God. |
| Galatians 3:14, NIV | He redeemed us in order that the blessing given to Abraham might come to the Gentiles through Christ Jesus, so that by faith we might receive the promise of the Spirit. |

# Prostitution, Nightclubs, and Strip Bars

If your way of life involves prostitution or working in a nightclub or strip bar, God has a better plan for your life. He said, "I have good plans for you, not plans to hurt you. I will give you hope and a good future" (Jeremiah 29:11, NCV). God wants to raise you up and out of your current situation. He has given you gifts and talents that are waiting to be discovered.

No one is beyond the love of God. In the Bible, a prostitute named Rahab helped save the Israelite people (Joshua 2:1) and is listed as an ancestor of Jesus in the first chapter of Matthew. James describes her as someone who "was shown to be right with God by her actions" (James 2:25, NLT). In other words, God did not see a prostitute when He saw Rahab; He saw a woman who could change her life by following God—and even be a blood relative of His Son, Jesus.

Your lifestyle will rob you of your freedom, even convincing you that you can escape the violence, disease, and other destructive problems it brings. Yet you may feel like you are trapped. Money is deceptive. It will never define your self-worth and it will never meet the emotional and spiritual needs that you have.

God knows your beauty, value, and worth. Will you allow His empowering love to restore your self-confidence, self-respect, and dignity? In doing so, God will take away your bitterness, shame, and pain.

When you are ready, pray this simple but powerful prayer.

*God, I need Your help. Protect me and rescue me from this hurtful lifestyle. Take away my pain and restore my life. I give You my fears and the mess that my life is in. I want You with all of my heart. Help me to discover a joyful and radiant new life in Christ. In Jesus's name. Amen.*

*For other helpful categories, see pages 13, 118, 153, 156, 174, 177, 375, 381.*

| | |
|---|---|
| Joshua 2:1, NKJV | Now Joshua the son of Nun sent out two men from Acacia Grove to spy secretly, saying, "Go, view the land, especially Jericho." So they went, and came to the house of a harlot named Rahab, and lodged there. |
| Psalm 25:20, NLT | Protect me! Rescue my life from them! Do not let me be disgraced, for in you I take refuge. |
| Psalm 38:22, NLT | Come quickly to help me, O Lord my savior. |
| Psalm 59:1, NLT | Rescue me from my enemies, O God. Protect me from those who have come to destroy me. |
| Psalm 103:12, NLT | He has taken our sins away from us as far as the east is from west. |
| Psalm 118:5, NLT | In my distress I prayed to the LORD, and the LORD answered me and set me free. |
| Psalm 141:4, NIV | Let not my heart be drawn to what is evil, to take part in wicked deeds with men who are evildoers; let me not eat of their delicacies. |
| Psalm 142:6, NCV | Listen to my cry, because I am helpless. Save me from those who are chasing me, because they are too strong for me. |
| Jeremiah 29:11, NCV | "I know what I am planning for you," says the LORD. "I have good plans for you, not plans to hurt you. I will give you hope and a good future." |

| | |
|---|---|
| Matthew 6:13, NIV | Lead us not into temptation, but deliver us from the evil one. |
| Romans 5:8, NLT | God showed his great love for us by sending Christ to die for us while we were still sinners. |
| Romans 7:15, NLT | I don't really understand myself, for I want to do what is right, but I don't do it. Instead, I do what I hate. |
| Romans 8:38-39, NIV | I am convinced that neither death nor life, neither angels nor demons, neither the present nor the future, nor any powers, neither height nor depth, nor anything else in all creation, will be able to separate us from the love of God that is in Christ Jesus our Lord. |
| 1 Corinthians 6:15, NIV | Do you not know that your bodies are members of Christ himself? Shall I then take the members of Christ and unite them with a prostitute? Never! |
| 1 Corinthians 6:18, ESV | Flee from sexual immorality. Every other sin a person commits is outside the body, but the sexually immoral person sins against his own body. |
| 1 Corinthians 7:23, CEV | God paid a great price for you. So don't become slaves of anyone else. |
| 1 Corinthians 10:13, NIV | No temptation has seized you except what is common to man. And God is faithful; he will not let you be tempted beyond what you can bear. |

But when you are tempted, he will also provide a way out so that you can stand up under it.

Ephesians 2:10, NKJV

We are His workmanship, created in Christ Jesus for good works, which God prepared beforehand that we should walk in them.

James 1:13-15, NIV

When tempted, no one should say, "God is tempting me." For God cannot be tempted by evil, nor does he tempt anyone; but each one is tempted when, by his own evil desire, he is dragged away and enticed. Then, after desire has conceived, it gives birth to sin; and sin, when it is full-grown, gives birth to death.

James 2:25, NLT

Rahab the prostitute is another example. She was shown to be right with God by her actions when she hid those messengers and sent them safely away by a different road.

# PROTECTION

In ancient times, God made a covenant of protection with His people (Isaiah 41:10-13). This covenant, like all divine covenants, was a sacred promise backed by the full faithfulness of God. He *would* fulfill it.

As God's children, we are privileged to be included under the covenant of protection. It is in His Word. Here are some pieces of this promise:

- He will watch over the "way of the righteous" (Psalm 1:6, NIV).
- He will keep His people from snares (Proverbs 3:26).
- He will deliver us from destruction (Psalm 107:20).

In place of fear, God's promised us peace. In place of danger, safety. In place of destruction, protection. Doesn't that sound wonderful?

If you are facing risky circumstances, don't be anxious. "God has not given us a spirit of fear, but of power and of love and of a sound mind" (2 Timothy 1:7, NKJV). Put on the full armor of God and stand in His name, trusting Him (Ephesians 6:10-17).

As you pray, remind God of the covenant of protection that He has made with His people. Pray a hedge of protection around you and your loved ones (Job 1:10). Then thank God for the protection He gives!

*For other helpful categories, see pages 132, 153, 311, 329.*

| Deuteronomy 28:7, NIV | The LORD will grant that the enemies who rise up against you will be defeated before you. They will come at you from one direction but flee from you in seven. |
|---|---|
| Deuteronomy 33:12, NIV | Let the beloved of the LORD rest secure in him, for he shields him all day long. |
| Deuteronomy 33:27, NCV | The everlasting God is your place of safety, and his arms will hold you up forever. He will force your enemy out ahead of you, saying, "Destroy the enemy!" |
| Joshua 1:9, NIV | Have I not commanded you? Be strong and courageous. Do not be terrified; do not be discouraged, for the LORD your God will be with you wherever you go. |
| Job 1:10, NKJV | Have You not made a hedge around him, around his household, and around all that he has on every side? You have blessed the work of his hands, and his possessions have increased in the land. |
| Psalm 1:6, NIV | The LORD watches over the way of the righteous. |
| Psalm 4:8, NIV | I will lie down and sleep in peace, for you alone, O LORD, make me dwell in safety. |
| Psalm 5:11, NIV | Let all who take refuge in you be glad; let them ever sing for joy. Spread your protection over them, that those who love your name may rejoice in you. |

Psalm 91:1-3, NIV   He who dwells in the shelter of the Most High will rest in the shadow of the Almighty. I will say of the LORD, "He is my refuge and my fortress, my God, in whom I trust." Surely he will save you from the fowler's snare and from the deadly pestilence.

Psalm 97:10, NCV   People who love the Lord hate evil. The Lord watches over those who follow him and frees them from the power of the wicked.

Psalm 121:7-8, NIV   The Lord will keep you from all harm—he will watch over your life; the LORD will watch over your coming and going both now and forevermore.

Proverbs 3:26, NCV   The Lord will keep you safe. He will keep you from being trapped.

Proverbs 18:10, NIV   The name of the LORD is a strong tower; the righteous run to it and are safe.

Isaiah 41:13, NKJV   I, the LORD your God, will hold your right hand, saying to you, "Fear not, I will help you."

Isaiah 59:19, NKJV   When the enemy comes in like a flood, the Spirit of the LORD will lift up a standard against him.

2 Timothy 1:7, NKJV   God has not given us a spirit of fear, but of power and of love and of a sound mind.

# Religions

As the demographics of our country change, Christians might easily find themselves living next door to Hindus, buying their groceries at a shop owned by Muslims, and having their nails done by Buddhists.

Along with this increasing religious diversity has come a tendency toward "tolerance" (defined as accepting all beliefs as equally true) and "syncretism" (combining religious beliefs). Are tolerance and syncretism the loving way to respond to others?

The truth is that, while you must respect religious liberty and should welcome the opportunity to get to know people with other beliefs, all religions were *not* created equal. Jesus said it plainly in John 14:6: "I am the way and the truth and the life. No one comes to the Father except through me" (NIV).

We were all created with spiritual hunger—that explains why people around the world have religious beliefs of some kind. But if you feed the spirit with anything but God's Word, you will be deceived.

Take your acquaintance with followers of other religious beliefs as God-given opportunities to let these people know about the Savior who died for them. But don't give in to the tendency to accept their religious beliefs at face value or to graft those beliefs onto your own. Instead, follow these three guidelines:

1. Search God's Word and let Him show you the truth that will set you free ( John 8:32).
2. Pray and renounce ties that you have had with other religions.
3. Search for a church whose foundation is built on Scripture (Luke 6:47-48).

*For other helpful categories, see pages 80, 243, 257, 352, 449.*

Deuteronomy 18:14, NKJV — These nations which you will dispossess listened to soothsayers and diviners; but as for you, the LORD your God has not appointed such for you.

Psalm 115:2-4, NIV — Why do the nations say, "Where is their God?" Our God is in heaven; he does whatever pleases him. But their idols are silver and gold, made by the hands of men.

Isaiah 43:11-12, NIV — "I, even I, am the LORD, and apart from me there is no savior. I have revealed and saved and proclaimed—I, and not some foreign god among you. You are my witnesses," declares the LORD, "that I am God."

Isaiah 47:13, NCV — You are tired of the advice you have received. So let those who study the sky—those who tell the future by looking at the stars and the new moons—let them save you from what is about to happen to you.

Luke 6:47-48, NKJV — Whoever comes to Me, and hears My sayings and does them, I will show you whom he is like: He is like a man building a house, who dug deep and laid the foundation on the rock. And when the flood arose, the stream beat vehemently against that house, and could not shake it, for it was founded on the rock.

John 8:32, NIV — Then you will know the truth, and the truth will set you free.

John 14:6, NKJV — I am the way, the truth, and the life. No one comes to the Father except through Me.

| | |
|---|---|
| John 15:12, NKJV | This is My commandment, that you love one another as I have loved you. |
| 2 Corinthians 6:14, NKJV | Do not be unequally yoked together with unbelievers. For what fellowship has righteousness with lawlessness? And what communion has light with darkness? |
| 2 Corinthians 6:15, NCV | How can Christ and Belial, the devil, have any agreement? What can a believer have together with a nonbeliever? |
| 2 Corinthians 6:16, NCV | The temple of God cannot have any agreement with idols, and we are the temple of the living God. As God said: "I will live with them and walk with them. And I will be their God, and they will be my people." |
| 2 Corinthians 6:17, NCV | Leave those people, and be separate, says the Lord. Touch nothing that is unclean, and I will accept you. |
| 1 Timothy 6:3-5, CEV | Anyone who teaches something different disagrees with the correct and godly teaching of our Lord Jesus Christ. Those people who disagree are proud of themselves, but they don't really know a thing. Their minds are sick, and they like to argue over words. They cause jealousy, disagreements, unkind words, evil suspicions, and nasty quarrels. They have wicked minds and have missed out on the truth. |

# RESTORATION

God is a God of restoration. In the book of Job we see that Job lost his possessions, family, and health to the devil, but God restored twice as much to him (Job 42:10). In the book of Joel, God promises to "restore to you the years that the locust [has] eaten, the cankerworm, and the caterpillar, and the palmerworm" (Joel 2:25, KJV).

When Jesus came to earth, the people knew Him as the One who brings both physical and spiritual restoration (Acts 10:38). Today, Jesus can heal and restore your life and your body from pain, sickness, and disease.

As the storms of life come and leave their mark on your soul, you can believe that God will restore your mind, will, and emotions (Psalm 23:3). Isaiah 40:31 says,

> Those who hope in the LORD
>     will renew their strength.
> They will soar on wings like eagles;
>         they will run and not grow weary,
>         they will walk and not be faint. (NIV)

As you apply God's Word to your life, you will see the power of restoration take over your life. Restoration is more than being restored to the former place. God's restoration is restoring you to the place where He originally intended you to be.

*For other helpful categories, see pages 171, 193–196, 207, 223, 289, 343.*

| | |
|---|---|
| Deuteronomy 30:3, NIV | Then the LORD your God will restore your fortunes and have compassion on you and gather you again from all the nations where he scattered you. |
| Job 33:26, NIV | He prays to God and finds favor with him, he sees God's face and shouts for joy; he is restored by God to his righteous state. |
| Job 42:10, NIV | After Job had prayed for his friends, the LORD made him prosperous again and gave him twice as much as he had before. |
| Psalm 23:3, NIV | He restores my soul. He guides me in paths of righteousness for his name's sake. |
| Psalm 51:12, NIV | Restore to me the joy of your salvation and grant me a willing spirit, to sustain me. |
| Isaiah 38:16, NLT | Lord, your discipline is good, for it leads to life and health. You restore my health and allow me to live! |
| Isaiah 40:31, NIV | Those who hope in the LORD will renew their strength. They will soar on wings like eagles; they will run and not grow weary, they will walk and not be faint. |
| Isaiah 57:18, NIV | I have seen his ways, but I will heal him; I will guide him and restore comfort to him. |

| | |
|---|---|
| Jeremiah 31:3-4, NIV | I have loved you with an everlasting love; I have drawn you with loving-kindness. I will build you up again and you will be rebuilt. |
| Lamentations 5:21, NIV | Restore us to yourself, O LORD, that we may return; renew our days as of old. |
| Joel 2:25, KJV | I will restore to you the years that the locust has eaten, the cankerworm, and the caterpiller, and the palmerworm, my great army which I sent among you. |
| Acts 10:38, NKJV | God anointed Jesus of Nazareth with the Holy Spirit and with power, and He went about doing good and healing all who were oppressed by the devil, for God was with Him. |

# Salvation—
## Sharing the Good News

Jesus died for the sins of people from all nations (John 3:16). In His final words to His disciples, Jesus gives a clear command to tell others the Good News and make disciples for the kingdom. This Great Commission is an instruction to all believers, not just to those who may have the gift of evangelism (Matthew 28:19)

As you talk with others about Christ, remember that it is God's power and grace that saves people, not your efforts. All that is required of you is your obedience to the leading of the Holy Spirit.

Your role in speaking about Christ has a direct effect on your own life. Jesus said, "Whoever acknowledges me before men, I will also acknowledge him before my Father in heaven. But whoever disowns me before men, I will disown him before my Father in heaven" (Matthew 10:32-33, NIV).

If you are feeling shy or uncertain, pray for God's confidence and boldness. Then by faith speak truth in love to those who are not saved. As Paul wrote, "I am not ashamed of the gospel, because it is the power of God for the salvation of everyone who believes" (Romans 1:16, NIV). As you listen to the leading of the Holy Spirit, you will experience the joy of sharing God's Good News with others.

*For other helpful categories, see pages 171, 193–196, 239, 257.*

| | |
|---|---|
| Proverbs 11:30, NKJV | The fruit of the righteous is a tree of life, and he who wins souls is wise. |
| Matthew 10:32-33, NIV | Whoever acknowledges me before men, I will also acknowledge him before my Father in heaven. But whoever disowns me before men, I will disown him before my Father in heaven. |
| Matthew 28:19, NIV | Go and make disciples of all nations, baptizing them in the name of the Father and of the Son and of the Holy Spirit. |
| Mark 11:24, NIV | Whatever you ask for in prayer, believe that you have received it, and it will be yours. |
| John 1:12, NLT | To all who believed him and accepted him, he gave the right to become children of God. |
| John 3:3, NIV | Jesus declared, "I tell you the truth, no one can see the kingdom of God unless he is born again." |
| John 3:16-17, NIV | For God so loved the world that he gave his one and only Son, that whoever believes in him shall not perish but have eternal life. For God did not send his Son into the world to condemn the world, but to save the world through him. |
| John 8:51, NIV | I tell you the truth, if anyone keeps my word, he will never see death. |
| John 14:6, NIV | I am the way and the truth and the life. No one comes to the Father except through me. |

John 15:8, NKJV    By this My Father is glorified, that you bear much fruit; so you will be My disciples.

Acts 4:12, NIV    Salvation is found in no one else, for there is no other name under heaven given to men by which we must be saved.

Acts 16:31, NKJV    Believe on the Lord Jesus Christ, and you will be saved, you and your household.

Romans 1:16, NIV    I am not ashamed of the gospel, because it is the power of God for the salvation of everyone who believes.

Romans 3:23, NKJV    All have sinned and fall short of the glory of God.

Romans 10:9-10, NKJV    If you confess with your mouth the Lord Jesus and believe in your heart that God has raised Him from the dead, you will be saved. For with the heart one believes unto righteousness, and with the mouth confession is made unto salvation.

Romans 10:13, KJV    Whosoever shall call upon the name of the Lord shall be saved.

Ephesians 1:18, NIV    I pray also that the eyes of your heart may be enlightened in order that you may know the hope to which he has called you, the riches of his glorious inheritance in the saints.

Ephesians 4:5, KJV    One Lord, one faith, one baptism.

| | |
|---|---|
| 1 Timothy 2:4, NIV | God our Savior wants all men to be saved and to come to a knowledge of the truth. |
| 1 Timothy 2:5, CEV | There is only one God, and Christ Jesus is the only one who can bring us to God. Jesus was truly human, and he gave himself to rescue all of us. |
| Titus 2:11, NLT | The grace of God has been revealed, bringing salvation to all people. |
| 2 Peter 3:9, NIV | The Lord is not slow in keeping his promise, as some understand slowness. He is patient with you, not wanting anyone to perish, but everyone to come to repentance. |
| 1 John 4:14, NIV | And we have seen and testify that the Father has sent his Son to be the Savior of the world. |

# SALVATION—PRAYING FOR SOMEONE WHO IS NOT SAVED

Are you praying for the salvation of a friend or loved one? There is a spiritual battle going on for the soul of that person in the spirit realm. The Bible says we don't "wrestle against flesh and blood, but against principalities, against powers, against the rulers of the darkness of this age, against spiritual hosts of wickedness in the heavenly places" (Ephesians 6:12, NKJV).

Praying for people to be saved can be a very long battle. You may have been praying for years for a relative or friend to know Jesus and you see no change. It is hard to keep praying when you don't see the fruit of those prayers. Jesus said in Luke 18:1 that we should always pray and not give up. Your prayers are powerful and they enter into the heart of God ( James 5:16).

The man on the cross next to Jesus prayed for salvation just before death, and Jesus welcomed him into paradise (Luke 23:43). Perhaps others thought that man would never know God. But God had not given up on him.

Pray that God will send laborers across your loved one's path as a witness for the gospel of salvation (Colossians 4:3). Pray that through God's grace He would give a hunger and thirst for His Word (Matthew 5:6). It is only by God's grace that anyone can be saved (Ephesians 2:8).

Whether you are praying for someone you love deeply or a stranger you want to love with Christ's love, when you pray for someone's salvation, you are joining a heavenly war. Arm yourself with the power of God's Word and the prayer of faith, and see the victory God can bring.

*For other helpful categories, see pages 65, 293, 314, 340, 343, 346.*

| | |
|---|---|
| Matthew 5:6, NIV | Blessed are those who hunger and thirst for righteousness, for they will be filled. |
| Matthew 10:33, NKJV | Whoever denies Me before men, him I will also deny before My Father who is in heaven. |
| Luke 15:21-24, NKJV | And the son said to him, "Father, I have sinned against heaven and in your sight, and am no longer worthy to be called your son." But the father said to his servants, "Bring out the best robe and put it on him, and put a ring on his hand and sandals on his feet. And bring the fatted calf here and kill it, and let us eat and be merry; for this my son was dead and is alive again; he was lost and is found." And they began to be merry. |
| Luke 18:1, NKJV | He spoke a parable to them, that men always ought to pray and not lose heart. |
| John 3:3, NIV | Jesus declared, "I tell you the truth, no one can see the kingdom of God unless he is born again." |
| Acts 4:12, NIV | Salvation is found in no one else, for there is no other name under heaven given to men by which we must be saved. |
| Acts 16:31, NKJV | Believe on the Lord Jesus Christ, and you will be saved, you and your household. |
| Romans 1:16, NKJV | I am not ashamed of the gospel of Christ, for it is the power of God to salvation for everyone who believes, for the Jew first and also for the Greek. |

| | |
|---|---|
| Romans 10:1, NIV | My heart's desire and prayer to God for the Israelites is that they may be saved. |
| Romans 10:13, KJV | Whosoever shall call upon the name of the Lord shall be saved. |
| 2 Corinthians 10:4-5, NKJV | The weapons of our warfare are not carnal but mighty in God for pulling down strongholds, casting down arguments and every high thing that exalts itself against the knowledge of God, bringing every thought into captivity to the obedience of Christ. |
| Ephesians 1:18, NIV | I pray also that the eyes of your heart may be enlightened in order that you may know the hope to which he has called you, the riches of his glorious inheritance in the saints. |
| Ephesians 2:8, NIV | For it is by grace you have been saved, through faith—and this not from yourselves, it is the gift of God. |
| Ephesians 6:12, KJV | We wrestle not against flesh and blood, but against principalities, against powers, against the rulers of the darkness of this world, against spiritual wickedness in high places. |
| Colossians 4:3, NIV | Pray for us, too, that God may open a door for our message, so that we may proclaim the mystery of Christ, for which I am in chains. |

| | |
|---|---|
| 1 Timothy 1:15, NIV | Here is a trustworthy saying that deserves full acceptance: Christ Jesus came into the world to save sinners—of whom I am the worst. |
| 1 Timothy 2:4, NIV | He wants all men to be saved and to come to knowledge of the truth. |
| Titus 2:11, NKJV | The grace of God that brings salvation has appeared to all men. |
| 2 Peter 3:9, NKJV | The Lord is not slack concerning His promise, as some count slackness, but is longsuffering toward us, not willing that any should perish but that all should come to repentance. |
| 1 John 1:8, NIV | If we claim to be without sin, we deceive ourselves and the truth is not in us. |
| 1 John 5:14-15, NIV | This is the confidence we have in approaching God: that if we ask anything according to his will, he hears us. And if we know that he hears us—whatever we ask—we know that we have what we asked of him. |

# SALVATION—PRAYING
# FOR YOUR HOUSEHOLD TO BE SAVED

If one or more members of your family do not know Christ, remember that your prayers can make a difference in their lives (James 5:16). Your loved ones must choose salvation on their own, but God also longs for them to choose Him (2 Peter 3:9).

Often, God shows His desire for spiritual protection through His provision of physical protection. Throughout the Bible, we see examples of household salvation that will encourage and build our faith.

- Noah prepared an ark for his family and in doing so provided physical salvation for his household (Hebrews 11:7). Although his children were not righteous before the Lord, God made provision for them to live and therefore have the opportunity to be right before Him (Genesis 7:1).
- Joseph was separated from his family, only later to be used by God to bring great deliverance to them (Genesis 45:7). This physical protection provided spiritual protection for the nation of Israel.
- Rahab the harlot, hearing of the powerful Israelite God and sensing that He was a God worth trusting, asked for and was granted household salvation (Joshua 6:17).

God is looking to you to pray for your family. If your children, parents, grandparents, or extended family of aunts, uncles, or cousins are not saved, praying the prayer of faith for them can usher in the will of God for household salvation. Remember, you activate the promises of God by speaking them out of your mouth. Be bold and declare in the face of your enemy: "As for me and my house we will serve the LORD" (Joshua 24:15, NASB).

*For other helpful categories, see pages 140, 293, 329, 343, 346.*

| | |
|---|---|
| Genesis 7:1, NKJV | The LORD said to Noah, "Come into the ark, you and all your household, because I have seen that you are righteous before Me in this generation." |
| Genesis 19:15, NIV | With the coming of dawn, the angels urged Lot, saying, "Hurry! Take your wife and your two daughters who are here, or you will be swept away when the city is punished." |
| Joshua 6:17, NKJV | Now the city shall be doomed by the LORD to destruction, it and all who are in it. Only Rahab the harlot shall live, she and all who are with her in the house, because she hid the messengers that we sent. |
| Joshua 24:15, NIV | But as for me and my household, we will serve the LORD. |
| Isaiah 49:25, NKJV | I will save your children. |
| Isaiah 54:13, NKJV | All your children shall be taught by the LORD, and great shall be the peace of your children. |
| Luke 19:9, NIV | Today salvation has come to this house, because this man, too, is a son of Abraham. |
| John 4:53, NIV | The father realized that this was the exact time at which Jesus had said to him, "Your son will live." So he and all his household believed. |
| Acts 16:14-15, NCV | One of the listeners was a woman named Lydia from the city of Thyatira whose job was selling purple cloth. She worshiped God, and he opened |

her mind to pay attention to what Paul was saying. She and all the people in her house were baptized.

Acts 18:8, NKJV — Crispus, the ruler of the synagogue, believed on the Lord with all his household.

1 Corinthians 1:16, NKJV — I also baptized the household of Stephanas.

2 Peter 3:9, NIV — The Lord is not slow in keeping his promise, as some understand slowness. He is patient with you, not wanting anyone to perish, but everyone to come to repentance.

# Satan—Who Satan Is

Christians have a real enemy. His fallen name is Satan. He is also known by his angelic name *Lucifer* and by *the devil*. Satan is the accuser and "the tempter" (Matthew 4:3, NKJV). He is also called "evil one" (Matthew 13:38, NIV), the "great dragon," and the ancient "serpent of old" (Revelation 12:9, NKJV).

It's important to know who your enemy is, how he operates, and what his strengths and strategies are:

- Satan was created as a holy angel (Isaiah 14:12).
- Satan was created as a cherubim, the highest created angel (Ezekiel 28:12-14).
- He became arrogant in his beauty and status and wanted to sit on a throne above God (Isaiah 14:13-14; Ezekiel 28:15; 1 Timothy 3:6).
- Satan's pride led to his fall (Isaiah 14:12-15). Because of Satan's sin, God barred Satan from heaven.
- Satan became the "ruler of this world" ( John 12:31, NKJV) and the "prince of the power of the air" (Ephesians 2:2, NKJV).
- Satan was cast out of heaven (Revelation 12:7-9) and still seeks to elevate his throne above God.

Satan will do anything and everything in his power to oppose God and those who follow God. But God is more powerful than Satan (1 John 4:4)! It is important both to believe that Satan is real and to know that his destiny—an eternity in the "lake of fire"—is already sealed (Revelation 20:10).

*For other helpful categories, see pages 257, 346, 356, 398.*

| | |
|---|---|
| Isaiah 14:12, NKJV | How you are fallen from heaven, O Lucifer, son of the morning! How you are cut down to the ground, you who weakened the nations! |
| Isaiah 14:13-15, NIV | You said in your heart, "I will ascend to heaven; I will raise my throne above the stars of God; I will sit enthroned on the mount of assembly, on the utmost heights of the sacred mountain. I will ascend above the tops of the clouds; I will make myself like the Most High." But you are brought down to the grave, to the depths of the pit. |
| Ezekiel 28:12, NIV | You were the model of perfection, full of wisdom and perfect in beauty. |
| Ezekiel 28:13, NIV | You were in Eden, the garden of God; every precious stone adorned you: ruby, topaz and emerald, chrysolite, onyx and jasper, sapphire, turquoise and beryl. Your settings and mountings were made of gold; on the day you were created they were prepared. |
| Ezekiel 28:14, NIV | You were anointed as a guardian cherub, for so I ordained you. You were on the holy mount of God; you walked among the fiery stones. |
| Ezekiel 28:15, NIV | You were blameless in your ways from the day you were created till wickedness was found in you. |
| Matthew 4:3, NKJV | When the tempter came to Him, he said, "If You are the Son of God, command that these stones become bread." |

| | |
|---|---|
| Matthew 13:38, NIV | The field is the world, and the good seed stands for the sons of the kingdom. The weeds are the sons of the evil one. |
| John 12:31, NKJV | Now is the judgment of this world; now the ruler of this world will be cast out. |
| Ephesians 2:2, NKJV | You once walked according to the course of this world, according to the prince of the power of the air, the spirit who now works in the sons of disobedience. |
| Revelation 12:7-8, NKJV | War broke out in heaven: Michael and his angels fought with the dragon; and the dragon and his angels fought, but they did not prevail, nor was a place found for them in heaven any longer. |
| Revelation 12:9, NKJV | The great dragon was cast out, that serpent of old, called the Devil and Satan, who deceives the whole world; he was cast to the earth, and his angels were cast out with him. |
| Revelation 20:10, NKJV | The devil, who deceived them, was cast into the lake of fire and brimstone where the beast and the false prophet are. And they will be tormented day and night forever and ever. |

# SATAN—WHAT SATAN DOES

Satan counterfeits all that God does, hoping to gain the worship of the world and encourage opposition to God's kingdom.

- He is the ultimate source behind every false cult and false religion (1 Corinthians 10:20 and 1 John 4:3).
- He steals, kills, and destroys (John 10:10).
- Lying is his "native language" (John 8:44, NIV).
- He knows and uses Scriptures to promote false doctrine and deceptions (Matthew 4:1-11).
- He takes away the Word of God from the hearts of His people (Luke 8:10-13).
- He is like a "roaring lion" seeking someone to devour (1 Peter 5:8-9, NKJV).
- He can sift people like wheat (Luke 22:31-33).
- He is capable of deceiving the whole world (Revelation 12:8-9).
- His kingdom is the "dominion of darkness" (Acts 26:16-18 and Colossians 1:13, NIV).
- He has angels (Revelation 12:7-9).
- He disguises himself as an "angel of light" (2 Corinthians 11:14, NKJV).
- He can fill your heart, leading you to lie to the Holy Spirit (Acts 5:3).
- He can perform "counterfeit miracles, signs, and wonders" (2 Thessalonians 2:9-10, NIV).
- He wants you to wear his mark on your forehead or hand (Revelation 14:9).

Don't give Satan "a way to defeat you" (Ephesians 4:27, NCV). *Know who you are fighting and use the authority that Jesus Christ gave you to put Satan in his place.* Know and speak God's Word. It is your powerful weapon against the devil and his cohorts.

*For other helpful categories, see pages 257, 346, 395, 402, 421.*

| Genesis 3:1, NIV | Now the serpent was more crafty than any of the wild animals the Lord God had made. He said to the woman, "Did God really say, 'You must not eat from any tree in the garden'?" |
|---|---|
| Matthew 4:5-7, NKJV | The devil took Him up into the holy city, set Him on the pinnacle of the temple, and said to Him, "If You are the Son of God, throw Yourself down. For it is written: 'He shall give His angels charge over you,' and, 'In their hands they shall bear you up, lest you dash your foot against a stone.'" Jesus said to him, "It is written again, 'You shall not tempt the LORD your God.'" |
| Luke 8:12, NKJV | Those by the wayside are the ones who hear; then the devil comes and takes away the word out of their hearts, lest they should believe and be saved. |
| Luke 22:31, NKJV | The Lord said, "Simon, Simon! Indeed, Satan has asked for you, that he may sift you as wheat." |
| John 8:44, NIV | You belong to your father, the devil, and you want to carry out your father's desire. He was a murderer from the beginning, not holding to the truth, for there is no truth in him. When he lies, he speaks his native language, for he is a liar and the father of lies. |
| John 10:10, NKJV | The thief does not come except to steal, and to kill, and to destroy. |
| Acts 5:3, NIV | Peter said, "Ananias, how is it that Satan has so filled your heart that you have lied to the Holy |

Spirit and have kept for yourself some of the money you received for the land?"

Acts 26:17-18, NKJV — I will deliver you from the Jewish people, as well as from the Gentiles, to whom I now send you, to open their eyes, in order to turn them from darkness to light, and from the power of Satan to God.

2 Corinthians 11:14, NLT — Satan disguises himself as an angel of light.

Ephesians 4:27, NCV — Do not give the devil a way to defeat you.

2 Thessalonians 2:9-10, NIV — The coming of the lawless one will be in accordance with the work of Satan displayed in all kinds of counterfeit miracles, signs and wonders, and in every sort of evil that deceives those who are perishing. They perish because they refused to love the truth and so be saved.

1 Peter 5:8, NKJV — Be sober, be vigilant; because your adversary the devil walks about like a roaring lion, seeking whom he may devour.

1 John 3:8, NKJV — He who sins is of the devil, for the devil has sinned from the beginning. For this purpose the Son of God was manifested, that He might destroy the works of the devil.

Revelation 12:7-9, NKJV — The dragon and his angels fought, but they did not prevail, nor was a place found for them in heaven any longer. So the great dragon was cast out, that serpent of old, called the Devil and

Satan, who deceives the whole world; he was cast to the earth, and his angels were cast out with him.

Revelation 14:9-10, NKJV    If anyone worships the beast and his image and receives his mark on the forehead or on the hand, he himself shall also drink of the wine of the wrath of God.

# SIN

Overcoming the deceitfulness of sin begins with making an honest evaluation of your actions. If you find yourself justifying or sugar-coating your behavior, you will be held back from spiritual victory—the victory of walking in the peace, purpose, and plan of God.

The consequences of sin are separation from God, guilt, shame, fear, blame, and even physical or spiritual death (Romans 6:23). But remember: the same spirit that raised Christ from the dead dwells in you (Romans 8:11)!

If you are struggling with the temptation of sin, change your atmosphere. Don't go to the familiar places that make you compromise. Take a closer look at the people you are associating with—they could be leading you in the wrong direction. You should not feel comfortable in or around sin. As you become more like Christ, you will acquire God's ability to overcome the desire to sin.

Most importantly, feed yourself Scripture! Renew your mind with His Word (Romans 12:2). Meditate on His Word day and night (Psalm 1:2). Hide His Word in your heart so that you will not sin against Him (Psalm 119:11). When you confess and renounce known sin, it will weaken its grip on your life. With the power of God's Word within you, you are well able to overcome the power of sin!

*For other helpful categories, see pages 199, 257, 398, 421.*

| | |
|---|---|
| Psalm 119:11, NKJV | Your word I have hidden in my heart, that I might not sin against You. |
| Proverbs 1:10, NIV | My son, if sinners entice you, do not give in to them. |
| Proverbs 13:20, CEV | Wise friends make you wise, but you hurt yourself by going around with fools. |
| Proverbs 26:11, NIV | As a dog returns to its vomit, so a fool repeats his folly. |
| Matthew 26:41, NIV | Watch and pray so that you will not fall into temptation. The spirit is willing, but the body is weak. |
| Romans 6:6-7, NIV | We know that our old self was crucified with him so that the body of sin might be done away with, that we should no longer be slaves to sin—because anyone who has died has been freed from sin. |
| Romans 6:18, NIV | You have been set free from sin and have become slaves to righteousness. |
| Romans 6:22, NIV | Now that you have been set free from sin and have become slaves to God, the benefit you reap leads to holiness, and the result is eternal life. |
| Romans 6:23, NKJV | The wages of sin is death, but the gift of God is eternal life in Christ Jesus our Lord. |

Romans 8:2, NIV — Through Christ Jesus the law of the Spirit of life set me free from the law of sin and death.

Romans 8:6-8, NIV — The mind of sinful man is death, but the mind controlled by the Spirit is life and peace; the sinful mind is hostile to God. It does not submit to God's law, nor can it do so. Those controlled by the sinful nature cannot please God.

Romans 8:10, NIV — If Christ is in you, your body is dead because of sin, but your Spirit is alive because of righteousness.

Romans 12:2, NKJV — Do not be conformed to this world, but be transformed by the renewing of your mind, that you may prove what is that good and acceptable and perfect will of God.

1 Corinthians 10:13, NIV — No temptation has seized you except what is common to man. And God is faithful; he will not let you be tempted beyond what you can bear. But when you are tempted, he will also provide a way out so that you can stand up under it.

Galatians 5:16-18, NIV — Live by the Spirit, and you will not gratify the desires of the sinful nature. For the sinful nature desires what is contrary to the Spirit, and the Spirit what is contrary to the sinful nature. They are in conflict with each other, so that you do not do what you want. But if you are led by the Spirit, you are not under law.

Ephesians 1:7, NKJV

In Him we have redemption through His blood, the forgiveness of sins, according to the riches of His grace.

James 4:8, NIV

Come near to God and he will come near to you. Wash your hands, you sinners, and purify your hearts, you double-minded.

1 John 1:8, NKJV

If we say that we have no sin, we deceive ourselves, and the truth is not in us.

1 John 4:4, NIV

You, dear children, are from God and have overcome them, because the one who is in you is greater than the one who is in the world.

# SLEEP—INSOMNIA

If you struggle to get a good night's sleep, you know that sleep is a gift from God. God designed sleep as an essential time of rest and rejuvenation that benefits your mind and body. Sleep helps your mood, memory, and concentration and strengthens your immune system, your nervous system, and your development.

Stress or an overly busy schedule often causes insomnia. In the midst of a fast-paced lifestyle, it is difficult to "shut off" our worries or plans at the end of the day.

Luke 8 describes Jesus's busy lifestyle as He traveled from one town to another. He cast out demons, taught large crowds, spent time with His family, and discipled His friends. Yet He was able to sleep—even once while a storm raged outside His boat. It was His traveling companions who couldn't sleep in the midst of the storm. They woke Jesus, saying, "Master, Master, we're going to drown!" (Luke 8:24, NIV).

When you feel as if you are in the midst of a storm physically or emotionally, remember that God promises rest for your soul. Jesus invites you, "Come to me, all you who are weary and burdened, and I will give you rest" (Matthew 11:28, NIV).

God's rest can come through making practical changes in your life. Sometimes certain medications and even vitamins cause insomnia, for instance. Be sure to check with your physician to see if any of the medications you are on might be causing you to lose your sleep.

Sleep is one of the few times in your life when you truly are out of control. Your heart continues to beat, your mind continues to work, and your body continues to function, but you are not "making" any of these things happen. Let yourself rest in the knowledge that God is giving you breath every day and night, whether you know it or not. He is caring for you, including all your concerns and fears, even as you sleep.

*For other helpful categories, see pages 62, 132, 153, 311, 428.*

Esther 6:1, ESV

On that night the king could not sleep. And he gave orders to bring the book of memorable deeds, the chronicles, and they were read before the king.

Psalm 3:5, CEV

I sleep and wake up refreshed because you, LORD, protect me.

Psalm 4:8, NIV

I will lie down and sleep in peace, for you alone, O LORD, make me dwell in safety.

Psalm 14:5, MSG

Night is coming for them, and nightmares, for God takes the side of victims. Do you think you can mess with the dreams of the poor? You can't, for God makes their dreams come true.

Psalm 91:1, NIV

He who dwells in the shelter of the Most High will rest in the shadow of the Almighty.

Psalm 116:7, NIV

Be at rest once more, O my soul, for the LORD has been good to you.

Psalm 127:2, NIV

In vain you rise early and stay up late, toiling for food to eat—for he grants sleep to those he loves.

Proverbs 10:24, MSG

The nightmares of the wicked come true; what the good people desire, they get.

Ecclesiastes 5:12, NCV

Those who work hard sleep in peace; it is not important if they eat little or much. But rich people worry about their wealth and cannot sleep.

| | |
|---|---|
| Isaiah 32:18, NIV | My people will live in peaceful dwelling places, in secure homes, in undisturbed places of rest. |
| Matthew 11:28, NIV | Come to me, all you who are weary and burdened, and I will give you rest. |
| 1 Peter 5:7, NKJV | Casting all your care upon Him, for He cares for you. |

# SLEEP—NIGHTMARES

Nightmares are usually reflections of stress and fear. Satan wants to use anything he can to get you to walk in fear. If you don't know what to do with nightmares, Satan can use them as a stronghold that will affect your life. Satan would like nothing better than for you to speak words of fear and dread about your dreams.

If you have frequent nightmares, you may find these guidelines helpful:

1. Take authority over your dreams. "You have been given fullness in Christ, who is the head over every power and authority" (Colossians 2:10, NIV). Declare out loud, "No weapon formed against me will prosper. Every voice [a dream has a voice] that is raised against me will be condemned. This is my inheritance as a servant of the Lord" (adapted from Isaiah 54:17, NKJV).

2. Trust God to take care of your daily concerns. "Give all your worries to him, because he cares about you" (1 Peter 5:7, NCV).

3. Remember that you have control over your thought life! Choose to forget the dream. Tell yourself, *I'm not going to remember that dream.* Scriptures tell you to "be transformed by the renewing of your mind" (Romans 12:2, NKJV).

4. Be aware that some medications can cause nightmares or intense dreams. Contact your doctor to see if the medication you are on could be causing this side effect.

5. Never forget that your eyes and ears are the gateways to your heart. Guard yourself against destructive outside influences. Television, news reports, video games, and the Internet can plant seeds of worry, doubt, and confusion. "I will set before my eyes no vile thing. The deeds of faithless men I hate; they will not cling to me" (Psalm 101:3, NIV).

6. Ask the Lord if the dream is from Him. You can have a dream that seems like a nightmare, but it may be a warning from God.

*For other helpful categories, see pages 9, 65, 218, 343, 343, 398.*

| Job 3:13, NIV | For now I would be lying down in peace; I would be asleep and at rest. |
| Psalm 4:8, NIV | I will lie down and sleep in peace, for you alone, O LORD, make me dwell in safety. |
| Psalm 14:5, MSG | Night is coming for them, and nightmares, for God takes the side of victims. Do you think you can mess with the dreams of the poor? You can't, for God makes their dreams come true. |
| Psalm 101:3, NIV | I will set before my eyes no vile thing. The deeds of faithless men I hate; they will not cling to me. |
| Proverbs 10:24, MSG | The nightmares of the wicked come true; what the good people desire, they get. |
| Matthew 11:28, NKJV | Come to Me, all you who labor and are heavy laden, and I will give you rest. |
| Ephesians 6:12, KJV | We wrestle not against flesh and blood, but against principalities, against powers, against the rulers of the darkness of this world, against spiritual wickedness in high places. |
| Colossians 2:10, NIV | You have been given fullness in Christ, who is the head over every power and authority. |
| 1 Peter 5:7, NCV | Give all your worries to him, because he cares about you. |
| 1 John 3:8, KJV | For this purpose the Son of God was manifested, that he might destroy the works of the devil. |

# STRENGTH

God promises to give us strength to meet our challenges, but He doesn't promise to eliminate challenges. Instead He walks beside us, giving us firm footing to walk in His strength no matter what we face.

If you are feeling weak today, God's Word can strengthen your spirit and bring your life into clear focus. He knows about the difficulties and problems you face. He tells you in His Word to "seek the LORD and his strength" no matter what is happening around you (1 Chronicles 16:11, ESV).

That means going to His Word and gaining the knowledge you need to overcome. There are Scriptures that will bring hope and strength for every need that you're facing right now. Learn them. Memorize them. Let them sink into your heart and mind so they will come to your thoughts when you need a reminder that God is strong even when you are weak. You are strong because the Word of God is in you (1 John 2:14)!

"The LORD gives strength to his people," David writes. "The LORD blesses his people with peace" (Psalm 29:11, NIV). When circumstances overwhelm you, knowing God's strength is in you will give you peace. A personal and close relationship with God and His Word will give you the confidence that will sustain you. Consistent fellowship with Him will give you the spiritual vitality that will help you to weather the storms of life. Abiding in God's presence empowers you to stay on course whenever you face challenges.

*For other helpful categories, see pages 9, 11, 196, 289, 333.*

| | |
|---|---|
| 2 Samuel 22:40, NCV | You gave me strength in battle. You made my enemies bow before me. |
| 1 Chronicles 16:11, NIV | Look to the LORD and his strength; seek his face always. |
| Nehemiah 8:10, NIV | The joy of the LORD is your strength. |
| Psalm 18:39, NIV | You armed me with strength for battle; you made my adversaries bow at my feet. |
| Psalm 28:7, NIV | The LORD is my strength and my shield; my heart trusts in him, and I am helped. My heart leaps for joy and I will give thanks to him in song. |
| Psalm 29:11, NIV | The LORD gives strength to his people; the LORD blesses his people with peace. |
| Psalm 46:1, KJV | God is our refuge and strength, a very present help in trouble. |
| Psalm 84:5, NIV | Blessed are those whose strength is in you, who have set their hearts on pilgrimage. |
| Psalm 118:14, NIV | The LORD is my strength and my song; he has become my salvation. |
| Psalm 138:3, NKJV | In the day when I cried out, You answered me, and made me bold with strength in my soul. |
| Proverbs 24:5, NIV | A wise man has great power, and a man of knowledge increases strength. |

| | |
|---|---|
| Proverbs 27:17, NIV | As iron sharpens iron, so one man sharpens another. |
| Isaiah 30:15, NKJV | In returning and rest you shall be saved; in quietness and confidence shall be your strength. |
| Isaiah 40:29, NKJV | He gives power to the weak, and to those who have no might He increases strength. |
| Isaiah 40:31, NIV | Those who hope in the LORD will renew their strength. They will soar on wings like eagles; they will run and not grow weary, they will walk and not be faint. |
| Isaiah 41:10, NLT | Don't be afraid, for I am with you. Don't be discouraged, for I am your God. I will strengthen you and help you. I will hold you up with my victorious right hand. |
| Ephesians 6:11, NIV | Put on the full armor of God so that you can take your stand against the devil's schemes. |
| Philippians 4:13, NKJV | I can do all things through Christ who strengthens me. |
| 1 John 2:14, NIV | I write to you, young men, because you are strong, and the word of God lives in you, and you have overcome the evil one. |

# Suicide—Suicidal Thoughts

Do you sometimes—or most of the time—feel that death would be better than life? Eternal life with God *will* be more wonderful than you can imagine. But it is up to God to determine when we will receive that eternal life (Job 14:5, NIV).

If you feel that something more powerful than yourself is darkening your thoughts and heart, remember that you "do not wrestle against flesh and blood, but against principalities, against powers, against the rulers of the darkness of this age, against spiritual hosts of wickedness in the heavenly places" (Ephesians 6:12, NKJV). It's true that you are wrestling a powerful force—but not a force more powerful than God's love. Seek help. You have reached a place that requires the arms of someone else to hold you up and wrestle with you. Your life *can* be stable again. You *will* overcome the feelings of being trapped and hopeless. You *will* be free from this pain. You *will* sleep soundly again. You are not alone. Others have walked a similar path, and are there to walk alongside you now.

One psalmist writes, "The troubles of my heart have enlarged; bring me out of my distresses! Look on my affliction and my pain, and forgive all my sins" (Psalm 25:17-18, NKJV). We overcome negative thoughts by renewing our mind with God's Word. When a harmful thought comes into your mind, say out loud, "The troubles of my heart have enlarged, but God, You will bring me out of my distresses! You look on my affliction and my pain, and You forgive all my sins. I will not be sad or upset. I will put my hope in You and keep praising You, my Savior and my God." No matter what you feel right now, the Word of God and the reality of God's love for you have not changed.

*For other helpful categories, see pages 13, 106, 236, 239, 289, 311, 333, 336, 343.*

National Suicide Hotline: 800-273-TALK (8255)

| | |
|---|---|
| Job 14:5, NIV | Man's days are determined; you have decreed the number of his months and have set limits he cannot exceed. |
| Psalm 18:4-6, NIV | The cords of death entangled me; the torrents of destruction overwhelmed me. The cords of the grave coiled around me; the snares of death confronted me. In my distress I called to the LORD; I cried to my God for help. From his temple he heard my voice; my cry came before him, into his ears. |
| Psalm 25:17-18, NKJV | The troubles of my heart have enlarged; bring me out of my distresses! Look on my affliction and my pain, and forgive all my sins. |
| Psalm 31:7, NIV | I will be glad and rejoice in your love, for you saw my affliction and knew the anguish of my soul. |
| Psalm 43:5, ESV | Why are you cast down, O my soul, and why are you in turmoil within me? Hope in God; for I shall again praise him, my salvation and my God. |
| Psalm 86:13, NIV | Great is your love toward me; you have delivered me from the depths of the grave. |
| Psalm 119:116, NKJV | Uphold me according to Your word, that I may live; and do not let me be ashamed of my hope. |
| Psalm 146:8, NKJV | The LORD raises those who are bowed down; The LORD loves the righteous. |
| Jeremiah 29:11, CEV | I will bless you with a future filled with hope—a future of success, not of suffering. |

Matthew 11:28, NIV        Come to me, all you who are weary and burdened, and I will give you rest.

Romans 8:38-39, NIV       I am convinced that neither death nor life, neither
angels nor demons, neither the present nor the
future, nor any powers, neither height nor depth,
nor anything else in all creation, will be able to
separate us from the love of God that is in Christ
Jesus our Lord.

Romans 15:13, NIV         May the God of hope fill you with all joy and
peace as you trust in him, so that you may over-
flow with hope by the power of the Holy Spirit.

1 Corinthians 6:19-20, NKJV  Do you not know that your body is the temple of
the Holy Spirit who is in you, whom you have
from God, and you are not your own? For you
were bought at a price; therefore glorify God in
your body and in your spirit, which are God's.

1 Corinthians 10:13, ESV  No temptation has overtaken you that is not
common to man. God is faithful, and he will not
let you be tempted beyond your ability, but with
the temptation he will also provide the way of
escape, that you may be able to endure it.

Ephesians 6:12, NKJV      We do not wrestle against flesh and blood, but
against principalities, against powers, against the
rulers of the darkness of this age, against spiritual
hosts of wickedness in the heavenly places.

1 Thessalonians 5:8, NIV    But since we belong to the day, let us be self-controlled, putting on faith and love as a breast-plate, and the hope of salvation as a helmet.

2 Timothy 1:7, NKJV    God has not given us a spirit of fear, but of power and of love and of a sound mind.

James 5:16, NIV    The prayer of a righteous man is powerful and effective.

# Suicide—When a Christian Commits Suicide

Many people who have lost a loved one to suicide struggle with guilt and the thought *If only I had...* Bring these thoughts to God whenever they grip you. Place them before His throne, believing that He understands the depths of your pain and regret and wants to take those feelings from you. God can heal, even now.

You can rest in knowing that the character of God is loving, compassionate, and understanding. Jesus said that once we are in His hands, our future is also in His hands. He is faithful to keep us in His care, even when we are faithless. If your loved one committed his or her life to the Lord Jesus Christ, the Scripture says of this one, "I give them eternal life, and they shall never perish; no one can snatch them out of my hand. My Father, who has given them to Me, is greater than all; no one can snatch them out of My Father's hand" (John 10:28-29, NKJV).

It may seem that depression or anger or difficult circumstances literally snatched your loved one from you through suicide. Any time someone dies suddenly, it is tempting to dwell on the decisions made just before that death. God knows and cares about your sorrow. He loves your loved one even more than you do. Instead of dwelling on the circumstances, pray for God's help in focusing on the joy and new life that he or she has now.

*For other helpful categories, see pages 150, 171, 196, 226, 230.*

Numbers 6:26, NKJV

The LORD lift up His countenance upon you, and give you peace.

Judges 16:29-30, NIV

Samson reached toward the two central pillars on which the temple stood. Bracing himself against them, his right hand on the one and his left hand on the other, Samson said, "Let me die with the Philistines!" Then he pushed with all his might, and down came the temple on the rulers and all the people in it. Thus he killed many more when he died than while he lived.

Nehemiah 9:17, NIV

You are a forgiving God, gracious and compassionate; slow to anger and abounding in love.

Proverbs 3:5, NKJV

Trust in the LORD with all your heart, and lean not on your own understanding.

John 3:16, NKJV

For God so loved the world that He gave His only begotten Son, that whoever believes in Him should not perish but have everlasting life.

John 10:28-29, NKJV

I give them eternal life, and they shall never perish; neither shall anyone snatch them out of My hand.

Romans 3:23, NKJV

All have sinned and fall short of the glory of God.

Romans 8:38-39, NKJV

I am persuaded that neither death nor life, nor angels nor principalities nor powers, nor things present nor things to come, nor height nor depth, nor any other created thing, shall be able to separate us from the love of God which is in Christ Jesus our Lord.

Romans 10:13, NKJV — Whoever calls on the name of the LORD shall be saved.

1 Corinthians 14:33, NKJV — God is not the author of confusion but of peace, as in all the churches of the saints.

1 John 3:19-20, NIV — This then is how we know that we belong to the truth, and how we set our hearts at rest in his presence whenever our hearts condemn us. For God is greater than our hearts, and he knows everything.

# TEMPTATION

It is never wrong to express your true feelings to God. If you are being tempted, your first instinct might be to "hide" your feelings from Him. But God already knows the temptations you face. He has given you a powerful tool—His Word—to stand up to them.

All of us will encounter some sort of temptation at one time or another. Jesus asked the disciples to pray that they would not fall into temptation because He knew that He would soon be leaving them. He knew they would need extra strength to face the temptation ahead—temptation to run away or to deny their relationship with Him (Luke 22:40).

Temptation itself is not sin. It's only when we give in to a temptation that it becomes sin. So be on guard and keep the lines of communication open with God about temptations in your life. Remember that Satan is the great deceiver, so "don't blame God when you are tempted! God cannot be tempted by evil, and he doesn't use evil to tempt others" (James 1:13, CEV).

God's Word is your defense against temptation. He has given you this power and authority over your spirit, mind, and body. Meditate on His Word and declare Scriptures that cause this temptation to fall—instead of you falling for it.

*For other helpful categories, see pages 199, 236, 257, 289, 346, 402.*

| | |
|---|---|
| Psalm 138:3, CEV | When I asked for your help, you answered my prayer and gave me courage. |
| Psalm 143:10, CEV | You are my God. Show me what you want me to do, and let your gentle Spirit lead me in the right path. |
| Proverbs 1:10, NKJV | My son, if sinners entice you, do not consent. |
| Matthew 6:13, NIV | Lead us not into temptation, but deliver us from the evil one. |
| Matthew 26:41, NIV | Watch and pray so that you will not fall into temptation. The spirit is willing, but the body is weak. |
| Luke 17:1, AMP | Temptations (snares, traps set to entice to sin) are sure to come, but woe to him by or through whom they come! |
| Luke 22:40, NKJV | Pray that you may not enter into temptation. |
| Romans 8:26, NIV | The Spirit helps us in our weakness. We do not know what we ought to pray for, but the Spirit himself intercedes for us with groans that words cannot express. |
| 1 Corinthians 10:13, NCV | The only temptation that has come to you is that which everyone has. But you can trust God, who will not permit you to be tempted more than you can stand. But when you are tempted, he will also give you a way to escape so that you will be able to stand it. |

2 Corinthians 9:8, NIV — God is able to make all grace abound to you, so that in all things at all times, having all that you need, you will abound in every good work.

Ephesians 6:11, NIV — Put on the full armor of God so that you can take your stand against the devil's schemes.

2 Timothy 2:22, CEV — Run from temptations that capture young people. Always do the right thing. Be faithful, loving, and easy to get along with. Worship with people whose hearts are pure.

Hebrews 2:18, NIV — Because he himself suffered when he was tempted, he is able to help those who are being tempted.

Hebrews 4:15-16, NCV — Our high priest is able to understand our weaknesses. He was tempted in every way that we are, but he did not sin. Let us, then, feel very sure that we can come before God's throne where there is grace. There we can receive mercy and grace to help us when we need it.

James 1:12, NCV — When people are tempted and still continue strong, they should be happy. After they have proved their faith, God will reward them with life forever. God promised this to all those who love him.

James 1:13, CEV — Don't blame God when you are tempted! God cannot be tempted by evil, and he doesn't use evil to tempt others.

James 4:17, NLT — Remember, it is sin to know what you ought to do and then not do it.

# THANKFULNESS

Are you known more for counting your blessings or complaining about your problems?

God wants you to take note of all He's done for you and be grateful. "In everything give thanks," His Word says; "for this is the will of God in Christ Jesus for you" (1 Thessalonians 5:18, NKJV). When you come to God and pray, "enter his gates with thanksgiving" (Psalm 100:4, NIV).

And truthfully, all of us have a lot to be grateful to God for. Psalm 118:7 says, "The LORD is with me; he is my helper. I will look in triumph on my enemies" (NIV). The enemies of sin, sickness, death, fear, poverty, pain, and heartache have all been defeated by the power of God's Word!

True gratitude, indeed, is being thankful even when bad things happen to us. In hardship and suffering, disappointment and mistreatment, we can still be thankful—because God is good to us!

Consistent gratitude like this not only delights the heart of God but also is good for us. There is power in having an orientation toward thanksgiving. It helps us to stay focused on what we have, not what we lack.

So stay in an attitude of gratitude. It will keep you from getting upset and feeling overwhelmed in the circumstances of life. And more than that, being thankful is a magnet for the favor and blessings of God!

*For other helpful categories, see pages 9, 150, 445.*

| | |
|---|---|
| 1 Chronicles 16:8, NIV | Give thanks to the LORD, call on his name; make known among the nations what he has done. |
| 1 Chronicles 16:34, NIV | Give thanks to the LORD, for he is good; his love endures forever. |
| Psalm 75:1, CEV | Our God, we thank you for being so near to us! Everyone celebrates your wonderful deeds. |
| Psalm 95:2, NIV | Let us come before him with thanksgiving and extol him with music and song. |
| Psalm 100:4, NIV | Enter his gates with thanksgiving and his courts with praise; give thanks to him and praise his name. |
| Psalm 106:1, NIV | Praise the LORD. Give thanks to the LORD, for he is good; his love endures forever. |
| Psalm 118:21, NIV | I will give you thanks, for you answered me; you have become my salvation. |
| 1 Corinthians 15:57, NIV | Thanks be to God! He gives us the victory through our Lord Jesus Christ. |
| Philippians 4:6, NKJV | Be anxious for nothing, but in everything by prayer and supplication, with thanksgiving, let your requests be made known to God. |
| 1 Thessalonians 5:18, NKJV | In everything give thanks; for this is the will of God in Christ Jesus for you. |

# TRAVEL

If your life requires a lot of traveling, you may spend countless hours in airports, train stations, and cars. The discomforts of traveling—missing loved ones, eating on the run, and hours of waiting—can grow old fast. You may feel a void from not having the time to commit to regular activities at home, at church, or in your community. Exhaustion can set in. Being in an unfamiliar environment can invoke temptations that would normally not prey on you.

Jesus understands the discomforts associated with traveling. He traveled from one town and village to another, carrying the good news of the gospel (Luke 8:1). He depended on the transportation of that day to help Him get from one place to another. He used boats to cross the sea, rode on the colt of a donkey into Jerusalem, and had dusty feet from all His walking.

You can use this season in your life to go deeper with your Savior. If you're waiting for long periods of time for your transportation, take advantage of our current technology and download Scripture memorizations or praise music to strengthen your spirit. Teaching CDs can help you to keep your mind centered in the right place. You can often visit a church in the city where you are staying. Meeting others in a different part of the country or world who love God is inspiring and rewarding.

Knowing that we live in perilous times, you or those you leave at home might have heightened concerns when you are away. Covering yourself in prayer and trusting in God's Word for protection is not just an option but a necessity. Just as God was with Jesus in His travels, so God will be with you. As one psalmist declares, "If I rise with the sun in the east and settle in the west beyond the sea, even there you would guide me. With your right hand you would hold me" (Psalm 139:9-10, NCV).

*For other helpful categories, see pages 329, 375, 384, 406, 411.*

| | |
|---|---|
| Genesis 28:15, NKJV | Behold, I am with you and will keep you wherever you go, and will bring you back to this land. |
| Psalm 139:9-10, NCV | If I rise with the sun in the east and settle in the west beyond the sea, even there you would guide me. With your right hand you would hold me. |
| Isaiah 45:2, NKJV | I will go before you and make the crooked places straight; I will break in pieces the gates of bronze and cut the bars of iron. |
| Luke 8:1, NCV | While Jesus was traveling through some cities and small towns, he preached and told the Good News about God's kingdom. The twelve apostles were with him. |
| Colossians 4:5-6, ESV | Walk in wisdom toward outsiders, making the best use of the time. Let your speech always be gracious, seasoned with salt, so that you may know how you ought to answer each person. |
| James 4:13-15, NKJV | Come now, you who say, "Today or tomorrow we will go to such and such a city, spend a year there, buy and sell, and make a profit"; whereas you do not know what will happen tomorrow. For what is your life? It is even a vapor that appears for a little time and then vanishes away. Instead you ought to say, "If the Lord wills, we shall live and do this or that." |

# TRUST

You often hear people say in difficult circumstances, "All we can do now is pray." In other words, "We can't control this. We have to trust God now."

The truth is, you are never in control of circumstances. Discover the freedom of trusting God *first* in your life, instead of trusting Him as a last resort. God alone is worthy of our total trust.

"Commit everything you do to the LORD. Trust him, and he will help you" (Psalm 37:5, NLT). God loves you and wants to help you with all of your cares and concerns. In Isaiah 41:13, God says, "I am the LORD, your God, who takes hold of your right hand and says to you, Do not fear; I will help you" (NIV). God offers His help. Are you willing to trust Him and take hold of His hand?

Are you ready to commit every aspect of your life to God? Do you believe that you can trust Him? Make a declaration today: "The LORD is my strength and my shield; my heart trusts in him, and I am helped. My heart leaps for joy and I will give thanks to him in song" (Psalm 28:7, NIV).

*For other helpful categories, see pages 132, 199, 218, 236.*

| Psalm 9:10, CEV | Everyone who honors your name can trust you, because you are faithful to all who depend on you. |

Psalm 9:10, CEV — Everyone who honors your name can trust you, because you are faithful to all who depend on you.

Psalm 13:5, NCV — I trust in your love. My heart is happy because you saved me.

Psalm 20:7, CEV — Some people trust the power of chariots or horses, but we trust you, LORD God.

Psalm 22:5, NCV — They called to you for help and were rescued. They trusted you and were not disappointed.

Psalm 25:2, NIV — In you I trust, O my God. Do not let me be put to shame, nor let my enemies triumph over me.

Psalm 28:7, NIV — The LORD is my strength and my shield; my heart trusts in him, and I am helped. My heart leaps for joy and I will give thanks to him in song.

Psalm 31:14, NIV — I trust in you, O LORD; I say, "You are my God."

Psalm 34:8, NKJV — Oh, taste and see that the LORD is good; blessed is the man who trusts in Him!

Psalm 37:3, NCV — Trust the Lord and do good. Live in the land and feed on truth.

Psalm 37:5, NLT — Commit everything you do to the LORD. Trust him, and he will help you.

Psalm 52:8, NIV — I am like an olive tree flourishing in the house of God; trust in God's unfailing love for ever and ever.

| | |
|---|---|
| Psalm 56:3, NIV | When I am afraid, I will trust in you. |
| Psalm 62:8, NCV | People, trust God all the time. Tell him all your problems, because God is our protection. |
| Psalm 84:12, NIV | O LORD Almighty, blessed is the man who trusts in you. |
| Psalm 86:2, NIV | Guard my life, for I am devoted to you. You are my God; save your servant who trusts in you. |
| Psalm 112:7, NIV | He will have no fear of bad news; his heart is steadfast, trusting in the LORD. |
| Psalm 118:8, NCV | It is better to trust the LORD than to trust people. |
| Proverbs 3:5-6, NIV | Trust in the LORD with all your heart and lean not on your own understanding; in all your ways acknowledge him, and he will make your paths straight. |
| Jeremiah 17:7-8, NIV | But blessed is the man who trusts in the LORD, whose confidence is in him. He will be like a tree planted by the water that sends out its roots by the stream. It does not fear when heat comes; its leaves are always green. It has no worries in a year of drought and never fails to bear fruit. |
| John 14:1, NIV | Do not let your hearts be troubled. Trust in God; trust also in me. |

# WEIGHT CONTROL

Anyone who struggles with weight control knows that one of the hardest parts of dieting is the "yo-yo effect." You lose a few pounds and feel great. But if you gain it back, you feel like a failure. You wonder if it's worth trying at all.

If you base your identity on how much you weigh, your self-image will yo-yo with your weight. This affects, not only your relationship with other people, but also your relationship with God.

Remember this: God's love for you has *nothing* to do with how much you weigh. When you are free to accept this truth, you can lean into God's design for your body, your eating habits, and your health. Maybe that means eating more. Or less. Let God direct those decisions, perhaps through the counsel of others, rather than relying on your feelings or conflicting desires.

Knowledge is a powerful tool that can help you keep your weight under control. Learning how to change your dietary *lifestyle* will help you to change your eating habits and will put you on course for a life of good health and continued success in your weight management.

Look for a support group that is right for you. Surround yourself with people who celebrate your decision to become physically healthy. Be in control of your environment. Plan your food ahead of time so that when you get hungry your meal will fit into the healthy lifestyle that you have chosen.

The Psalms tell us that all creatures look to God "to give them their food at the proper time. When you give it to them, they gather it up; when you open your hand, they are satisfied with good things" (Psalm 104:27-28, NIV). With God in control of your eating, you will be satisfied. Your cravings will come under His control as well. And you will experience a new delight in the "good things" He gives you to sustain and refresh your body.

*For other helpful categories, see pages 13, 129, 180, 196, 411, 421.*

Psalm 51:6, NCV — You want me to be completely truthful, so teach me wisdom.

Psalm 63:5, NLT — You satisfy me more than the richest feast.

Psalm 104:27-28, NIV — These all look to you to give them their food at the proper time. When you give it to them, they gather it up; when you open your hand, they are satisfied with good things.

Isaiah 55:1, NCV — The LORD says, "All you who are thirsty, come and drink. Those of you who do not have money, come, buy and eat! Come buy wine and milk without money and without cost."

Isaiah 55:2, NCV — Why spend your money on something that is not real food? Why work for something that doesn't really satisfy you? Listen closely to me, and you will eat what is good; your soul will enjoy the rich food that satisfies.

Matthew 11:28, NIV — Come to me, all you who are weary and burdened, and I will give you rest.

Romans 12:1, NLT — Dear brothers and sisters, I plead with you to give your bodies to God because of all he has done for you. Let them be a living and holy sacrifice—the kind he will find acceptable. This is truly the way to worship him.

Romans 12:2, NLT — Don't copy the behavior and customs of this world, but let God transform you into a new person by changing the way you think. Then you will learn to know God's will for you, which is good and pleasing and perfect.

1 Corinthians 6:19-20, NIV — Do you not know that your body is a temple of the Holy Spirit, who is in you, whom you have received from God? You are not your own; you were bought at a price. Therefore honor God with your body.

1 Corinthians 10:31, CEV — When you eat or drink or do anything else, always do it to honor God.

2 Corinthians 12:9, NIV — My grace is sufficient for you, for my power is made perfect in weakness.

Philippians 4:13, NKJV — I can do all things through Christ who strengthens me.

Colossians 3:2, NLT — Think about the things of heaven, not the things of earth.

# WIDOWS

Early in the Old Testament, the Scripture reveals the heart and plan of God to-ward the widow. "Cursed is the man who withholds justice from…the widow," God told the Israelites (Deuteronomy 27:19, NIV). A psalmist declared God to be "a protector of the widows" (Psalm 68:5, AMP). Then and now, widows are under God's special attention and care.

Jesus reflected His Father's heart for widows. When He saw a widow grieving the death of her only son, "He had compassion on her" (Luke 7:13, NKJV). It is important to understand that whenever we see the heart of God, as in this passage, it is related to the grand purpose and plan of God. When the crowd around Jesus saw Him care for the widow, they said, "God has visited his people!" (Luke 7:16, ESV).

That is a word to you! God has come to help you in your hour of need. Pray and remind Him of the promises for your provision in this season to protect, defend, and comfort you. Ask Him to heal your heart and the hearts of your children (Psalm 147:3). Ask Him to go before you and "make the crooked places straight" (Isaiah 45:2, NKJV). He is your sustainer (Psalm 146:9).

*For other helpful categories, see pages 132, 153, 193,  223, 226, 230, 263, 289.*

| | |
|---|---|
| Exodus 22:22-23, NIV | Do not take advantage of a widow or an orphan. If you do and they cry out to me, I will certainly hear their cry. |
| Deuteronomy 10:18, NIV | He defends the cause of the fatherless and the widow, and loves the alien, giving him food and clothing. |
| Deuteronomy 27:19, NCV | Anyone will be cursed who is unfair to foreigners, orphans, or widows. |
| Psalm 68:5, AMP | A father of the fatherless and a judge and protector of the widows is God in His holy habitation. |
| Psalm 119:76, NLT | Now let your unfailing love comfort me, just as you promised me, your servant. |
| Psalm 146:9, NIV | The LORD watches over the alien and sustains the fatherless and the widow. |
| Psalm 147:3, NKJV | He heals the brokenhearted and binds up their wounds. |
| Proverbs 15:25, NCV | The Lord will tear down the proud person's house, but he will protect the widow's property. |
| Isaiah 45:2, NKJV | I will go before you and make the crooked places straight. |
| Isaiah 61:7, NIV | Instead of their shame my people will receive a double portion, and instead of disgrace they will rejoice in their inheritance; and so they will |

inherit a double portion in their land, and everlasting joy will be theirs.

Joel 2:25, NIV

I will repay you for the years the locusts have eaten—the great locust and the young locust, the other locusts and the locust swarm—my great army that I sent among you.

Zechariah 9:12, NIV

Return to your fortress, O prisoners of hope; even now I announce that I will restore twice as much to you.

1 Corinthians 7:39, NKJV

A wife is bound by law as long as her husband lives; but if her husband dies, she is at liberty to be married to whom she wishes, only in the Lord.

2 Corinthians 1:3, NIV

Praise be to the God and Father of our Lord Jesus Christ, the Father of compassion and the God of all comfort.

# Wisdom

Many people call the Bible the book of wisdom. The Bible is a great treasure of truth about God, about life, and about eternity. It shows you the difference between right and wrong based upon the infinite wisdom of Almighty God. Wisdom is the mind of God revealed.

Wisdom comes in two ways: as a gift and as the result of a passionate search. Wisdom's starting point is God and His revealed Word, the source of "knowledge and understanding" (Proverbs 2:6, NIV). In that sense, wisdom is God's gift. But He gives it only to those who seek it.

When Solomon was named king over Israel, God told him he could ask for anything he wanted. Solomon asked for wisdom (2 Chronicles 1:10). In response, God gave Solomon "wisdom and very great insight, and a breadth of understanding as measureless as the sand on the seashore" (1 Kings 4:29-31, NIV). Solomon was known as a man who could discern right from wrong.

Like Solomon, if you want wisdom, you must decide to go after it. Be determined and persistent. If you're in need of wisdom, "ask God, and it will be given to you. God is generous and won't correct you for asking" (James 1:5, CEV).

You can be confident in discerning God's wisdom because any guidance that comes from God "leads us to be pure, friendly, gentle, sensible, kind, helpful, genuine, and sincere" (James 3:17, CEV). God's wisdom will "lead you along straight paths" when you face hard decisions (Proverbs 4:11, NIV).

By knowing and applying God's Word to your life, you can live the way God wants you to live. He wants you to be strong, confident, and equipped to rely on His Word for daily living. He is eager to pour out His heart and make known His thoughts to you.

*For other helpful categories, see pages 9, 65, 132, 199, 340, 441.*

| | |
|---|---|
| Job 12:13, NIV | To God belong wisdom and power; counsel and understanding are his. |
| Psalm 37:30, NKJV | The mouth of the righteous speaks wisdom, and his tongue talks of justice. |
| Psalm 111:10, NIV | The fear of the LORD is the beginning of wisdom; all who follow his precepts have good understanding. To him belongs eternal praise. |
| Psalm 119:98, NIV | Your commands make me wiser than my enemies, for they are ever with me. |
| Proverbs 2:2, NCV | Listen carefully to wisdom; set your mind on understanding. |
| Proverbs 2:6-7, NKJV | The LORD gives wisdom; from His mouth come knowledge and understanding; He stores up sound wisdom for the upright; He is a shield to those who walk uprightly. |
| Proverbs 3:17, NCV | Wisdom will make your life pleasant and will bring you peace. |
| Proverbs 4:7, NIV | Wisdom is supreme; therefore get wisdom. Though it cost all you have, get understanding. |
| Proverbs 4:11, NIV | I guide you in the way of wisdom and lead you along straight paths. |
| Proverbs 9:11, NCV | I am Wisdom. If you follow me, you will live a long time. |

| Proverbs 9:12, NIV | If you are wise, your wisdom will reward you; if you are a mocker, you alone will suffer. |
| Proverbs 11:2, NCV | Pride leads only to shame; it is wise to be humble. |
| Proverbs 13:20, NLT | Walk with the wise and become wise; associate with fools and get in trouble. |
| Proverbs 14:24, NCV | Wise people are rewarded with wealth, but fools only get more foolishness. |
| Proverbs 15:33, NCV | Respect for the Lord will teach you wisdom. If you want to be honored, you must be humble. |
| Proverbs 19:11, NIV | A man's wisdom gives him patience; it is to his glory to overlook an offense. |
| Proverbs 21:30, NKJV | There is no wisdom or understanding or counsel against the LORD. |
| Daniel 2:21, NIV | He gives wisdom to the wise and knowledge to the discerning. |
| Ephesians 1:17, NCV | I have not stopped asking the God of our Lord Jesus Christ, the glorious Father, to give you a spirit of wisdom and revelation so that you will know him better. |
| Colossians 1:9, NKJV | We do not cease to pray for you, and to ask that you may be filled with the knowledge of His will in all wisdom and spiritual understanding. |

James 1:5, CEV

If any of you need wisdom, you should ask God, and it will be given to you. God is generous and won't correct you for asking.

James 3:17, CEV

The wisdom that comes from above leads us to be pure, friendly, gentle, sensible, kind, helpful, genuine, and sincere.

# WISE LIVING

The Bible teaches, corrects, rebukes, and trains you in righteousness (2 Timothy 3:16). In other words, it instructs you on how to live the type of life that is pleasing to God. Wise living begins when you acknowledge the value of God's Word and pattern your life in obedience to Him.

One of the most important points of the book of Proverbs is to live wisely: "My son, give attention to my words; incline your ear to my sayings. Do not let them depart from your eyes; keep them in the midst of your heart" (Proverbs 4:20-21, NKJV).

Incline your ears, eyes, and heart to wisdom in everything you do. One of the best ways to do this is to choose your companions carefully: "He who walks with the wise grows wise" (Proverbs 13:20, NIV). Do you spend most of your time with television, the Internet, or friends who lead you away from God's Word? Choose to spend time first in God's Word and with friends who speak God's truth. Then you will have a foundation from which you can reach out to others.

As you meditate on the following Scriptures, ask yourself, *Does my life line up with God's Word?* Having a passion for God Word will help you to live the wise life—a life that will bring you great joy and much fruit for His glory!

*For other helpful categories, see pages 199, 218, 402, 421, 437.*

| | |
|---|---|
| Exodus 20:13, NIV | You shall not murder. |
| Leviticus 19:11, NIV | Do not steal. Do not lie. Do not deceive one another. |
| Leviticus 19:28, NKJV | You shall not make any cuttings in your flesh for the dead, nor tattoo any marks on you: I am the LORD. |
| Deuteronomy 22:5, NIV | A woman must not wear men's clothing, nor a man wear women's clothing, for the LORD your God detests anyone who does this. |
| Psalm 119:9, NIV | How can a young man keep his way pure? By living according to your word. |
| Proverbs 4:20-21, NKJV | My son, give attention to my words; incline your ear to my sayings. Do not let them depart from your eyes; keep them in the midst of your heart. |
| Proverbs 6:32, NIV | A man who commits adultery lacks judgment; whoever does so destroys himself. |
| Proverbs 13:20, NIV | He who walks with the wise grows wise, but a companion of fools suffers harm. |
| Proverbs 15:27, NIV | A greedy man brings trouble to his family, but he who hates bribes will live. |
| Proverbs 20:1, NCV | Wine and beer make people loud and uncontrolled; it is not wise to get drunk on them. |

| Proverbs 20:3, NIV | It is to a man's honor to avoid strife, but every fool is quick to quarrel. |
|---|---|
| Proverbs 20:19, NIV | A gossip betrays a confidence; so avoid a man who talks too much. |
| Proverbs 23:9, NIV | Do not speak to a fool, for he will scorn the wisdom of your words. |
| Luke 20:34, AMP | Jesus said to them, The people of this world and present age marry and are given in marriage. |
| Romans 12:16, NIV | Live in harmony with one another. Do not be proud, but be willing to associate with people of low position. Do not be conceited. |
| Romans 12:17, NIV | Do not repay anyone evil for evil. Be careful to do what is right in the eyes of everybody. |
| Romans 13:13, NCV | Let us live in a right way, like people who belong to the day. We should not have wild parties or get drunk. There should be no sexual sins of any kind, no fighting or jealousy. |
| 1 Corinthians 5:11, NIV | You must not associate with anyone who calls himself a brother but is sexually immoral or greedy, an idolater or a slanderer, a drunkard or a swindler. With such a man do not even eat. |
| Galatians 2:20, NIV | I have been crucified with Christ and I no longer live, but Christ lives in me. The life I live in the body, I live by faith in the Son of God, who loved me and gave himself for me. |

Ephesians 5:15, AMP · Look carefully then how you walk! Live purposefully and worthily and accurately, not as the unwise and witless, but as wise (sensible, intelligent people).

2 Timothy 2:22, CEV · Run from temptations that capture young people. Always do the right thing. Be faithful, loving, and easy to get along with. Worship with people whose hearts are pure.

Titus 3:1-2, NCV · Remind the believers to yield to the authority of rulers and government leaders, to obey them, to be ready to do good, to speak no evil about anyone, to live in peace, and to be gentle and polite to all people.

James 1:27, NIV · Keep yourself from being polluted by the world.

1 Peter 4:2-4, NCV · Strengthen yourselves so that you will live here on earth doing what God wants, not the evil things people want. In the past you wasted too much time doing what nonbelievers enjoy. You were guilty of sexual sins, evil desires, drunkenness, wild and drunken parties and hateful idol worship. Nonbelievers think it is strange that you do not do the many wild and wasteful things they do, so they insult you.

# THE WORDS YOU SPEAK

Do you struggle with saying the wrong thing at the wrong time—and feeling as if your own mouth is out of control? If so, that's understandable! In fact, James said, "No man can tame the tongue" (James 3:8, NIV).

Only God can tame our tongue. Pray Psalm 19:14 out loud every day: "Let the words of my mouth and the meditation of my heart be acceptable in Your sight, O LORD, my strength and my Redeemer" (NKJV).

Consider the options you have:

| *Uncontrolled Tongue* | *Controlled Tongue* |
|---|---|
| Gossips | Praises God and others |
| Speaks evil | Speaks life |
| Lies and spreads lies | Speaks peace |
| Complains, grumbles, and quarrels | Speaks forgiveness |
| Uses negative words | Offers acceptance |
| Gives negative reports | Gives encouragement |
| Brags about self | Comes from faith |
| Says the first thing that comes to mind | Speaks in love |
| Hurts others with words | Uses wisdom |
| Spreads false teachings | Speaks God's Word |
| Is of the devil | Is pleasing to God |

God is eager to help you move from one column to the other. Ask Him for help and believe that He will do it.

*For other helpful categories, see pages 28, 180, 204, 218.*

| | |
|---|---|
| Exodus 20:7, NIV | You shall not misuse the name of the LORD your God, for the LORD will not hold anyone guiltless who misuses his name. |
| Deuteronomy 23:23, NIV | Whatever your lips utter you must be sure to do, because you made your vow freely to the LORD your God with your own mouth. |
| Deuteronomy 30:14, NIV | The word is very near you; it is in your mouth and in your heart so you may obey it. |
| Joshua 1:8, NIV | Do not let this Book of the Law depart from your mouth; meditate on it day and night, so that you may be careful to do everything written in it. Then you will be prosperous and successful. |
| Job 22:28, NKJV | You will also declare a thing, and it will be established for you; so light will shine on your ways. |
| Psalm 17:3, NIV | Though you probe my heart and examine me at night, though you test me, you will find nothing; I have resolved that my mouth will not sin. |
| Psalm 19:14, NKJV | Let the words of my mouth and the meditation of my heart be acceptable in Your sight, O LORD, my strength and my Redeemer. |
| Psalm 37:30, NIV | The mouth of the righteous man utters wisdom, and his tongue speaks what is just. |
| Psalm 40:3, NIV | He put a new song in my mouth, a hymn of praise to our God. Many will see and fear and put their trust in the LORD. |

| | |
|---|---|
| Psalm 49:3, NIV | My mouth will speak words of wisdom; the utterance from my heart will give understanding. |
| Psalm 141:3, NIV | Set a guard over my mouth, O LORD; keep watch over the door of my lips. |
| Psalm 149:6, NIV | May the praise of God be in their mouths and a double-edged sword in their hands. |
| Proverbs 18:21, NKJV | Death and life are in the power of the tongue, and those who love it will eat its fruit. |
| Ecclesiastes 5:2, NKJV | Do not be rash with your mouth, and let not your heart utter anything hastily before God. For God is in heaven and you on earth; therefore let your words be few. |
| Ecclesiastes 5:6, NIV | Do not let your mouth lead you into sin. |
| Matthew 12:34, NKJV | Out of the abundance of the heart the mouth speaks. |
| Matthew 12:37, NKJV | By your words you will be justified, and by your words you will be condemned. |
| Matthew 15:11, NIV | What goes into a man's mouth does not make him "unclean" but what comes out of his mouth, that is what makes him "unclean." |
| Ephesians 4:29, NIV | Do not let any unwholesome talk come out of your mouths, but only what is helpful for building others up according to their needs, that it may benefit those who listen. |

James 3:8, NIV          No man can tame the tongue. It is a restless evil, full of deadly poison.

James 3:10, NIV         Out of the same mouth come praise and cursing. My brothers, this should not be.

# Prayer of Salvation

Spiritual salvation is a gift that comes through faith in Jesus Christ and not through our own works of just being a good person. God is calling you to receive this gift. As Jesus said, "I am the way, the truth, and the life. No one comes to the Father except through Me" (John 14:6, NKJV). If you have never asked Jesus to come into your heart and be the Lord and Savior of your life, I invite you to say this simple but powerful prayer:

*Heavenly Father,*

*I come in the name of Jesus. I recognize that I am a sinner and I cannot save myself. I ask You to forgive me and cleanse me from all my sins. I believe in my heart and confess with my mouth that Jesus died for me. I believe that Jesus is the Son of God and that He was raised from the dead and now sits at Your right hand, interceding as my Advocate. Lord Jesus, thank You for being my Savior. I receive You now. Amen.*

Asking to receive Jesus Christ's salvation changes your whole life. You might not feel any different (or you might), but something has changed inside you. The Holy Spirit has come to dwell within you. Go tell someone about what just happened in your life. It's time to celebrate!

# Prayer Requests
## and Scripture Promises

| Name or Circumstances | Scripture Promise |
| --- | --- |
| _____ | _____ |
| _____ | _____ |
| _____ | _____ |
| _____ | _____ |
| _____ | _____ |
| _____ | _____ |
| _____ | _____ |
| _____ | _____ |
| _____ | _____ |
| _____ | _____ |
| _____ | _____ |

| Name or Circumstances | Scripture Promise |
| --- | --- |
| | |
| | |
| | |
| | |
| | |
| | |
| | |
| | |
| | |
| | |
| | |
| | |
| | |

| NAME OR CIRCUMSTANCES | SCRIPTURE PROMISE |
|---|---|
| _____ | _____ |
| _____ | _____ |
| _____ | _____ |
| _____ | _____ |
| _____ | _____ |
| _____ | _____ |
| _____ | _____ |
| _____ | _____ |
| _____ | _____ |
| _____ | _____ |
| _____ | _____ |
| _____ | _____ |
| _____ | _____ |
| _____ | _____ |

| NAME OR CIRCUMSTANCES | SCRIPTURE PROMISE |
| --- | --- |
| | |
| | |
| | |
| | |
| | |
| | |
| | |
| | |
| | |
| | |
| | |
| | |
| | |

| Name or Circumstances | Scripture Promise |
|---|---|
| | |
| | |
| | |
| | |
| | |
| | |
| | |
| | |
| | |
| | |
| | |
| | |
| | |

| NAME OR CIRCUMSTANCES | SCRIPTURE PROMISE |
| --- | --- |
| _____ | _____ |
| _____ | _____ |
| _____ | _____ |
| _____ | _____ |
| _____ | _____ |
| _____ | _____ |
| _____ | _____ |
| _____ | _____ |
| _____ | _____ |
| _____ | _____ |
| _____ | _____ |
| _____ | _____ |
| _____ | _____ |

# ABOUT THE AUTHOR

Dee Chernicky is a teacher, conference speaker, and ordained minister. A graduate of Victory Bible Institute in Tulsa, Oklahoma, Dee is the founder of One Heart One Voice Ministries. Her Say the Word™ CD series has inspired many to memorize and speak the Word of God. You are invited to contact Dee at www.oneheartonevoiceministries.org. Please include your prayer request and comments when you write.